WAX TRASH AND VINYL TREASURES: RECORD COLLECTING AS A SOCIAL PRACTICE

Wax Trash and Vinyl Treasures: Record Collecting as a Social Practice

ROY SHUKER
Victoria University of Wellington, New Zealand

ASHGATE

Published by
Ashgate Publishing Limited
Wey Court East
Union Road
Farnham
Surrey, GU9 7PT
England

Ashgate Publishing Company
Suite 420
101 Cherry Street
Burlington
VT 05401-4405
USA

www.ashgate.com

British Library Cataloguing in Publication Data
Shuker, Roy.
    Wax trash and vinyl treasures : record collecting as a social practice. – (Ashgate popular and folk music series)
    1. Sound recordings – Collectors and collecting – Social aspects. 2. Collectors and collecting – Social aspects. 3. Sound recordings – Collectors and collecting.
    I. Title II. Series
    306.4'87–dc22

Library of Congress Cataloging-in-Publication Data
Shuker, Roy.
    Wax trash and vinyl treasures : record collecting as a social practice / Roy Shuker.
        p. cm.—(Ashgate popular and folk music series)
    Includes bibliographical references.
    ISBN 978-0-7546-6782-7 (hardcover : alk. paper)
    1. Sound recordings—Collectors and collecting. 2. Collectors and collecting—Social aspects. I. Title.

    ML111.5.S46 2010
    780.26'6075—dc22

                                                                                    2009030058

ISBN 9780754667827 (hbk)
ISBN 9780754699163 (ebk)

Mixed Sources
Product group from well-managed forests and other controlled sources
www.fsc.org Cert no. SA-COC-1565
© 1996 Forest Stewardship Council
FSC

Printed and bound in Great Britain by
MPG Books Group, UK

Contents

General Editor's Preface

The upheaval that occurred in musicology during the last two decades of the twentieth century created a new urgency for the study of popular music alongside the development of new critical and theoretical models. A relativistic outlook replaced the universal perspective of modernism (the international ambitions of the 12-note style); the grand narrative of the evolution and dissolution of tonality was challenged, and emphasis shifted to cultural context, reception and subject position. Together, these have conspired to eat away at the status of canonical composers and categories of high and low in music. A need has arisen, also, to recognize and address the emergence of crossovers, mixed and new genres, to engage in debates concerning the vexed problem of what constitutes authenticity in music, and to offer a critique of musical practice as the product of free, individual expression.

Popular musicology is a vital and exciting area of scholarship, and the *Ashgate Popular and Folk Music Series* aims to present the best research in the field. Authors are concerned with locating musical practices, values and meanings in cultural context, and draw upon methodologies and theories developed in cultural studies, semiotics, poststructuralism, psychology and sociology. The series focuses on popular musics of the twentieth and twenty-first centuries. It is designed to embrace the world's popular musics from Acid Jazz to Zydeco, whether high tech or low tech, commercial or non-commercial, contemporary or traditional.

Derek B. Scott
Professor of Critical Musicology
University of Leeds, UK

Acknowledgements

This study has had a lengthy gestation, and I am grateful for the patience of those interested in the topic, who have supported me along the way, and who have had a long wait. I initially became interested in undertaking an academic study of record collecting after reading the novel *High Fidelity* (1995) by Nick Hornby, and then seeing the feature film based on it (*High Fidelity*, 2000). As a collector myself, and with many friends who considered themselves collectors, I felt both the novel and the film tended to caricature the 'record collector'. Accordingly, through 2001–02, I interviewed 67 record collectors (see Appendix 1 for details). The results of this survey were incorporated into: a circulated 'Report' to the interviewees; some preliminary presentations at several academic conferences; a contribution to the first volume of *The CONTINUUM Encyclopedia of Popular Music of the World* (Shepherd et al., 2003); and an article, 'Beyond the High Fidelity Stereotype', published in *Popular Music* (Shuker, 2004).

The idea of a full-length book gradually emerged, and initial research on broader aspects of the topic, especially the historical development of record collecting, was undertaken during periods of research leave in 2002 and 2003. A number of developments then delayed and thwarted the project: in 2003 I took up a new and extremely demanding academic job, which also involved a family relocation and two house moves; I developed a serious health problem (now resolved!); and the collecting study was put on hold while I undertook other publishing commitments. In 2008–09 I returned to the project, 'updating' a number of the earlier interviews, adding others and revisiting the literature. To those who have periodically asked 'where is the book at?', here is my answer.

I am especially grateful to all those who took the time to complete my on-line survey, and respond to follow up questions, or were interviewed in person: Ray Alcock, Neil Ames, Malcolm Bancroft, Keith Beattie, Albert Bell, Michael Bollotin, John Book, Phillip Braithwaite, Marc Brennan, Catherine Brown, Norma Coates, Gregg Crossan, William Dart, Peter Dawson, Susan Fast, Michelle Flannery, Lee Ann Fullerton, Liz Giuffre, Matt Glesne, Barry Grant, Warren Green, Joel Hayward, Michelle Henry, Shane Homan, Hasse Huss, Jonathon Ibell, Tina Janering, Bruce Johnson, Anti-Ville Karja, Danny Keenan, Keir Keightley, Joe Kellich, Brett Loper, Colin McLeay, Steven Mallet, Lee Marshall, Jo Mason, Shawn Mawer, Allen Meek, Grant Mitchell, Tony Mitchell, Craig Morrison, Terry Newman, Andre Nuchelmans, Andrew Njsse, Paul Oliver, Shane Palmer, Gonny Pasaribu, Nick Plimmer, Aaron Regev, Motti Regev, Jane Roscoe, David Sanjek, Ian Shirley, Gary Shuker, Andrew Stafford, Geoff Stahl, Yngvar Steinbolt, Juliette Taylor, Mark Vanderdrift, Laura Vroomen, Steve Waksman, Oliver Wang,

Michelle Wauchope, Michael Weber, Martin Webster, Lisa Wheeler, Craig Wilson, Joel Wing and Brennon Wood.

One of the pleasures of the research has been eventually meeting a number of these collectors, in several cases, visiting them in their homes, viewing their collections and enjoying their hospitality.

Copies of their unpublished work on record collecting were generously supplied by Lee Marshall (his PhD study of bootleggers and tape traders), Ed Montano (his dissertation on collecting The Shadows; thanks also to David Horn for alerting me to it), Julie Bogle (her graduate paper on women record collectors; thanks also to Nabeel Zuberi for alerting me to this), Lee Ann Fullerton (her conference papers on women collectors and the independent record shop) and Jonathon Kelso (his graduate project on on-line record collecting).

The initial development of the project was shaped by informal chats with Henry Barnard, Tom Gati, Simon Hay, Peter McLennan, Allen Meek, and Dave Laing and John Shepherd. It was subsequently extended through discussions, in some cases on-going since 2002, with Peter Dawson, Susan Fast, Haase Huss, Craig Morrison, Andre Nuchelmans, Michael Pickering, Gary Shuker, Geoff Stahl, Simon Sweetman, Jim Urry and Tom Weber. Tim Anderson alerted me to the work of Robert Crumb and Harvey Pekar. Most recently, Gabor Valyi, Mikey Vallee and Johannes Brusila provided helpful references and insights on the history of vinyl and its current revival. Alan Lewis, the editor of *Record Collector*, was very helpful in clarifying my use of the magazine, and providing me with a personal perspective on his own collecting and career in the music press. Ian Shirley, the editor of the *Rare Record Price Guide 2010*, and writer of a regular column in *Record Collector*, provided extensive replies to my questions about the current state of record collecting.

Useful feedback on 'work in progress' was made by those attending my papers at IASPM (the International Association for the Study of Popular Music) conferences in Turku, Finland in June 2001, Montreal in 2003 and Wellington, New Zealand in 2006, and at seminars at Victoria University in 2006 and 2008 and Otago University in 2008. Helpful commentary on various early drafts of material has been provided by Keith Beattie, Ed Montano and Mary Jane Shuker.

At Ashgate, Derek Scott provided insightful comments on the initial proposal and Heidi Bishop proved extremely patient as I stumbled towards providing the final manuscript. My thanks also to Jonathan Hoare, for exemplary copy-editing.

Roy Shuker
Wellington, New Zealand

Introduction

This study examines the historical development of record collecting, its contemporary status, and the infrastructure within which it functions.[1] I refer to it as *a social practice* since the characteristics, motivations and practices exhibited by record collectors are social activities. I focus on the questions of *who* collects, and *why, what* is being collected and the *process* of collecting, including sites of acquisition, the thrill of the chase and the 'find'. I also consider the context created by the music industry, especially the role of the music press and record companies in both shaping and responding to record collecting.

In considering these questions, I draw on the general literature on collecting, along with previous studies of record collecting, historical and contemporary profiles of record collectors, including a number of personal interviews (see Appendix 1), and other relevant secondary literature on popular music. In addition, I have utilized the music press, primarily the collector oriented publications. As a long-time collector (see Appendix 2), I also draw on my own experiences, in part through a 'participant observer' study of what can be termed sites of acquisition: record shops, record fairs, and thrift shops, and through the internet. Reflecting the location of the collectors I talked to, my coverage is restricted largely to record collecting in the United Kingdom and the United States, with some examples from Canada, Europe, Israel, Australia and New Zealand.

Let me begin with some indications of the scope of collecting popular music and the widespread interest in it, as both an economic and cultural commodity, during 2007–08:

- In early 2008, the 'World's Greatest Record Collection' was offered for sale on eBay, with a starting bid of (US) $3 million, and an estimated value of $50 million. By the end of March 2008, more people had window-shopped the collection than any other item offered in eBay's history. Consisting of an estimated six million recordings, it had been put together by its owner Paul Mawhinny, over some fifty years, and stored in his 16,000 square

---

[1] This is not a book about which records – and associated musical artefacts – are collectable, where to find these and how much they are worth. These topics are necessarily engaged with here, but extensive information on them is readily available from introductions such as Dave Thompson's excellent The Music Lover's Guide to Record Collecting (Backbeat, San Francisco, 2002), the various Record Price Guides, the main collector magazines, notably the UK-based Record Collector and, in the United States, Goldmine (see Chapter 6); and collector websites such as the Record Collectors Guild.

foot, climate controlled combination record shop and archive in Pittsburgh, United States.[2]

- The 10th edition of the *Rare Record Price Guide* was published, now a massive tome of 1,408 pages, and featuring colour illustrations. The rarest listings included the two-LP set *The Beatles* (Apple, 1968) at £5–7,000.[3]
- In 2008, the opening, due for 2009, of the Abba Museum in Stockholm was announced. Capitalizing on the continued fascination with the Swedish pop quartet, the most commercially successful group of the 1970s, the new museum will feature the gold and platinum discs of former band members.[4]
- Guinness Publications issued *California Dreaming: Memories and Visions of LA 1966–1975*, by photographer Henry Diltz, in a print run of 2,000 copies; the signed, handmade limited edition book was available for £225 (*Record Collector*, January 2008: 20).
- Auction house Christies, New York, November 2007 sale of rock'n'roll memorabilia included a signed copy of Jimi Hendrix's *Axis Bold as Love* vinyl album, along with related photos, which sold for US$23,000.
- Long-established music fairs in the United Kingdom, Europe and the United States attracted large numbers of collectors.
- Despite the continued decline of the record industry, the reissues labels were stronger than ever, with a plethora of individual reissues and boxed sets from record companies such as Ace, Cherry Red and Rhino (De Whalley, 2007).
- A week in the life of a collector, April 2008: I purchased a copy of Lester Bangs's extremely scarce book on Blondie, from local web auction site Trade Me (cost NZ$10); obtained a June 2004 issue of *MOJO* – the Morrissey cover – needed to complete a run of the magazine, from a second hand bookstore (NZ$2); and found a near-mint copy in a local thrift shop of Iron Butterfly's 1970 *Live* album (NZ$3), featuring the extended version of the band's 'In-A-Gadda-Da-Vida', a catalyst in establishing 'progressive' FM radio programming.[5]

---

[2]   http://www.thegreatestmusiccollection.com. The collection was not sold, and was subsequently purchased privately.

[3]   Often referred to as 'The White Album', it is the unique numbering system that makes this the most collectable UK album; the album was released with its sleeves numbered consecutively for the first 500,000 copies, each number embossed on the cover. This valuation was for copies numbered between 1 and 10 (Rare Record Price Guide 2010, 10th edition, published at the end of 2008). Number 00010 was sold at a Christies auction in 2001 for £6,000.

[4]   http://www.abbathemuseum.com (Abba broke up in 1982).

[5]   This illustrates the role of the search and 'the find', especially at a bargain price, as central to the enjoyment of collecting. All of these were obtainable on the web, but at greater cost.

As these examples suggest, I am using the term 'record collecting' as shorthand for a variety of distinct but related practices. 'Record collecting' can be pursued via the collection of particular formats, genres, performers, record labels, producers or some combination of these. It can also embrace the use of – and sometimes collecting of – related print materials: the music press generally, but especially the specialist collector magazines, fanzines, discographies and general guidebooks; the recording industry targeting of collectors (reissue labels; promotional releases, remixes, boxed sets); and dedicated sites of acquisition (record fairs, second-hand and specialist shops, eBay and high-profile auctions). The term 'records' is often used to refer to vinyl recordings, but here I use it to include sound recordings in any format, most notably shellac 78s, vinyl LPs and 45s, audiotapes, CDs and as digital downloads.

A brief history of record collecting

Record collecting has a now extensive, although largely unexplored history. During the mid-to-late nineteenth century, a mix of capitalism and consumerism, increased leisure time, disposable income and nostalgia made collecting a significant aspect of the social identity for the new middle classes of Europe, Britain and its colonies, and the United States. Record collecting as a social practice was a logical extension of such activities.

At the end of the nineteenth century sound became 'a thing', a material product for sale in the market (see the discussion in Chapter 1). Its subsequent reproduction as a cultural and economic artefact has produced the 'sound recording' in its various historical formats, along with related technology, memorabilia and literature. Record collectors who were active during the period 1903 to the 1950s and the advent of vinyl collected 78s and, in some cases, cylinders as well. This group established 'record collecting' as a major form of collecting, with its own set of practices and related literature. These early collectors were associated with the emergence of what can be termed a gramophone culture, which embraced a number of *sites*: physical and social spaces, and institutions which facilitated and shaped the production and consumption of recorded music. These included the early recording companies, record clubs and appreciation societies, music retail outlets and the second-hand market, and the music press. By the introduction of vinyl records in the 1950s, record collecting was already a well-established 'hobby'.

Record collecting since the1960s has seen the steady expansion of the overarching infrastructure within which the hobby was already embedded: the rise of record fairs, specialist record shops (independent and second hand), increased major label interest in reissues and their back catalogue, specialist reissue labels, and a collector press. Well documented in the United Kingdom and the United States, such developments are also evident internationally. Looking back in 1996, Peter Doggett observed:

> As we discovered, there was no such thing as a pop or rock'n'roll collector until the 1960s. Only then did dealers start importing material from the US, and loyal R&B fans began to flood into places like Soho market in London every weekend, searching through piles of old 45s and 78s in the hopes of finding an obscure rockabilly or blues gem. (Doggett, 1996a: editorial)

From there, a small but dedicated collectors' network began to spread across the country.

> By the early 1970s, there were specialist shops, mail order dealers, and a bunch of soul, rnb and r'n'r fanzines. Around the same time, the reissue market – which had always been a purely low budget affair – started very slowly to get off the ground. (Doggett, 1987: 16)

A key moment was the establishment of *Record Collector* magazine, in 1979, which provided a focus for collectors.

A similar pattern was evident in the United States:

> What started as a small-time, largely underground hobby has expanded into a respected, full-fledged industry. In 1974, almost no one could make a living collecting music. Now [1994], with the advent of computer databases, new recording options and more, the hobby/industry is more efficient, lucrative and wide-reaching than it ever has been before. (Thompson, 1994)

The launch of *Goldmine* in 1974 did much to consolidate record collecting in North America.

The landscape of record collecting has changed dramatically in the past 15 to 20 years. The range of collectibles has increased, with promotional material and memorabilia more prominent. Record collecting has become more organized, more intense and, at times, more expensive. The internet has added a major new dimension to collecting, creating increased opportunity but also fuelling price rises. Reflecting such developments, the record collecting press has mushroomed, with a succession of ever-larger and more comprehensive magazines, guidebooks, price guides and discographies. Today, record collecting is a major form of collecting, with its own set of collecting practices.

Yet while record collecting is a significant social activity, it remains a relatively neglected aspect of the consumption of popular music. There is a plethora of guidebooks on record collecting, but these focus primarily on documenting artists and their collectable recordings, and their economic value, along with some attention to questions such as where to find records, the importance of condition and their care. In academia, general studies of music consumption, especially fandom, provide some insights, but more extended critical discussion is sparse. Accordingly, the topic is ripe for a fuller analysis, with particular attention to the motivations and characteristics of collectors as well as their collecting practices and the context within which these take place.

The following sections introduce some of the relevant literature on collecting more generally and, then, record collecting in particular. The themes and concerns evident here are ones that will be returned to throughout this study.

Collecting

We can point to the development of a collecting sensibility, linked to possessive individualism, historically present since the Greeks, but more fully realized under contemporary capitalism. As social anthropologist James Clifford puts it, in the Western world, 'collecting has long been the strategy for the deployment of a possessive self, culture, and authenticity' (Clifford, 1988: 218). Today, as Pearce observes, 'the gathering together of chosen objects for purposes regarded as special is of great importance, as a social phenomenon, as a focus of personal emotion, and as an economic force' (Pearce, 1995: Preface).

Collecting is a very common activity: in the contemporary Western world around a quarter to a third of adults are willing to identify themselves as collectors, and this 'collecting disposition' cuts across class and gender boundaries (Belk, 2001; Pearce, 1995; 1998). The extensive Leicester Collecting Project amply demonstrated, with the exception of the financially very expensive collectibles (Old Master paintings and suchlike), that every kind of collection occurs in every kind of social background (Pearce, 1997). In examining the social location of collectors there has been very limited attention paid to the role of ethnicity and class, but the 'gendering' of collecting has attracted considerable attention. While there is convincing survey evidence that the majority of collectors are women, male collectors and their preferred collectibles usually are given more public prominence. The studies by Pearce, Belk and others show that most children collect, and both boys and girls are equally likely to be avid collectors before their teenage years. During adolescence collecting declines for both boys and girls, but especially for girls. There is a tendency for men to renew collecting in middle age – a trend not seen to the same extent among women. In general, women's emotional investment in the collecting process, and the nature of the artefacts collected, differs from that of men, with a greater emphasis on domestic-related collectibles, while men are more interested in the investment rationale of collecting. As Belk argues, 'collecting is most often a highly gendered activity with the greatest social sanction for those collections and collector traits that fit masculine sex-role stereotypes' (Belk, 2001: 99). Characteristic collector traits include those identified as 'masculine': aggressiveness, competitiveness, desire for mastery over a symbolic realm; and those seen as 'feminine': preservation, creativity and nurturance. These can, of course, be combined: collecting is one of the few socially sanctioned opportunities for men to be expressive, while at the same time being aggressive and competitive.

Given its social prominence, it is hardly surprising that collecting has been the subject of considerable theoretical speculation and empirical study, with major contributions from sociology, anthropology, history, social psychology, museum studies and market research, especially consumer studies. Most recently, collecting is an aspect of the study of material culture, which has defined itself as a distinct area of academic inquiry. Key questions addressed in this body of work include: In what ways do we interact with material things? How do material objects affect the way we relate to each other? What are the connections between material things and social processes? (See Miller, 1998; 2006; Tilley et al., 2006.)

The literature on collecting embraces a now fairly standard set of motifs and an associated vocabulary. Collectors and the collecting process are variously associated with: longing, desire and pleasure; ritualistic, near-sacred and repetitive acquisition; passionate and selective consumption; stewardship and cultural preservation; and obsession and linked pathologies such as completism, accumulation and a preoccupation with collection size. The collection exhibits a series of attributes: it is a source of pleasure; an economic investment; an exhibition of logic, unity and control; an indicator of cultural and social capital; and a socially sanctioned form of materialist and competitive consumption, consumer culture taken to excess As shall be demonstrated later, all of these are present among record collectors and their collecting.

Record collecting

Belk provides a working definition of 'collecting', which is essentially compatible with others in the literature: 'the process of actively, selectively, and passionately acquiring things removed from ordinary use and perceived as part of a set of non-identical objects or experiences' (Belk, 2001: 67). This is essentially to distinguish collecting from acquisitiveness and accumulation, though elements of both may be part of the collector's persona and collecting practices. However, elements of Belk's definition of collecting are awkward in relation to record collecting. Sound recordings are largely mass-produced artefacts, and therefore hardly non-identical in that individual copies exist even if from the same master recording.[6] Further, even when collected, recordings will frequently retain a strong element of use value – people will play them – thereby placing them not too distant from 'ordinary' use.

More useful for my purposes is the work of Pearce, who distinguishes three co-existing modes of the relationship of collectors to the collected object: souvenir, fetishistic and systematic. In souvenir collecting, 'the individual creates a romantic life-history by selecting and arranging personal memorial material to create

---

[6]   It is, however, the exceptions to the mass-produced recordings that are often the most sought-after and valuable collectibles, such as unique album covers, promos, acetates and test pressings.

what ... might be called an object autobiography, where the objects are at the service of the autobiographer'. In contrast, in fetishistic collecting 'the objects are dominant and ... are allowed to create the self of the collector, who responds by obsessively collecting as many items as possible'. Thirdly, systematic collecting is characterized by an 'intellectual rationale', with the emphasis placed on the completeness of the collection (Pearce, 1995: 32). Pearce stresses that the three approaches are not exclusive, and can coexist in each collection. Each of these collecting modes are represented among record collectors, broadly corresponding to varying emphases: on recordings as part of identity formation and life history (souvenir collecting); accumulation and completism (fetishistic collecting); and discrimination and connoisseurship (systematic collecting).

Muesterberger, a psychoanalyst, claims, 'Collectors themselves – dedicated, serious, infatuated, beset – cannot explain or understand this all-consuming drive ... is it an obsession? An addiction? Is it a passion or urge, or perhaps a need to hold, or possess, to accumulate?' (Muesterberger, 1994: 3). This is an overstatement. While it is true that many collectors find it difficult to pinpoint the precise set of motivations that drive their collecting, they are frequently well aware of the various explanations offered for it (see, for example, the biographical accounts in Blom, 2002; Elsner and Cardinal, 1994). This was particularly evident among my record collectors, whose responses to two central questions covering self-definition and perceptions of collectors and the collecting process showed considerable awareness of the 'High Fidelity' stereotype, along with a concern to distance personal practice from this. As Chapter 2 shows, their responses suggest a range of characteristics associated with the label 'record collector', while demonstrating that the concept is far from a unitary one.

Given that record collectors can be regarded as a type of fan, the literature on fandom is relevant to a consideration of record collecting. The traditional view of fandom has situated it in terms of pathology and deviance, reserving the label 'fans' for teenagers who are generally presented as avidly and uncritically following the latest pop sensation. These fans have been unfairly denigrated in most writing on popular music and, indeed, by many other consumers. Their behaviour is often described as a form of pathology, and the terms applied to it have clear connotations of condemnation and undesirability: 'Beatlemania', 'teenyboppers', 'groupies' (Lewis, 1992). As Nick Hornby's novel *High Fidelity* (1995) suggests, a similar labelling process can be seen in the tendency to associate record collecting with paradigms of obsession and addiction, arrested adolescence and social awkwardness. This image of the record collector as anti- or a-social has been reinforced by the manner in which the phenomenon is treated in other popular texts, including the film *Ghost World*, and the cartoons by Robert Crumb and Harvey Pekar featuring record collectors.

The contributors to Lewis's classic study showed fandom to be a complex phenomenon, related to the formation of social identities, especially sexuality. This view of fandom as an active process has been confirmed by later studies, which essentially view fandom as a form of sustained affective consumption (Sandvoss,

2005; for accounts from fans themselves, see Aizelwood, 1994; Hunter, 2004; Smith, 1995). This approach is evident in several accounts of popular music fans, notably Cavicchi's detailed ethnography of Bruce Springsteen fans, whose collecting of Springsteen recordings, including bootlegs, was a significant aspect of many of their lives (Cavicchi, 1998). Such fandom offers its participants membership of a community not defined in traditional status terms.

We can usefully extend the term fan to embrace those who see themselves as 'serious' devotees or aficionados of particular musical styles or performers. These are fans in terms of the word's origins in 'fanatic', but their fanaticism is usually at more of an intellectual level and focused on the music *per se* rather than on the persona of the performer(s). Indeed, such individuals would often not describe themselves as 'fans', preferring instead to describe themselves as 'into' particular performers or genres, or as 'music lovers' or, indeed, as 'record collectors'. Adopting this distinction is not to perpetuate an aesthetically-based, discriminatory view of the former group (fans in the traditional sense). Both categories of fan engage in fandom as an active process, and both often display impressive knowledge of their preferred genres or performers. My argument is that their emotional and physical investments are different, as are the social consumption situations in which their fandom operates.

As Campbell observes, 'A record collection does not a record collector make' (Campbell, 2001). This is to make a central distinction between (simply) liking the music – in the sense of a fan, or music lover – and methodically seeking out and acquiring it. Consequently, possessing an abundance of records is a necessary but not sufficient condition for the self-recognition of a 'collector'. The central factor is the systematic approach to acquiring new material for the collection, a characteristic commonly seen as distinguishing collecting: 'In the collecting form of consumption, acquisition is a key process. Someone who possesses a collection is not necessarily a collector unless they continue to acquire additional things for the collection' (Belk, 2001: 66). While fans will collect records, record collectors are more often characterized by what can be termed 'secondary involvement' in music, activities beyond 'simply' listening to the music: the seeking out of rare releases, such as the picture discs and bootlegs; the reading of fanzines in addition to commercial music magazines; concert going; and an interest in record labels and producers as well as performers.

As this brief discussion has indicated, attempts to define (record) collecting and the (record) collector are fraught. Such concepts are far from unitary, and should be regarded as a set of motifs and social practices, themes that shall be returned to throughout this study.

Investigating the record collector

There are a small number of studies of record collectors and record collecting. The best known of these is Will Straw's contribution to *Sexing the Groove*. Drawing on some of the considerable general literature on collecting and collectors, Straw usefully speculates on the psychology of record collecting as a social practice, especially its largely male character. He identifies several characteristics of record collecting 'which are more easily recuperable': hipness, connoisseurship, bohemianism and the adventurous hunter. These are related to the record collector's 'obscurantist interest in the marginal', a stance which clearly resonates with 'rock culture's mythic emphasis on oppositionality'. The valorizing of the obscure is linked to trash fandoms generally, and the consequent discourse surrounding these is a feature of the homosocial world of young men (Straw, 1997a).

While frequently convincing, Straw's analysis arguably lacks any systematic embedding in the views of the collectors themselves. Collectors feature more prominently in a number of recent academic studies: Hayes (2006) on young Canadian vinyl collectors in the digital age; Dougan (2006) on canon formation and blues record collecting; Hosokawa and Matsuoka's historical analysis (2004) of vinyl record collecting in Japan; and Marshall's study of bootleggers and tape traders (2005). Unpublished graduate research studies include Bogle (1999) on women who collect records; Kelso (2007) on digital collecting; and Montano (2003) on Cliff Richard record collectors. Other published accounts include *Incredibly Strange Music*, profiling collectors of exotica (Vale and Juno, 1993; 1994); Milano's study of well-known vinyl collectors (Milano, 2003); and Dean's account of 78 collector Joe Bussard (Dean, 2001). There is also an on-going series on individual collectors in the magazine *Record Collector*; and the documentaries *Vinyl*, by Canadian film-maker and collector Alan Zweig, and *Desperate Man Blues* (on Joe Bussard). An entertaining and informative account of the hunt aspect of record collecting is provided by Blecha (2005), and there are several accounts of 'digging in the crates' (for example, Schloss, 2004).[7]

In addition to the academic literature and popular journalism, the representation of record collectors and collecting in various popular culture texts has been important in establishing a stereotypical view. As already indicated, popular discourse around record collectors and collecting, in common with discussions of collecting generally, construct a dominant representation of record collectors as obsessive males, whose passion for collecting is often a substitute for 'real' social relationships, and who exhibit a 'trainspotting' mentality toward popular music, a concern with the details of recordings. This is very much the case in the best-known representation of record collectors, the novel *High Fidelity* (Hornby, 1995), and the subsequent film of the same name, directed by Stephen Frears and starring John Cusack, released in 2000.

With some reference to the above literature, this study draws primarily on 70 extensive 'interviews' with record collectors, mostly undertaken in 2002–03, with some follow ups and new interviewees in 2007–08 (see Appendix 1 for details).

---

[7]   In addition to this body of work in English, there is Robert Haagsma's Vinylfanaten, a study of 22 avid vinyl collectors from Holland and Belgium; see Record Collector, September 2007: 10–11.

My opportunity sample fell into two groups of record collectors, although with some overlap between them:

1. An older group (largely 40 plus) who collect rock and pop recordings, primarily within the period 1945 to 1980, with a marked preference for vinyl. This group is almost exclusively male. Their preferred genres include reggae, '60s guitar rock, psychedelia/garage, rockabilly and surf. While love of music is central to their collecting, there is some concern with the rarity and associated economic value of the recordings.
2. A younger group (under 40) who primarily collect popular music on CDs, although with some attention to vinyl. Their genre preferences at times include the 1950s through to and into the '70s, but their collecting focus is usually on genres of the last 20 years, especially non-mainstream styles such as punk, goth, new wave and rap. While males are still in the majority here, there are a number of women collectors within this group. While several of these collectors are aware of rarity and economic values, and may even spend considerable amounts on particular recordings, they are arguably more concerned with the aesthetic qualities of the recordings: the music as such.

The 'social practices' of both groups, shared by other record collectors, presents an interwoven narrative of desire and identification, alongside notions of cultural and economic value, which characterize many collectors' accounts of their passion.

Book structure

Chapter 1: The 78 era: creating a collector constituency

The chapter covers the early development of record collecting, following the advent of sound recording and the rise of a gramophone culture. It considers the early collectors of 78s, their motivations and collecting practices, and the context in which they collected: the role of record labels, record clubs and the music press, especially the collector magazines, and music retail. The chapter then sketches the post-1960 collecting of 78s.

Chapter 2: The contemporary collector: beyond the High Fidelity *stereotype*

Contemporary record collectors are shown to demonstrate a complex mix of characteristics: a love of music; obsessive-compulsive behaviour, accumulation and completism, selectivity and discrimination; and self-education and scholarship.

As a social practice, contemporary record collecting presents itself as a core component of individual social identity and a central part of the lifecycle, related to issues of cultural consumption, social identity and 'the construction of self' in contemporary society.

Chapter 3: Formats, collectors and the music industry

The focus here is on the development of successive recording formats, along with the collecting of each. Individual collector preferences relate to an amalgam of the age of the collector and associated notions of nostalgia, historicism and authenticity; availability, collector ambition and cost; and aesthetics, in terms of preferred artists and genres, sound quality, and aspects such as album cover art. The chapter begins with an examination of the historical development of the various recording formats, moving from these to the collecting of each. It then considers the role of the music industry in both responding to and shaping the record collecting market.

Chapter 4: Taste, the canon and the collectable

This chapter considers the issues of taste and cultural capital, and what is 'collectable'. Intersecting with personal taste is the key notion of 'collectable', with the collecting process and what is collectable shaped by considerations of demand and availability; condition and cost; aura and authenticity; and rarity and value. Taste and what is collectable are historically contingent, reflecting generational and demographic trends in collecting, and both engage with varying forms of cultural capital. The complex interaction of these various factors is illustrated through a consideration of collectable artists, genres and recent top-selling recordings. What is collectable can also be informed by a strong sense of discrimination, in part based on views of which artists, recordings and genres have musical/aesthetic value: a canon. There are also collectable fields which are not (necessarily) so informed by these collecting principles, but which are subsumed under the broad rubric of 'record collecting'. Examples of these are the collecting of chart number 1 hits, compilations, bootlegs, memorabilia and music magazines; these are underpinned by different inflections of taste and collectability.

Chapter 5: Collecting practices

Hunting metaphors abound in the general literature on collecting, and collectors frequently refer to notions of pleasure and desire in the pursuit of items for their collection. This is a process involving competition, effort (as with visiting sites of acquisition and the physical act of sorting through records) and choice (between desired items, especially if budget is a consideration), underpinned by a strong element of compulsion. The chapter examines the collectors hunt for new material, and the various sites for its acquisition. Also considered are issues and practices around the storage and cataloguing of the collection, whether or not to lend recordings, and the public and private display of the collection.

Chapter 6: Record collecting and the music press

The music press is a key part of the infrastructure of record collecting. Record collectors are among the readers of the music press in general, but also consume a number of publications aimed more specifically at them. These include general collecting guides, price guides, discographies, and magazines such as *Record Collector* and *Goldmine*. As the field of collecting has grown, there has been a proliferation of this literature, along with increased specialization among its titles. This chapter examines the historical development of these publications since 1970, their emphases and the use made of them by record collectors.

Chapter 7: Collector profiles

In 'cut and pasting' individual collectors across the various chapters and topics covered, rarely does a sense of 'the whole collector' – the individual voice – emerge. Accordingly, this last chapter includes a series of ten collector profiles. Most are collectors with whom I have had on-going contact over the past eight or nine years, in some cases, even longer. This time frame demonstrates the shifting physical and emotional investments made by collectors in the hobby, as their musical interests and life circumstances change. I have chosen them to represent a range of collecting interests, ages and geographic locations.

Conclusion

The conclusion to this study draws on the seven chapters to make some general observations on record collectors and their collecting practices and the context within which these take place. It also considers collecting in relation to the wider study of collecting. As the general discussion and the extended profiles (Chapter 7) show, it is difficult to sustain a unitary definition of the record collector and record collecting. Rather, given the different emphases and practices taken on over time by individual collectors, I argue that it makes more sense to speak of 'a career' in record collecting.

Chapter 1

The 78 era: creating a collector constituency

This chapter begins with the early development of record collecting, as the advent of recorded sound at the end of the nineteenth century created a new form of music collectible, associated with the emergence of what can be termed a gramophone culture. Record collectors active during the period 1903 to the 1950s and the advent of vinyl collected 78s and, in some cases, cylinders. This group established 'record collecting' as a major form of collecting, with its own set of practices, associated literature and appreciation societies. These collectors had a shared interest in sound recordings as both sources of listening pleasure and significant cultural artefacts, with associated notions of discrimination, musical canons and rarity. They also shared the dominant characteristics of collectors more generally, albeit with particular inflections of these: the thrill of the chase; obsession, linked to accumulation and completism; at times a preoccupation with rarity and economic value; and a concern for cultural preservation. The concern involved self-education and public, vernacular scholarship, drawing on the collection as a resource. These traits were subsumed into collecting as a significant aspect of social identity, involving the acquisition of cultural capital, overlaid with a patina of nostalgia.

Gramophone culture operated within a context that shaped the emergence and subsequent development of a collecting constituency and record collecting as a social practice. While there is frequent overlap between them, especially through their respective roles in shaping taste and discrimination (including canon formation), this context included a number of *sites*: physical and social spaces, practices and institutions which facilitated and shaped the production and consumption of recorded music and its collectors. These sites were:

- sites of production and promotion: the role of the early recording companies;
- sites of appreciation: record clubs and societies;
- sites of acquisition: music retail, and the second-hand market; and
- sites of mediation: the music press.

A consideration of these forms the second part of the chapter.

What I have termed the 78 era was over by 1960. The 78 was supplanted by vinyl during the 1950s, and the gramophone replaced by new forms of sound reproduction. But the passing of the 78 recording did not end interest in the era and its music. The recordings and the equipment used to play them have remained highly collectable. Since the 1960s, there has been a proliferation of interest in the period, with a considerable amount of scholarship devoted to documenting its music and the associated technologies. A good deal of this research has been undertaken by collectors. Today, there is an active network of 78 collector societies, specialist dealers and auction houses, and publications, with much of this accessible through the internet. The last section of the chapter briefly considers 78 collecting and collectors since the early 1960s.

The rise of gramophone culture

Collecting was a prominent part of the social life of the new middle classes, emerging along with industrialization and urbanization during the mid-to-late nineteenth century, with the collector's 'cabinet of curiosities' a feature of many Victorian lounges (Blom, 2002). A mix of capitalism and consumerism, increased leisure time, disposable income and nostalgia made collecting a significant aspect of social identity for the middle classes of Europe, Britain and its colonies, and the United States. The state art galleries, museums and libraries of the Victorian era owed much to the generosity of those collectors who endowed and funded them.

Music was already well established as a form of collectible by this time. Prominent collectors had built up libraries of music publications, especially sheet music (Hermann, 1999; King, 1963); the collecting and publication, and in some cases field recording, of traditional folk songs had emerged as a major movement, initially in England and on the European continent, then in North America and throughout the world (Oliver, 2003); and both private collectors and institutions had long collected musical instruments. Record collecting as a social practice was a logical extension of such activities. Indeed, collecting 'sound recordings' was an activity accessible to a wider, more socially democratic constituency, since it did not necessarily require the same levels of capital investment as traditional music collectibles.

Edison invented the phonograph, a 'talking machine', in November 1877, a device which used cylinders to record and reproduce sound. The first commercially marketed recordings were produced by several companies, most notably Columbia. These early impressed tin foil records were very restricted in use, since they were destroyed once removed from the supporting metal cylinder. As such, they hardly made ideal collectibles. After some initial development, Edison abandoned the fledgling phonograph for a decade, turning instead to the development of electricity, but he eventually produced a considerably improved phonograph in 1887. Around the same time, Berliner further developed the new technology with his gramophone (1888), using a flat disc technique instead of the cumbersome cylinder. He tried several materials for the accompanying discs, before utilizing shellac in 1891, a compound derived from a natural resin secreted by the lac beetle. The shellac 78 became the industry standard, a position it maintained over the next half century. (On the development of sound recording, its technological and social impact, see Chanan, 1995; Copeland, 1991; Day, 2000; Millard, 1995.)

As Fabrizio observes, 'A period of nearly 20 years elapsed between the invention of sound recording/replay and the point at which the majority of Americans could afford to buy a talking machine' (Fabrizio, 1999). The resurrected phonograph was to be a business machine, but this application proved limited. However, an enterprising dealer equipped the phonographs with a coin-operated mechanism that played a cylinder, featuring a popular tune or comic monologue, through a set of ear tubes to the patron. These caught on hugely in the early 1890s, and were part of many public spaces and entertainment venues. In 1896, Edison and the Columbia label introduced the first machines targeting the home entertainment market in the United States.

The phonograph represented the true beginning of recorded sound technology, replacing 'the shared Victorian pleasures of bandstand and music hall with the solitary delight of a private world of sound' (Millard, 1995: 1). By 1900, several large commercial recording companies were operating on a stable national basis, and listening to the various new 'talking machines' was a popular pastime. A strong link between hardware and software was established from the start of sound recording, with companies marketing both their models of the phonograph and the recordings to be played on it. The terms 'phonograph' and 'gramophone' were initially both widely used, indicating the different models, but the latter came to denote all forms of 'record player'. By the early 1900s, it had emerged as the fashion accessory of the day and was recognized as a familiar object in the home.

The recording industry took off around the turn of the century. In 1899, 151,000 phonographs were produced in the United States alone, and there was now a steady, though limited, supply of discs and pre-recorded cylinders. In 1897 only about 500,000 records had been sold in the United States, but by 1899 this number had reached 2.8 million, and continued to rise. In the United States, the period 1889–1912 saw the production of over 8,000 masters of Edison's 'Two-Minute Cylinders', with total production running into the millions. Spoken word recordings by leading figures of the period formed an important part of the repertoire, which was associated with a concern with fidelity; 'the illusion of real presence', as *Scientific American* magazine termed it in 1877 (Thompson, 1996: 3). During the 1920s over 100 million records were sold in the United States alone, before the Depression brought the recording industry to the verge of collapse (Gronow, 1983).

The gramophone, as various historians of recorded sound have observed, played a role in defining modernity, being put to use in ways that sharply changed the culture of music in the home and turning music into a 'thing' (see Eisenberg, 1988; Kenney, 1999). The domestication of recorded sound increased the musical repertoire available to the home listener, while freeing up the experience of music from its physical location in place and time. As Gronow put it, 'the musician became immortal' (Gronow, 1983: 54).

The first record collectors

Those who first began collecting recordings, primarily 78s, although in some cases cylinders as well, established 'record collecting' as a major form of collecting, with its own set of collecting practices and associated literature. They also helped form the dominant image of the record collector as an obsessive personality, although this must be strongly qualified in relation to their sense of community, their role in cultural preservation and their sociability.

These first record collectors are difficult to profile extensively, since biographical material is sparse. My account is reliant on a handful of previously published profiles and recollections, scattered across a range of monographs, biographies and journal articles. Most are of collectors initially active in the 1940s. As might be expected, more material is available on collectors whose activities had a wider profile, through the writings and recordings they produced drawing on their collections. These include the folk collectors Alan Lomax and Harry Smith, blues aficionados John Hammond and Jerry Wexler, classical music collectors such as Compton McKenzie and Michael Corenthal, and prominent jazz collectors such as Brian Rusk.

They were concentrated in those countries and areas subject to the greatest penetration of gramophone culture, especially the United States, England and Western Europe, but also in Japan, New Zealand and Australia. As a group, it would appear that they were exclusively male and often of middle-class backgrounds. Of course this claim must be related to the point that it is usually members of socially dominant groups who leave the majority of surviving historical traces.

The field of record collecting was initially largely a male preserve. The biographies and recollections I have accessed are all by and about men, and few saw fit to comment on the absence of women from their collecting activities. Explanations for this situation include the point that time and disposable income, even more so than now, were more available to males. It would also have been difficult for women to break into the masculine peer groups who dominated early record clubs and societies. The gendered nature of related psychological and personality attributes have seen the subsequent common perception of record collecting as a male activity (see Chapter 2, for discussion of the gendered nature of contemporary record collecting).

This also appears to be very much a white group in the United States, where in the 1920s there was only a tiny black middle class, and they did not represent enough disposable income to be catered for by most recording companies. As the existence of 'race records' and associated labels (from Okey in the 1920s) indicates, black people bought records, but if any collected in any systematic way, no traces of this activity have survived. The middle-class location of collectors is supported by the professional backgrounds of the collectors profiled, while the earliest known American collectors of jazz and blues were university students. John Hammond, who studied at Yale, later reflected on the appeal of black culture: 'All music fascinated me, but the simple honesty and convincing lyrics of the early blues singers, the rhythm and creative ingenuity of the jazz players, excited me most – certainly all those I liked best – were black' (Hammond, 1977: 30).

What was collected?

The genre interests of these early record collectors in both the United States and the United Kingdom can be divided into two broad groups, with little overlap between them:

1. Those collecting in the classical repertoire, especially vocal (opera). Initial collecting interest was largely in this genre, in part as classical music was already a well-established and valued art form.
2. Those collecting within 'popular music', often collectively termed 'Early American music' or 'old time music', and including the various genres which progressively emerged: jazz, big band, c&w (country and western), r&b (rhythm and blues – usually referred to as 'race' music until the 1950s) and the various 'ethnic' musics associated with American immigrant groups.

While the classical collectors valorized the aesthetic qualities of recordings, the 'popular' collectors more frequently valued scarcity, combined with associated notions of authenticity. I draw here on both groups for examples of collecting practices.

Behind the collecting impulse

The early record collectors were motivated by a mix of motives: a love of the music, a concern with cultural preservation, scholarship and education. Michael Corenthal provides an evocative example of a love of the music of the 78 era and its performers:

> Amid the usual assortment [of an accumulation of discs left by a husband to his widow] was a small box of these superb Wisconsin black and blue label Paramount recordings. Keep talking. Well, I [Corenthal] wasn't about to let history go down the tubes so I captured these rare Black stylists of the 1920's jazz and blues performances. One item of memorable fondness was Paramount #12252. This was a Paramount recording from October 1924 featuring Ma Rainey and her Georgia Jazz band. It wasn't a bad little band at that, accompanying the principals were Louis Armstrong on cornet, Buster Bailey on clarinet, and Fletcher Henderson on piano. Right on. I can [now] appreciate Ma Rainey because I've had the opportunity to appreciate her extraordinary recordings. (Corenthal, 1986: 12)

At times lurking alongside such enthusiasms were usually less lauded, psychological tendencies: compulsion and addiction, with their associated tendencies of accumulation and completism, and the emphasis on the 'hunt' aspect of collecting. The case of Dr John Grams illustrates such a mix. In 1946, the release of the Columbia picture *The Jolson Story* led John to collect Al Jolson's recordings.

> Temporarily, he was satisfied owning the Jolson recordings on Decca Records released from the film and newer releases such as the Anniversary Song. One day, while visiting a radio store in Sheboygan, John saw jutting out of a wire rack a Brunswick release #4033 issued in 1928 featuring the younger Jolson performing at the height of his career *Sonny Boy* and *There's a Rainbow 'Round My Shoulder*. John simply had to have this record, quite scratched and very dusty. When he approached the proprietor about this matter, the fellow seemed quite annoyed by his interest and demanded the astronomical sum of $2.00 for this shellac beater. (Corenthal, 1986: 123)

John was stunned, since new 78s were then selling at 53¢, but still bought it: 'A collector was born and without any clue or system, John began addressing the problem of how to find other Jolson recordings from the past.' Eventually he had them all.

Cultural preservation, education and scholarship

As Corenthal's reference to 'history' indicates, cultural preservation was a major theme in the collecting activities of this group. Purchasing sound recordings was an important way for American immigrants to preserve their own folk culture, and motivated several prominent collectors, such as Ford Porter, 'The Polka King' (Corenthal, 1986: 98ff.). The collections they built up provided an invaluable archive for later compilations and re-releases of early American music, which otherwise would have been lost. In several cases, they also recorded and documented the music, as did blues collector Samuel Charters, John Lomax and his son Alan, and Joe Bussard.

Perhaps the best known example of cultural preservation during this early period of collecting is Harry Smith's *Anthology of American Folk Music*. Born in 1923 in Portland, Oregon, Smith grew up in and around Seattle, Washington. In 1940 he began to collect commercially released blues and country 78s from the 1920s and 1930s, records which were often cheaply available in thrift shops. In 1952, by which time his collection numbered tens of thousands, he assembled 84 discs by mostly forgotten performers on an anthology he entitled *American Folk Music*. Including recordings originally released by such still active labels as Columbia, Brunswick and Victor, the compilation was released by Folkways

Records as three double LPs, re-titled the *Anthology of American Folk Music* (Cantwell, 1996; Dougan, 2006: 7–8).[1]

In 2000, a decade after Smith's death in 1990, an intended fourth volume finally appeared, issued on two CDs (Revenant); the liner notes include a 1968 interview with Smith. In 2007 a tribute album indicated the Anthology's continued legacy.

Obsessive-compulsive behaviour

As the various collector clubs/societies (below) indicate, there was a clear collegiality and sense of community among record collectors. While examples of competition, one-upmanship and social dislocation are present, more commonly their collecting provided the basis for enduring friendships. At times, however, the collecting practices of some early collectors, along with their general social habits, lend themselves to the classic images of collectors as obsessive personalities.

Acquiring vast quantities of recordings, regardless of aesthetic value, was less evident in this early period, presumably reflecting a combination of the relatively high cost of records along with their more limited availability. Completism was more common. It included wanting every imaginable version of a particular tune; wanting all one artist's output; and collecting every recording within a particular series:

> One of my early addictions [note the metaphor] was the Meditation Theme from the opera Thais. I [Corenthal] was enchanted by the violin solo by Mischa Elman on the single faced Victor Red Seal and would have rested my case if I hadn't noticed another version by Fritz Kreisler on this same Victor Red Seal label and had to compare the two great violin virtuosos. The Victor Company really loved this tune because in a few months the Thais Meditation appeared to me again and this time the artist was Maude Powell. [this is pre-1920] … Thus a new aspect of collecting was opened up to me. Later on as a collector-dealer, I stumbled into a goodly number of variations of a tune called Tiger Rag introduced in 1917 by the Original Dixieland Jazz Band. Now I became a serious fanatic. I scoured through stacks and stacks of records to come up with every conceivable rendition and just my luck, there were hundreds of recorded versions. (Corenthal, 1986: Introduction)

With his dealer's hat on, Corenthal also participated in such a search for a collector 'desperately seeking' to complete a Wayne King collection:

---

[1]   The set became a foundation stone for the American folk music revival of the 1950s and 1960s, influencing performers such as Bob Dylan, Roger McGuinn (the Byrds) and Jerry Garcia (the Grateful Dead). It has continued to exert an influence, especially among folk revivalists.

He had searched high and low in his career to locate everything Wayne King had ever recorded. He even convinced Wayne King himself to part with rare transcriptions after agreeing to have everything placed on tape. And yet with his devotional search and dedicated effort, one disc had eluded him. This was a Wayne King selection on a 1931 Victor Orthophonic recording of Stardust coupled with Ted Weem's version of My Favorite Band. The recording issued at the height of the depression was only moderately successful and eventually dropped from the catalogue [Victor later reissued it around 1934 but with a different coupling]. The fellow in fact had several of these but was adamant about owning Victor #22656 containing the original issue. Finally I obtained the record. The fellow arrived with a record album containing space for ten discs from the beginning of Wayne King's career. One slot was vacant and this was the pocket for Victor #22656. Once he stuck Stardust in the slot, I doubt if he ever went back to look at those records. That's just part of the strange phenomenon of collecting. (Corenthal, 1986: Introduction)

These examples illustrate the key role played by the hunt in collecting, its obsessional overtones, and the attraction of 'the aura' of the original recording; I will have more to say about these in later chapters.

In addition to collecting particular artists and styles of music, completists began collecting whole series of releases. Prominent examples of this were the Victor company's Red Seal recordings, and the 'Black Platties', blues and jazz records by black artists, produced by Paramount in the 1920s.

Discrimination, authenticity and value

Among collectors of classical music, there was an emphasis on discrimination. This is strongly evident in the editorial columns and other contributions in *The Gramophone* (UK, 1923 on) and in several early collector guides. For example, Boris Semeonoff's *Record collecting; a guide for beginners*, published in 1949, regarded collecting as a process involving discrimination, rather than simply personal taste: 'Record collecting is a term used loosely to imply no more than the acquiring of a library of recorded music. Collecting, *in the proper sense*, implies taste, discrimination, and, increasingly, knowledge.' And: 'Mere quantity counts for little. Quality in the true sense is what counts, and quality and rarity are by no means synonymous (Semeonoff, 1949: 1). This discrimination is almost entirely predicated on aesthetic criteria, with some reference to the condition of the recording. Here collecting becomes part of the acquisition of middle-class cultural capital and its potential contribution to upward social mobility.

On the other hand, among many collectors of early popular music, discrimination is not so much on aesthetic grounds, as on a preoccupation with authenticity and the aura of the artefact: in some cases the more obscure the recording the better. Again the collection provides a major source of cultural capital, though usually among one's collecting peers rather than a larger social group. This leads to a preoccupation with rarity, condition and economic value. The last was not the primary motivation of early collectors, since prices in the 1920s and '30s were largely still within the reach of most collectors' pockets. However, this changed as the dynamics of supply and demand shifted. While there was still a plethora of 78s available to the collector in the 1940s, some labels, performers and styles were already extremely rare. Semeonoff documented how, following the Second World War, this increased interest in and development of record collecting was evident in the current 'Exchange and Mart' section of *The Gramophone*, compared to a decade earlier. He observed that not only had the number of advertisements greatly increased, but so had prices – 'very considerably' (Semeonoff, 1949: 19). Paradoxically, however, while many early collectors were now prepared to pay large sums for the scarcer recordings, typically more pleasure remained in obtaining an item very cheaply, usually from a seller who has no idea of its 'real' value.

The collecting context

I turn now to the context within which early record collecting took place: the role of the industry, record clubs and societies, and the music press in manipulating and mediating the collecting process; and the hunt for records.

Marketing to collectors

A range of marketing practices emerged amongst the early recording companies. While these were oriented towards the general market, most also targeted the music collector, several almost exclusively so. The most obvious marketing strategy was the production of catalogues and other advertising material. Both of these are themselves now very collectable, and linked to the continued interest in collecting 78s, along with antique phonographs. Victor, Zonophone and Columbia all published catalogues and monthly record supplements from the early 1900s. These alerted retailers and collectors to what was available, and also to what was not; consequently, collectors often lobbied companies to release recordings of particular repertoires/performers.

An important promotional strategy was the production of 'celebrity' discs (by better-known artists), which were sold at a higher price, adding to their cultural cachet. The Gramophone Company of Great Britain released a number of these between 1920 and 1925. They featured different coloured labels, representing different prices, 'which in turn reflected the eminence of the performers' (Copeland, 1991: 39). Perhaps the best-known example of this music industry practice is the well-documented Red Seal recordings. A related marketing practice, since it frequently featured celebrity recordings, was the very successful subscription service introduced in the United Kingdom by HMV in 1931. This collected subscription advances for great but as yet unrecorded classical compositions, making them only when the required commercially viable number of subscribers had been reached, a strategy especially appropriate in the depression years (Chanan, 1995). A further strategy was the release of picture discs, first produced in the 1920s, by companies in Germany, Great Britain and the United States. The best known are those later released by Vogue, in 1946–47, in a limited series (of 74) which became highly collectable. The often visually striking picture discs appealed to collectors attracted by their aesthetics. They also attracted the interest of those who wanted a fuller collection of their preferred performer(s), and had the appeal of a bounded series, with at least the possibility of completion. Usually available commercially, picture discs became a more extensive and established part of the industry's promotional apparatus in the 1980s.

In sum, early retailing strategies and recordings aimed to create and serve record collectors, with industry practices reinforcing the notion of collecting as a selective process, especially in the classical repertoire.

Sites of appreciation

Record appreciation societies were similarly important for fostering collecting as a selective activity, involving the acquisition of discrimination, discernment and cultural capital. Initially, this was especially the case in relation to classical music and, in particular, opera singers. Later, jazz, while originally a populist genre (the Jazz Age of the 1920s), proved increasingly attractive to those looking to explore a more musically complex style of popular music.

A key example of this process was the U.K. Gramophone Society. A number of local groups came together in 1923 to form a national association, linked to a new publication, *The Gramophone*, edited by Compton McKenzie. A 1933 survey of the Society showed it to have 33 member societies, with approximately 1,500 members. Four had existed prior to 1914, but most had formed during the previous few years. Initially there was an emphasis on the intricacies of sound reproduction and its technologies, but later there was a marked shift towards musical appreciation: 'The new societies are generally small groups of intelligent music lovers ... it is the aim of nearly every society to effect an interchange of ideas on nearly every type of music, thus promoting an all-round appreciation of the musical art.'[2] In the United States, the hot jazz clubs and jazz societies of the 1930s (Lopez, 2002) played a similar role for their sub-genre, as did those in the United Kingdom (Parsonage, 2005)· In Japan, the initial development of record collecting emphasized 'the appropriation of foreign music'. Listening clubs, established around 1915–16, and guides to Western classical music, which first appeared in the 1920s, guided the early collectors 'toward the Western sensibility; the [musical] connoisseurship was thus "borrowed" and authenticated' (Hosokawa and Matsuoka, 2004: 151, 153).

---

[2]   *The Gramophone*, 1936, 14 (158): 86.

Sites of acquisition

Where collectors acquired recordings depended to an extent on what styles of music were being collected, and the initial appearance of these. Reflecting its early dominance of recordings, the classical repertoire, especially its vocalists, was the first genre to have been systematically collected. Jazz collecting became prominent in the 1930s, with some emergent interest in early blues. However, most early American popular music remained a neglected form through the 1930s, with very few collectors and extremely limited resources to facilitate their efforts.

So, where did the early record collectors obtain their recordings? Two main sites were utilized: conventional retail, including mail order, and a variety of second-hand sources. Sheet music retailers quickly moved into selling recorded music, and mail order was available from the late 1890s. Record company catalogues, and the adverts in early issues of *The Gramophone* and the jazz-oriented *Melody Maker* (1926 on) provide evidence of both. In the case of the classical repertoire, retail and mail order were the main sources for additions to the collection. Given the relatively easy availability of classical recordings, and their largely middle-class consumers, the culture of classical collecting did not need to associate with the 'down market' practice of scavenging through thrift stores and such like.

Recordings in the popular repertoire were also available through retail music shops, but their circulation was more restricted. Jazz and blues records had limited distribution and sales through the 1920s and much of the '30s as most record stores were limited in the labels they sold. Collecting hot jazz records, therefore,

> ... meant generally rummaging for jazz records in remainder bins at furniture shops, junkyards, or Salvation Army depots located mostly in black neighbourhoods. More committed collectors would roam black neighbourhoods door to door [referred to as canvassing], or take autos, buses, and trains to different parts of the country searching for jazz records. (Lopez, 2002: 160)

John Hammond relates his regular search through New York stores for records, as a teenager in the early 1920s:

> I was paid $1 a week as my allowance, and for that I could take the bus down Fifth Avenue to 37th Street, spend an hour at the Widener store listening to new Columbia and Okeh releases on which most of the early Negro and country artists appeared. Then I spend half an hour at the Hardman-Peck store, where Brunswicks were sold, and finally I stopped for a couple of minutes at Landay's Victor Records store. I could spend seventy-five cents, which would buy one ten-inch Columbia or Brunswick record, take the bus home, and have a dime for the rest of the week. (Hammond, 1977: 30)

In the United States, the buyers of many earlier blues and jazz records were almost exclusively poor blacks, and the few records sold generally were played on inferior equipment, resulting in damage or destruction. Consequently, as Hilbert later observed in his guide to prices for such material: 'There are many jazz and blues records that exist only in a handful of copies' (Hilbert, 1998: Introduction). A few original collectors of popular genres bought off the shelf as the recordings were issued. Later, in the 1930s, used records could often be found by 'junking' or canvassing, searching a neighbourhood house by house, asking occupants if they had any old records (often holding up a 78 to make clear what sort of records were sought). This practice continued into the 1950s, although there were decreasing returns by the 1960s, as the sources and numbers of surviving recordings dried up and became fully exploited.

There developed among collectors of early American/old time music a major emphasis on this hunt aspect of collecting, with frequent tales of canvassing, trawling for material and finds of rare recordings. Jerry Wexler[3] recalls: 'We were record collectors, fierce and indefatigable. To discover, in the back of some basement in far Rockaway, a carton of unopened, still-in-original wrappers sets of Black Swan – a label owned by W. C. Handy and responsible for Ethel Waters first recordings – was an experience second only to orgasm' (cited in Lopez, 2002: 261) – and one gets the impression that some collectors gave their collections the higher priority!

Richard Nevins recalls how rare records like Champion 16,000s could usually only be found by canvassing, knocking on doors in rural southern locales where old blues country records had originally been predominately sold:

> Many of the great collectors in the eastern U.S. were put together with a great deal of canvassing back in the 1950s and 60s when 78s were still in the same houses in which they had been purchased in the 1920s and 30s. The folks who had bought them originally still had them, but stored them away after LPs and 45s became the current formats. We used to knock on doors and ask folks if they had any old records that they didn't play anymore and would consider selling. Just about any house in the South in which people over 60 lived still had records from 40 to 50 years ago, and most were happy to sell the old unplayed discs. (Nevins, 2006)

Through the 1930s, hot jazz clubs ran swap meets, and some began to run auctions. By the early 1940s there were jazz record stores, which usually had a bin or two of used records in addition to new stock. But the wider hunt aspect remained vital, as Harriet Hershe (in 1940) shows in her lament on life married to a hot jazz collector:

> He collects every available record in every available spare moment … he can make the necessary excursions to the darkest part of the city and countryside,

---

[3] Jerry Wexler, 1917–2008, went on to have a high-profile and very successful career in the music industry, primarily as a producer for Atlantic from 1954 to 1979.

canvass the basements of second-hand stores, and Salvation Army outlets ... He goes about with a haggard, hazy look, a copy of *Downbeat* in one hand, and a record catalogue in the other. (Lopez, 2002: 159)

Sites of mediation: the music press

The experience of Harriet Hershe's husband, with its reference to *Downbeat*, hints at the importance of the music press to the avid record collector. We now tend to take for granted an extensive literature serving record collectors, including general guidebooks, discographies, critics 'best of' and consumer record guides, and collector-oriented magazines. Together these are involved in creating and maintaining a set of collecting practices and conventional wisdom, especially notions of the canon – what is/should be collectable (see Chapter 4). Early collectors had far less available to help them, and often produced the forerunners of today's plethora of publications. Here I refer briefly to several of these early efforts, and the manner in which they consolidated a number of central themes in collecting.

Publications on recordings of classical music strongly emphasized discrimination, almost entirely predicated on aesthetic criteria, although with some reference to condition. This is particularly evident in the editorial columns and other contributions in *The Gramophone* (UK, 1923), where collecting becomes part of cultural capital and upward social mobility. It has justifiably been viewed as 'the first magazine in any language to treat recorded music as seriously as the great British literary reviews examined the written word' (LeMahieu, 1988: 172). After selling an impressive 500 copies a month in its first year, by the late 1920s its sales had reached 12,000 per issue. Its own survey of readers (in 1931) showed them to be largely a broad cross-section of the professional middle classes. *The Gramophone* reviewed new releases, disseminated information on technical developments in sound reproduction, and encouraged record companies to produce and the public to buy 'serious music', a label essentially equated with the classical canon.

Several early collector guides offered additional advice and information to the classical collector. EMG Hand Made Gramophones Ltd published a series on 'The Art of Record Buying' (available free prior to the Second World War; the last appeared in 1940). Johnson refers to it as 'Probably one of the first selected record catalogues to be issued, and one of the best' (Johnson, 1954). More significant was Morton Moses' *The Record Collector's Guide: American Celebrity Discs*, first published in 1936 as a 44-page pamphlet. The first edition was followed by a fuller version in 1949, in which Moses observed that 'the interest in collectors' recordings has increased tremendously' since his earlier guide.

The period covered by Moses (in his 1949 edition) is between the release of the first Columbia celebrity discs in April 1903, and the issuance of the first complete Victor catalogue in January 1912: the era of acoustical recording. The catalogue is arranged alphabetically, by artist, from Bessie Abbot to Nicola Zerola. Moses stressed the educational role of his guidebook, and the esoteric nature of record collecting and the role of specialized knowledge was already evident. He observed that the would-be collector of rare records must learn to distinguish between five types of Victor labels: the early Monarch (10 inch) and De Luxe (12 inch) labels; the Grand Prize label, adopted 1 December 1905; the Patents label, adopted in 1908, with three variants to the endings of the patent numbers at the bottom of the label; the No-Patents label, adopted in 1914; and the Victrola label of subsequent single- and double-faced issues.

> Anyone with an interest in opera and its greatest stars should find this information valuable. To know how many records an artist made, what selections he sang, how old he was at the time, cannot be regarded as unimportant. To be stimulated by this knowledge to a further investigation of the achievements of some of the world's most talented musicians would be an even greater compliment to the purposes of this book. (Moses, 1949 [1936]: Preface)

Moses refers to the increasing scarcity and value of many of these recordings, especially where the master recordings were soon destroyed. The majority of Columbia records included in his book fell within this category. His guide has remained in print, and second-hand copies continue to fetch good prices, indicative of the continued interest in 78 collecting.

Discrimination continued to be emphasized by the post-war guides; for instance, Blanks detailed overview of Western classical recordings is subtitled *A Record Collector's Guide to Music Appreciation* (Blanks, 1968). In such views, 'planning a record collection is more than a matter of personal taste ... as well as being curtailed by economy, personal taste must also be limited by selectiveness' (Gillies, 1966: 7). As Bryant (1962: 22) observed, guidelines were necessary given the vast selection of recordings already available.

Accordingly, such guides provided guidance on 'the best' of the available recordings. Gillies sought to 'deepen our awareness of the range of music offered on records', in the process aiming to provide 'a realistic selection from the music of every period' (Gillies 1966: Introduction).

As noted earlier, Semeonoff observes that the rapid expansion of collecting can be seen by comparing the 'Exchange and Mart' section of a current issue of *The Gramophone* with a pre-war issue. Not only are there an increased number of listings, but 'prices have increased very considerably' (Semeonoff, 1949: 2). However: 'Music lovers do not know how to set about increasing the scope of their collections, nor what pitfalls are to be avoided. It is to the beginner that this book is addressed. No attempt has been made to cater for the specialist or the advanced collector' (Semeonoff, 1949: Introduction). His chapters indicate the scope of such guides, dealing with the history of recording; formats (from the acoustical to the electrical age), with reference to the numbering systems used by the early recording companies; Good and Bad Recordings; Dating and Identification; the Condition of Records; Storage and Indexing; Gramophone Societies; Literature;

including periodicals, yearbooks, and company catalogues; Shops and Buying by Post. Later chapters cover Singers; Instrumentalists; Conductors and Orchestras; and Jazz (a chapter contributed by Alexander Ross).

The hunt, and the chance of a 'find', is central to these accounts: 'One never knows when something one has been looking for months or even years, is going to turn up. There is, too, the chance of finding records one did not know even existed' (Semeonoff, 1949: 2). This was a possibility underpinned by the unsystematic operating practices of the early record companies, and made knowledge central to building the collection. Gillies suggests that having obtained a player and a few records, the novice collector's 'next step should be a subscription to a good record review' (Gillies, 1966: Introduction). Following this advice himself, Blanks praises *The Gramophone* as a key source, referring to how he also went through all the back issues to become familiar with the available repertoire, and the recommended recordings contained in it (Blanks, 1968: 3).

The early recording companies were frequently very unsystematic in their operating practices, especially in terms of tracking inventory and cataloguing releases. While some catalogues were produced, there was a general lack of these, especially from the smaller companies, along with a failure to keep thorough records of releases. There was also the ephemeral nature of much of this material, which was then rarely kept in libraries and archives. This lack of systematic and accessible information on releases made collecting a challenge, a detective-like activity adding to the thrill of the chase: the hunt for elusive or even unknown or unrecorded items. In so doing, it fostered discography as an important aspect of collecting.

In 1934, the French critic Charles Delaunay was the first to publish a comprehensive discography, a word he coined. His *Hot Discography* was then published in English in 1936, while in 1935 the first such British compilation had been published: *Rhythm on Record*, by Hilton Schelman, assisted by Stanley Dance. These two books were 'a basis for and inspiration to later works of similar character' (Godbolt, 1984: 175). Through the later 1920s and through the 1930s, hundreds of discographies of early jazz and jazz-related recordings were produced by collector enthusiasts, often in home-produced magazines, sometimes in the pages of Britain's jazz-oriented *Melody Maker*, *Hot News* and *Swing Music*. At times, heated arguments raged over attribution and provenance of particular artists and recordings, and the intricacies of various labels' notation/cataloguing practices. This vernacular scholarship provided an essential resource for major compilations to come (see Godbolt, 1984; Lopez, 2002; Parsonage, 2005).

Beyond the 78 era

What I have termed the 78 era was over by 1960. The 78 as a format had been supplanted by vinyl by the end of the 1950s, and the gramophone replaced by new forms of sound reproduction. But the passing of the 78 recording did not end interest in the era and its music. The recordings and the equipment used to play them have remained highly collectable. A number of those who had begun their collecting during the 1940s and 1950s continued to do so, and were joined by younger collectors attracted by the 78s' associations with authenticity and romance. Indeed, since the 1960s, there has been a proliferation of interest in gramophone culture, with a considerable amount of scholarship devoted to documenting its music and the associated technologies. A good deal of this research has been undertaken by collectors.

Who and why

Contemporary collectors of 78s display similar practices and behaviours as their earlier counterparts: a mix of a love of pre-1950 musical styles, completism and a concern for authenticity, rarity and value. The collectors of 78 recordings in the 1960s and 1970s were an older group. Many such collectors had grown up through the era of 78s, and became collectors at an early age: for example, Joe Bussard, born in 1936, started collecting at age ten; and Sam Charters, born in 1929, began buying old recordings by American blues musicians in his teens. In 1985, when Corenthal interviewed and recorded the recollections of six major collectors of 78s, five were in their 60s.

This aging constituency were now joined by younger collectors, attracted by the 78s' associations with musical authenticity and the romance of a nostalgic past. Soderbergh (1983) cites a 1980 survey of US collectors of 78s which showed that 32 per cent were not old enough to remember the 78 era, so they were presumably born around 1945–50. Some were collecting the CD and vinyl reissues of the 78 era, as well as the original recordings. Former rock musician Jeff Healey, with his band The Jazz Wizards, drew on Healey's lifelong love of 1920s jazz and his extensive collection for a new album of old standards: *Among Friends* (2002). Healy states why he was attracted to the project: 'It's a classic time period in American songwriting … I've always actively acquired records from the '20s and '30s. I now sit here with 25,000 78s and 4,000 CDs of material issues from that period, so there's a fair amount of material to choose from.'[4]

To play 78s, you need equipment that is much less commonly available now. To a degree, this presents a barrier to accessing the music the fragile shellac recordings contain, but it also forms part of their appeal: the ritual aspect of handling and playing them on gramophones (similar to the appeal of vinyl and turntables to collectors of vinyl recordings). There is also, to varying extent, an associated 'rejection' of the present era and its music: Corenthal refers to 'how misguided efforts [record price guides, which largely ignore pre-1950 music and 78s] can so monopolize and homogenize younger generations that they virtually eliminate competition of musical forms', replacing this with a preoccupation with

---

[4]   *Eye Music*, Toronto, 20 June 2002: 27. Healey died in 2008.

'sexuality, drugs and noise distortion' (Corenthal, 1986: 19). Joe Bussard profiler Dean recounts how

> ... a jeep packed with teenagers swings past the window, blaring bass-heavy rap that resonates for blocks around. 'Listen to that shit', hisses Bussard. 'Boom! Boom! Boom!' He begins to rail against the contemporary world anew, once again comparing it with the '20s, the zenith of Western civilization. He rhapsodizes about this lost age and its enduring artistry. (Dean, 2001)

As with the earlier collectors, cultural preservation and enjoyment of the music of the gramophone era are central themes. Many contemporary 78 collectors are involved in radio programmes, reissue-oriented recording companies, and historical research, especially the production of discographies. The editors of an extensive early bibliography noted how:

> On the research level, many full or part-time hobbyists have turned to constructing biographies, discographies, and comprehensive articles on the many available subjects which the era includes. Others are experimenting to re-record the finer material of the era on modern tape equipment for the dual purpose of reissue in LP form and preservation of what is now recognized as a dynamic part of the oral, social, historical, and musical heritage of America. (Betz and Betz, 1966)

A few brief examples of such contributions must stand here for a wider body of such work.

Dr John Grams, a collector of jazz recordings and a radio broadcaster, through the 1960s and '70s ran a five-hour radio show every Saturday evening, offering jazz appreciation for a new generation of collectors. He also prepared a series of short radio spots for public radio, chronologically highlighting developments in jazz history, and taught jazz courses at Marquette University (Corenthal, 1986). From 1956 to 1970, Joe Bussard ran the last 78 record label Fonotone, dedicated to releasing new recordings of old time music – in 2005, a five-CD anthology of Fonotone releases was issued by Dust-to-Digital. Bussard gladly shares his collection; he has long taped recordings for a nominal sum, and undertaken a number of radio programmes; recently he established his own website and he is also on MySpace. Walter Welsh was for many years a collector of early acoustical phonographs, records and related memorabilia. While a professor at Syracuse University, he invented and patented a system for reproducing acoustical recordings, co-wrote a key study of the early development of sound recording (Welsh and Burt, 1994) and developed the Syracuse Archive. Allen Koenigsberg, drawing on his own collection, and with the input of other collectors, produced a detailed history of the development of Edison cylinders (1988), and edited *The Antique Phonograph Monthly* (APM Press, Brooklyn, 1972–), a scholarly publication providing a forum for those interested in the 78 era. Finally,

Richard Nevins drew on his own collection and borrowed recordings from others to compile a collection of rare 78s:

> This 2 CD set is comprised of super rarities and unissued gems that would cause even the most advanced collectors to sit up and take notice – one might consider many of the tracks to be as revelatory in their domain as the Dead Sea Scrolls were in theirs. Indeed, a number of selections will be heard here for the very first time as no existing copies have been found before, while many others that survive only one known copy have lain hidden away out of common access. Some of the unissued test pressings used here have been sparsely heard before, but only in very poor sound quality that failed to impart their power and eloquence. Show a collector of old 78 records items like the Son House and Georgia Potlickers one-of-a-kind rarities that appear here and he'll tell you items like that are 'the stuff that dreams are made of.' (Nevins, 2006)

The tradition of the record collector as an archivist and cultural preserver has been an ongoing and influential one.

What is collected: rarity and value

Early cylinders are now extremely rare, and acoustical disc recordings prior to 1925 are also scarce. So too are early gramophones. Increased interest in pre-1950s recordings generally, combined with the relative scarcity of particular genres, artists and labels, meant that the rarer recordings had become economic investments by the 1980s. Soderbergh observed,

> ... the 78s that bring the stiffest prices are seldom the garden variety records such as you and I possess. If I were to characterize the most prized 78s on the current market, it would be a disc featuring black artists released on an uncommon label, recorded between 1920–1934, that did not sell a million copies, and was jazz or jazz-inflected (rather than of the pop swing persuasion). (Soderbergh, 1983: 11)

Writing in 1988, Hilbert noted that each year more of the fragile and easily-broken 78s are destroyed or lost: 'the supply dwindles, the demand sizzles and prices soar.' (Hilbert, 1988: Introduction). He was referring to jazz and blues 78s, but his comment was more generally applicable. Critical of the 'pricing books flooding the market' in the early 1980s, with their emphasis on 'eccentric oddities', Corenthal (1986: 18–20) offered his own selection of a dozen rare recordings from the 78 era. Drawing on various published guides, Soderbergh listed 132 records now priced at $50 or more in contemporary guides. He was astonished to find 'so many records with such lofty price tags'. 'Had I lowered that figure to $10, there would be at least 500 items on the list.' He emphasized that top prices held only for a record that's condition is 'clearly excellent' (Soderbergh, 1983).

More recently, the advertising in collector magazines such as *Discoveries* and *Goldmine*, and the bidding wars on sites such as eBay, illustrate how many items are now beyond the reach of all but the wealthiest collectors. The market for blues 78s by artists such as Robert Johnson continues to be strong: in 2007 a copy of his 'Preaching Blues' sold for £3,332 on eBay, despite its B-side 'Love in Vain' being graded at E (*Record Collector*, 344, Christmas 2007). Rock'n'roll 78s have become one of the hottest commodities in the record-collecting world. 'In general, the rarest rock 78s are the most obscure issues on the best-loved labels – early Sun, Chess, and Vee-Jay releases, for example. The most expensive, on the other hand, tend to be those by the best-known artists' (Thompson, 2002: 101), as with the Everly Brothers 78s released in the British market, but not released in the United States.

Sites of acquisition

Although there are still finds to be made, the days of 'junking' are now largely over. Accordingly, record dealers have become more important as a source of recordings for collectors. The first national directory of collectable-record dealers, published in 1980, could already include over 250 dealers in over 40 American states (Felton, 1980). Collectors' magazines such as *Goldmine*, *Discoveries* [now defunct] and the UK-based *Record Collector* include extensive dealer advertising, usually listing records for auction or set sale (at fixed prices), so also collectors' (and dealers') 'wants lists'. Only a small proportion of this is for 78s, but they remain an important niche market. Record fairs and conventions, some now very large in scale, still include dealers specializing in 78s, as do some auction houses. The internet has added a new locale for these activities (see Chapter 5).

Literature serving 78 collectors

As interest in collecting 78s, along with their associated players and memorabilia, continued into the 1960s, a range of publications catered to it. An example was *The Record Finder*, published ten times per annum, out of Vermont in the United States. Regular features included 78 auction announcements, set sales, trade news, want ads and record collector convention dates and locations. Soderbergh (1983: 49) suggested, 'Becoming an avid reader of *Record Finder* is an excellent way to penetrate the veil that separates sane people from 78 rpm lovers.' The best-known price guide remains Les Dock's key reference on early American music generally: the *American Premium Record Guide*, included 45,000 recordings from 1915 to the early 1960s, with guidelines regarding condition and grading of records, and a large selection of label illustrations. First published in 1980, the volume became the key guide in the field, with subsequent editions (up to a 6th edition published in 2002).

As 78 collectors became more numerous and more organized, there was an increased availability of information and guidance on various collectable genres. In the jazz field, for example, the International Association of Jazz Record Collectors, *Joslin's Jazz Journal* (US) and *Vintage Jazz Market* (UK), and new discographies, such as those by Brian Rust, assisted in the creation of a world-wide market. As Hilbert himself claimed, guides such as his own marked an important step toward changing jazz record collecting from a relatively obscure 'underground' hobby into an investment opportunity by establishing accurate pricing on jazz and ragtime records (Hilbert, 1988: Introduction). Several early books on the development of sound recording (especially Gellat, 1977), laid the foundations for subsequent scholarship on this topic. The collecting of antique gramophones and phonographs has been stimulated by several comprehensive and attractive studies (Fabrizio and Paul, 1997; 2000). These scholars are record collectors and active members of the 78 societies.

Conclusion

The emergence and subsequent development of record collecting parallels the development of the music industry during the gramophone age. This was primarily in relation to recording formats and sound reproduction, but also with the emergence of music retail and the music press. The historical developments and examples sketched here laid the groundwork for later collecting practices. The 78 era established 'record collecting' as a major activity, with its own set of collecting practices, associated literature and appreciation societies. Collectors and collecting since the gramophone age have continued to exhibit these earlier preoccupations and trends, though with new inflections. It is to these contemporary collectors that I now turn.

Chapter 2

The contemporary collector: beyond the *High Fidelity* stereotype

The popular image of contemporary record collectors is of obsessive males, whose 'trainspotting' passion for collecting is often a substitute for 'real' social relationships. I have termed this 'the *High Fidelity* stereotype' (Shuker, 2004), after the novel by Nick Hornby. It is one that can draw on some support from academic discussions of collectors and collecting, but it represents only a partial account of record collectors. Interviews with self-identified contemporary collectors, along with reference to a number of other published profiles of record collectors (see Appendix 1), show they demonstrate a complex mix of characteristics: a love of music; obsessive-compulsive behaviour, accumulation and completism; selectivity and discrimination; and self-education and scholarship. These are, of course, very much the set of characteristics identified with the collectors of the 78 era (see Chapter 1); they are further explored here, while the associated collecting practices introduced are returned to in subsequent chapters. As a social practice, contemporary record collecting presents itself as a core component of individual social identity and a central part of the life cycle.

Social location

As indicated in my introduction, collecting in general is an activity that cuts across social class, gender and ethnicity. But how accurate is that general situation for record collectors? My own opportunity sample consisted largely of academics and graduate students, along with a few working as journalists and in the music industry. The collectors profiled in *Record Collector*, *Goldmine* and elsewhere largely work within the music industry (as DJs, musicians, label owners, graphic artists) or in professional occupations. Those featuring in other published discussions of record collectors also seem to be largely from the middle class.[1] The middle-class/ professional location of these collectors raises questions as to their typicality. Their emphasis on discrimination, along with frequent reference to the size, rarity and economic value of their collections (see the discussion below), arguably may well distinguish them from other 'classed' collecting constituencies.

---

[1]   This tentative assertion is based on the jobs they occupy. The extent of a working-class constituency of record collectors, and the nature of their collecting practices, warrants further investigation.

The social variable that has received the greatest attention in discussion of record collectors is gender.[2] Unlike collecting in general, record collecting is usually perceived as a male-dominated activity. The available evidence supports the popular image of 'the male record collector'. Record collectors active on related websites appear to be mainly males, although the use of gender neutral or 'misleading' email addresses make it difficult to claim this with total authority. A Record Collector's Guild poll in 2004 on the gender of members elicited only 77 responses. Only 14 of these were women, suggesting a ratio of only around 18 per cent of the membership, which then included 296 users. The readership of the *Record Collector* is 95 per cent male,[3] while its feature 'The Collector' is dominated by males. My own original interviews included only 11 women, roughly 16 per cent of my total collector group. *Vinyl*, a Canadian documentary on record collectors (dir. Alan Zwieg, 2000), included only five females among its 100 subjects.

Popular culture texts reinforce this pattern and image of a male dominated field. Fictional record collectors, as with the main protagonists of *Ghost World*, *High Fidelity* and those in the comics by Robert Crumb (a collector himself; see Milano, 2003) and Harvey Pekar are men. The huge success, especially among male readers, of Nick Hornby's novel *High Fidelity*, suggested considerable empathy with Rob Fleming, a record shop owner who is a committed record collector. His shop, Championship Vinyl, 'for the serious record collector', only gets by because of mail order, and 'the people who make a special effort to shop here Saturdays – young men – always young men' (Hornby, 1995: 38). The majority of my collectors, especially the males, drawing on personal observation, agreed that record collecting is largely a male activity:

- 'Yes, it's definitely a male pursuit. If you go to record conventions, look at DJs, etc. it's probably 95% male dominated.' (Joel Wing)
- 'It is a fact that most people I know that collect records are male.' (Andre Nuchelmans)
- 'It does seem to be a male pastime, I've only once met a female record collector.' (Peter Dawson)

Conversely, the majority of the women collectors were conscious of being in a visible minority:

'I would have to agree. The times I've spent attending record swaps, searching record stores I have found myself in the minority. There have been times I have had to "prove" to other collectors that I am not a girl who simply likes record

---

[2]   Ethnicity is rarely commented on in relation to record collecting. My own interviews included several Asian Americans, and a number of prominent Black American DJs are record collectors.

[3]   As stated at www.recordcollectormag.com/advertising (accessed November 2008).

collecting because their boyfriend got them into it ... which is frustrating and sad.' (Michelle Wauchope)

For male collectors, the social role of collecting appears to be a significant part of masculinity. Straw suggests:

> record collections, like sports statistics, provide the raw materials around which the rituals of homosocial interaction take shape. Just as ongoing conversation between men shapes the composition and extension of each man's collection, so each man finds, in the similarity of his points of reference to his peers, confirmation of a shared universe of critical judgment. (Straw, 1997a: 5)

In common with other forms of collecting, record collecting can represent a public display of power and knowledge, serving as a form of cultural capital within the peer group. As Straw puts it, record collecting can be regarded as 'either structures of control or the by-products of irrational and fetishistic obsession: as material evidence of the homosocial information-mongering which is one underpinning of male power and compensatory undertakings by those unable to wield that power' (Straw, 1997a: 4).

As Laura Vroomen observed, 'the definition of collecting that's usually employed relies on a particular type of collecting that is probably more common among men.' This was evident in the comments of male collectors, such as Andrew Stafford: 'Seeing High Fidelity, and thinking about my own friends, has brought it home to me that I know very few *genuine* female collectors' (my emphasis). His use of the term 'genuine' suggests a definition based on collection size and the 'serious' approaches taken by males to their collecting, a view also implicit in comments such as Keith Beattie's: 'I have to agree that it probably is a male activity. I rarely see females raking through the second hand bins with the same fervour as males, and I have rarely come across females with sizeable collections of music.' Here, the category of 'record collector' is clearly a socially constructed one.

Supporting Straw's analysis, the male need to display cultural capital was also acknowledged as a factor: 'Yes I agree but I have few ideas why, maybe men want to impress people more with their collecting ability' (Warren Green); a point also recognized by women collectors: 'perhaps men talk about music and their collections with more confidence, so that it seems as if that kind of activity is more common among them' (Laura Vroomen). Lee Ann Fullington, reflecting on her experiences working in an indie record shop, observed:

> 'We called the record collectors who were obsessive (white labels, obscurantists, completes, etc.) record psychos. These collectors, were MEN, always MEN, and they came in regularly and spent regularly pretty good proportions of their incomes on specific artists, genres, and pressings. While several women were just as passionate about collecting records/CDs, the obsession did not manifest

itself in their behaviour as obviously as it did for the men. Men were more likely
to enthuse or go on and on about a particular find.'

In her study of women record collectors, Bogle set out to challenge Straw's claim
that record collecting was a male dominated practice. Through two initial contacts,
and within a day, she found 11 women collectors, each of whom volunteered
further contacts for her study: 'The mere fact that, had I wanted to, I could have
communicated with as many as fifty or sixty women who collect records (mostly
in New Zealand, but with two in England, and another in Japan) certainly proves
the point that women collectors are out there.' What she found striking was the
tendency for women to play down the fact they are collectors. While passionate
about their collections, and the process of hunting down records, 'they are put off
by the term record collector, and its possible masculine, and even anal connotations'
(Bogle, 1999: 6).

This was true of most of the woman collectors I interviewed, and is illustrated
by Norma Coates, who characterized collecting as:

> 'Dweeby; very male-oriented. I couldn't care less about alternate takes or
> terribly obscure bands from the Raleigh, NC scene. I am a denizen of used-CD
> and vinyl stores when time permits, but to fill in holes in my knowledge rather
> than to search for some goodie. I see collecting as akin to being a fan of baseball
> or sports stats; kind of a useless pursuit, less driven by music or musical taste
> and more driven by the need to exert masculine power/knowledge.'

Explanations for the gendered nature of record collecting are complex, and fall
roughly into those emphasizing psychological/personality characteristics, and
those preferring social/cultural explanations.

Psychological/personality characteristics

My collectors frequently shared Straw's view that, for men, record collecting
embraced being in control, through competitive display demonstrating knowledge,
and asserting cultural capital and power:

- 'It's a need to control, to tame, to connect through artefacts to previous
  people, places, moods. Record people tend to be more intellectually
  centred, not so much emotionally centred, it's a neurotic thing, what do
  female neurotics do?' (Craig Morrison)
- 'It has to do with things like possessiveness, control and impracticality
  – very well-known traits of the modern bourgeois Western male.' (Motti
  Regev)
- 'Ownership of objects and arranging, cataloguing, counting, storing and
  getting on top of the collector's discourse, is a way of confirming control,

especially important when men are so indoctrinated to believe they must be.' (Bruce Johnson)

Knowledge and demonstrating mastery of a collectable field were seen as particularly important in relation to genre scenes traditionally gendered as male, most notably hard rock and heavy metal (see Leonard, 2007). Several male collectors observed that these genres are in the main aimed at a male audience, the majority of their successful artists are male, and males are usually regarded as being the most skilful rock musicians. Accordingly, they considered that for many males there is an element of identification with their 'heroes' through collecting their records and acquiring related cultural capital. Albert Bell observes how this is very evident in the case of heavy metal:

> 'In this case I guess it tends to reflect male predominance in the metal scene. Although, this has somewhat dissipated over the years I can't say that it has had any effect on the collecting process. Although audiences and artistes denote an increasing female involvement, collecting has remained at least in my experience a male activity. My guess is, at least when it comes to metal, that male involvement in the scene is much more intensive and long-lasting. Males also long for status within the (metal) scene and when it comes to metal this generally demands an extensive knowledge of the music and to be conversant with the diversity of genres and bands that constitute the music.'

Albert, who was heavily involved in Malta's metal scene, relates this to the constitution of male identity and masculine peer group bonding:

> 'I also feel that my collection resounds with my deeply entrenched bonds with the genre and the metal scene. To stop collecting items would be to severe these bonds, and that is something unthinkable for many who like me have a significant part of their identity moulded with the genre. Undoubtedly, female bonding with metal tends to be more peripheral and transient. In my view this is symptomatic of the fact that the motivations for female involvement in metal are somewhat dissimilar to those of males.' (Albert Bell)

Sociological and cultural factors

Many respondents referred to the range of social variables involved in shaping the gender imbalance in record collecting, including the points that men generally have more disposable income than women; they are perhaps less likely to feel obligated to spend 'their' money on home and children; rock music is a male dominated cultural sphere; and the way particular forms of knowledge, and modes of engaging with technology, have traditionally been encoded as 'masculine' within Western society. As Keir Keightley put it, 'women aren't driven to forms of "conspicuous seriousness" in the ways men are, in part because the very idea of seriousness has historically been gendered as masculine for a long time in Western culture.' For Michelle: 'If I had to find a reason why, I would probably say it's caught up in the notion that "serious" music is male music, and as only "serious" music is collected, by default only guys collect (Michelle Wauchope).

A further aspect here is the general male dominance of the record industry generally (see Leonard, 2007, for a helpful summary of the relevant literature), and particular collecting environments. That males make up the majority of customers at record fairs, second hand and specialist/indie record shops and other collecting sites, 'scares a lot of woman off' (Joe Kelich). This is also the case in particular music scenes, such as the DJ community: 'Part of it is self-perpetuating ... it's a very male environment and thus doesn't really encourage the entry of women into that space' (Oliver Wang).[4]

As already indicated, women collectors are frequently conscious of this labelling issue and the association of record collecting with males: 'I think that's true [that record collecting is perceived as primarily a male pursuit], but probably because of labels more than anything else' (Liz Giuffre). The question of what happens when girls/women collect is a fascinating one, and can be related to the question of the labels we put on things, including the differing conceptions of the 'fan' as compared to the 'collector'. As Steve Wakesman observes,

> 'what happens if we consider a 12-year-old girl's collection of N'Sync albums and other items as a significant form of record collecting? On that level, it may not be that women don't collect as that the modes of collecting in which girls and women have most often engaged aren't invested with the same sort of authority.'

My daughter Emma, at age ten regarded her 17 recordings – primarily by S Club 7 and Britney Spears – as a collection: 'When you are interested in a band you try to collect lots of stuff about them. You collect posters, CDs, videos, and look them up on the web' (Emma Shuker). Later, as a teenager, she referred to herself as 'a collector' (although now of film DVDs rather than music).

Several common themes emerged from my interviews with women collectors: they placed a greater emphasis on the 'use value' of their recordings, and showed less concern with collection size, rarity and value. It is worth noting, however, that many male collectors shared the same broad orientation. For example, Belgian collector Michelle (as in the English Michael) Henry observed 'Collectors have picture discs, sealed copies, etc. that can't be played or they lose their value. I love music – if I can't listen to it, I won't buy or keep it.' The explanations offered for why record collecting is male dominated are underpinned by different, gender inflected definitions of the field.

---

[4]   On the 'maleness' of the DJ community, see Brewster and Broughton (1999: esp. page 9). For the male orientation of indie record shops, see Chapter 5.

Defining the record collector

At this point, I turn to consider further the characteristics of 'the record collector'. As my discussion of gender has indicated, to see oneself as a collector is not as straightforward as might be supposed, often reflecting a reluctance to be associated with the negative behavioural characteristics popularly linked to the label. This reluctance has been noted in other studies of record collectors. For example, several of Montano's interviewees 'seemed reluctant to use the word (collector) itself, either avoiding its use completely, or placing it between inverted commas as a way of suggesting they were not entirely comfortable with its use' (Montano, 2003: 5). However, given an affirmative answer is presumed by their responding to my call for 'subjects', and then completing the initial questionnaire, it was hardly surprising that most of my original respondents simply said 'yes' to the question 'Do you consider yourself a record collector? Further, some (12/67) added emphasis to their response, with comments such as 'yes, definitely' and 'absolutely'.

At times, such ready acceptance was combined with particular conceptions of 'collector': 'Yep, I've got the completist disease' (Mark Vanderdrift); and 'Yes. I realize I'm not in the same league as some collectors. But I am obsessive and addicted to all formats, which is the hallmark of a collector' (Tony Mitchell). Some were at pains to widen the definition, as they collected not just recordings but a range of items associated with a particular musician or group, including videos, calendars, magazines, posters, t-shirts, tour programmes, promotional displays and books. And several were apologetic about it, with comments such as 'reluctantly yes'; 'yes, afraid so'; 'sadly, yes'. This generally foreshadowed their later identification of the typical record collector as an obsessive personality. Accordingly, there were attempts to distance personal practice from a perceived stereotype. This view was underpinned by a particular conception of the record collector, with an emphasis on completism and collection size. Indeed, the status of 'record collector' can be a shifting one, with changing levels of investment – economic, physical and emotional – in the process. (For more on this point, see the collector profiles in Chapter 7.)

A fundamental distinction emerged between the collector who 'loved music', and the collector who was preoccupied with collection size, rarity and economic value. 'I still cling to the belief that I'm a fan of music first, records second' (Keir Keightley). However, use value and exchange value were commonly held in tension. Those who claimed a love of music as central to their collecting were also proud of items they had paid high prices for, or were very valuable.

As suggested here, collectors themselves refer to an interwoven and overlapping set of characteristics and behaviours associated with record collectors and record collecting. A major characteristic identified with record collecting was a love of music, with attention also paid to questions of obsessive-compulsive behaviour; accumulation, completism and collection size; rarity and value; and selectivity, discrimination and cultural capital. These themes structure the discussion which follows.

A love of music

'The ones [collectors] I know truly love music in a visceral, personal way ... they derive an amazing amount of pleasure from finding, buying, sharing and talking about records.' (Oliver Wang)

The sheer appeal of the cultural artefact is sometimes overlooked in popular perceptions of collecting, with emphasis often on negative or socially suspect behaviours associated with collecting. The term 'passion' is at the heart of most accounts of collecting, both (auto-) biographical and critical, and is exemplified in the very titles of some studies: *To Have and to Hold* (Blom); *Collecting: An Unruly Passion* (Muesterberger). Collecting is 'highly involved passionate consumption' (Belk, 2001: 66), rather than a 'standard' form of consumption such as buying household food staples. Such passion includes the collecting *process* – the thrill of the chase and the find – and the pleasure of simply *having* the desired artefact. An emphasis on ownership characterizes some variants of collecting, for example, bibliomania: the book collector who simply collects books as objects; shelved and catalogued; they are collected not read. (Blom, 2002: 200ff.). But passion also embraces the pleasures of *use*.

As the 78 era showed (see Chapter 1), love of the music itself is at the heart of the passion of many collectors. 'To the collector music matters' affirms Stan Denski (Campbell, 2001: 4); you can listen and respond to it in a variety of situations; it has a use value. Many of my respondents used the word 'passion' to explain their love of record collecting:

'The passion I have for hip hop, funk, jazz, and soul is the same passion I read about in articles about 80-year-old collectors who feel no good music came out after 1930. The same passion I read about when a British collector visits Louisiana, enters a warehouse of old 78s, and says "how much for the warehouse?" The same passion a recording engineer has when he discovers an acetate of a recording session he thought was lost in time. Or the same passion young collectors like myself have when they take time to do their research, go out to meet these musicians, and to read about the views of the "young'uns" enjoying a song that was recorded 20 years before they were even born.' (John Book)

In this sense, record collecting is an accentuated, and more committed form of popular music fandom. The lived experience of music variously provides enjoyment and satisfaction – physical, emotional and aesthetic/intellectual – as well as catharsis and emotional support. Yet the use value of recorded music can provide a rationalization for ownership, since the love of music is compromised by the ability of the collector to play only a fraction of the quantity of recorded sounds which make up the collection. The realization that 'there's a limit to how many records it's possible to listen to' (Campbell, 2001: 9), is one that represents a critical point in a collector's life. This does raise some questions about the psychological mechanisms at work in the collecting process, and suggests use can function as a defensive screen for less socially sanctioned reasons for collecting.

Love of music extends beyond collecting and listening to recordings, with collectors demonstrating a strong interest in live music. A *Record Collector* readership survey in 2006 showed 15 per cent of its readers go to a gig once a week or more, while a further 36 per cent see live music at least once and up to three times a month.[5] A similar level of commitment was present among my collectors, although frequency of attendance varied, was related to opportunity and cost, and declined with age. Some saw it as a necessary complement to their collecting, expressing considerable passion for the live experience.

> 'Listening to music but not seeing and hearing music being performed is akin to a sort of cultural necrophilia in my mind. Despite what way too many hip cultural critics and academics say, music is a living breathing thing, not just because audiences listen to and consume and dance to it, but because MUSICIANS PLAY THE DAMN STUFF. It's amazing to me how often this basic fact is tossed aside as unimportant. Granted, the "liveness" of music is a bit more precarious in the digital age, but for me, it's of key importance.' (Steve Waksman)

Which performances were attended, hardly surprisingly reflected musical preferences:

> 'My concert going reflects my collecting: I will see all UK gigs by Dylan and the Stones, and will sometimes go abroad to see some. There are also a certain number of artists who I have a few records from who I like to see live, such as Pulp and Blur. The only one I have left to tick off now is Leonard Cohen. I don't much like concerts where I know nothing of the artist, or don't know the songs.' (Lee Marshall, in 2002; by 2009 he had seen Cohen)

There was at times a willingness to take a chance or check out someone relatively new (to the collector), or to support friends in bands, or who were DJing. Nine of my collectors had played in bands themselves at various times, and there were four who were DJs.

Live gig/concert going tended to decline with age and domestic situations:

- 'Hardly ever these days [has young child, and works shifts], but have been to 100s of them in previous years.' (Peter Dawson)

---

[5] *Record Collector*, December 2007: 123.

- 'Concerts are less frequent in my early 30s dotage; ... I find myself going to quieter shows like Ron Sexsmith (Canadian folk troubadour, wonderful) more often, but that's because the new music I like tends to be in the singer/ songwriter vein.' (Andrew Stafford)

Concert attendance was also restricted by opportunity and cost:

'Yes, whenever there is a band in town or in a neighbouring town that I know I like or that I think I would like, I attend the shows. Lately I've seen Neil Young with Crazy Horse and Queens of the Stone Age. As I live in Holland there aren't that many shows by international artists. I live in Amsterdam, but the shows I've seen were in Rotterdam and Utrecht.' (Andre Nuchelmans)

And for Liz Giuffre (in 2002):

'When I can. Again it's a money thing. I've been lucky this year and spread it out a bit. I saw AC/DC in January (that was an experience!), Neil Finn twice in June, the Whitlams about six times all around Sydney, Robbie Williams a couple of weeks ago (I was given that as a present).'

A few (7) did not, or very rarely, currently attend live performances. This reflected comfort (including the noise level) and, to various degrees, a preference for the recorded sound and control over the listening situation, rather than the live experience: 'Not often anymore. Bad ears and low tolerance for sweaty crowded clubs. Why risk seeing a shitty show when you can endlessly recreate that ideal (or approximation of) studio moment in your own home? *I find comfort in the predictability*' (Geoff Stahl; my emphasis). Similarly, for Greg Crossan: 'I've been to a few rock concerts, but find them too loud. I'd rather spend the money on a CD *I can listen to whenever I want*' (my emphasis). A further aspect of 'love of music' is the willingness of collectors to share their music, through lending and display (see Chapter 5).

Collectors as obsessive-compulsives

'Any collector has to have an acquisitive nature – it is not enough to hear a particular track, you want to own it as well.' (Tina Janeering)

The view of collectors as individuals characterized by obsessive-compulsive behaviour is a major component of popular conceptions, which can draw on a fair amount of support from academic studies. The literature on collecting abounds with metaphors of disease and individual pathology. Baudrillard (1994), for example, regarded the collector as an infantile and inadequate personality, while Freud – himself a collector – saw collecting as a by-product of childhood trauma. Other writers depict collectors as obsessive-compulsives, with their objects of desire providing a central organizing focus in their lives. For instance, Muesterberger (1994) argues that collecting is a way of overcoming childhood anxiety by creating a sense of order and completion, a process that can easily become obsessional and/ or compulsive. In such cases, the maintenance and expansion of their collections are frequently regarded as overshadowing the individual's social relationships. Unless, of course, these are with other collectors, and even these relationships may be characterized by jealousy, antagonism and even violence.

Obsessive-compulsive behaviour among collectors is often related to the thrill of the chase (an aspect which is the focus of Chapter 5). The metaphors of desire and the hunt are present in many biographical accounts of collecting (for instance, those in Danet and Katriel, 1994; Blom, 2002) and in numerous 'guidebooks' for collecting. Many record collectors carry around lists of recordings they are looking for, 'to fill gaps in the collection' (Gary Shuker). Key obsessional behaviours are accumulation, a preoccupation with collection size and completism. For example, Eisenberg (1988: 1–3) describes the case of 'Clarence', a New York record collector crippled with arthritis and now on welfare, living in an unlit, unheated 14-room house 'so crammed with trash that the door wouldn't open – and with three-quarters of a million (vinyl) records'. 'Clarence' had inherited the house from his parents, along with a considerable inheritance, now gone, which enabled him to pursue his dream of owning a complete collection of jazz, pop and rock recordings, along with ethnological field recordings and various recorded ephemera.

Campbell (2001) describes his 'nine of the heaviest' collectors as comprising 'one of the most interesting groups of driven, obsessive-compulsive loonies imaginable'. For Joe Bussard, self-proclaimed 'King of the record collectors', 'it was his life'; as his wife put it: 'he was always so busy with his music ... he hardly had time for anything else' (Dean, 2001: 185).

Elements of obsessive-compulsive behaviour were present in the collecting practices of a number of my respondents, and in their definitions of record collectors (both themselves and others), with the frequent use of various terms indicating individual pathology: 'my own sickness of record collecting', as Greg Crossan termed it. Similar observations about record collecting, and their own 'admissions', included:

- 'There is definitely an aspect of obsession about it.' (Craig Morrison)
- 'Obsessive, neurotic, compulsive, competitive, nerdy, very knowledgeable.' (Joe Kelich)
- 'Collecting anything is a slightly obsessive activity I suppose. It takes up an awesome amount of time if one lets it. I can waste hours in a record shop – secondhand or new.' (Tina Janeering)

In this respect, the respondents were following a common practice among collectors: the self 'use of the medical vocabulary of disease to justify the self-indulgence of collecting' (Belk, 2001: 80).

At the same time, however, there was frequently a deliberate attempt to distance oneself from this *High Fidelity* stereotype of the trainspotting obsessive. Two strategies were present here: first, an internalizing of this conception of collecting, in a knowing, self-mocking fashion: '[record collectors are] disturbed ... deeply, I suspect' (William Dart); second, the 'I'm not like everybody else' approach, separating out one's own collecting from the stereotyped caricature: 'Obsessive anal retentive losers who haven't got a life' [or] 'alternatively, people like me for whom music is a life support system' (Tony Mitchell). Compulsive collecting practices include the compulsive, regular and repetitive search for and purchase of items for the collection (see the discussion in Chapter 5).

'Size matters!'

'For some reason, despite being asked this question many times, I have avoided counting them. *I think the final number might scare me.*' (Michelle Flannery; my emphasis)

There is a common perception that collection size – the number of items owned – are a major determinant of 'the collector', as well as a significant indicator of the relative status of collectors. Yet this is applicable to relatively few collecting fields, and even within those to only a small segment of their collectors. In the collecting of books, art and stamps, for example, the emphasis is rather on discrimination and associated qualities such as historical significance and aesthetic merit, authenticity and condition. The extreme examples of collectors here are just that, an extreme: for example the nineteenth-century bibliomaniac Thomas Phillipps, whose stated ambition was 'to have one copy of every book in the world'. Many of his acquisitions never left the crates they were delivered in and most of the others were stacked and almost impossible to access (Blom, 2002: 201–5). Of course, such cases are highlighted in many discussions of collecting, reinforcing the preoccupation with size.

Certainly, published pieces on record collectors support this perception by focusing on those with large collections. Of Campbell's nine collectors, five had collections of 25–30,000 items, and one had 80,000 albums and 45,000 singles. Joe Bussard owns over 25,000 78s, and many of the exotica collectors profiled in *Incredibly Strange Music* (Vale and Juno, 1993; 1994) possessed considerable collections. The collectors featured in the British *Record Collector* magazine series 'The Collector', especially the older ones, have considerable numbers of recordings, while the magazine's readers owned an average of 2,144 vinyl albums and 1,046 CDs.[6] Indeed, Milano suggests that 8,000 records is an ideal size: 'a reasonable amount to absorb in one lifetime, and a small enough collection to keep in one room' (Milano, 2003: 72).

---

6   As stated at www.recordcollectormag.com/advertising (accessed November 2008).

On the other hand, roughly half of my collectors owned fewer than 1,000 items, suggesting that collection size was not as important to them as the focused nature of their collecting. Those who had relatively small collections, while identifying themselves as collectors 'in a small way', emphasized this point. Gender was a factor here, with the women stressing the use value of their collection:

> 'With a few exceptions, I don't just collect to have recordings. I know the vast majority of recordings in my collection intimately and have spent a good deal of time over each one. It takes me a while to digest a record and I can spend a few months listening only to a single recording.' (Susan Fast)

In terms of collection size, the number of sound recordings they (the 67 interviewees in 2001–02) then owned broke down as follows:

Less than 500	7 M; 3 F
500–1,000	18 M; 5 F
1,000–1,500	13 M; 2 F
1,500–5,000	9 M; 1 F
5,000–10,000	4 M; 0 F
10,000 plus	5 M; 0 F
Total	56 M; 11 F

Indeed, supporting this emphasis is the point that many collectors had only an approximate idea of the size of their holdings:

- 'I don't know exactly. I have stopped counting really. I would say that my collection runs well over a thousand items.' (Albert Bell)
- 'No sense of exact count; somewhere between 3,000 and 5,000.' (David Sanjek)

Others were able to be very specific about their holdings, including several of those with larger collections. In some cases this related to maintaining an up-to-date catalogue of the collection (see Chapter 5 for approaches to collection cataloguing), usually explained as necessary for insurance purposes. Former or current tape traders had a good idea of their holdings; as did several collectors who were DJs or ran radio shows: 'At one point in time when I was heavily into tape trading (*circa* ten years ago) I had compiled a detailed list of all my stuff which was imperative if you wanted to be taken seriously in tape-trading circles' (Albert Bell).

In the (all male) 10,000 plus group, three estimated their collections at approximately 10,000, one had 19,000 recordings and one 47,000. These collectors, as might be expected, had often been collecting longer (and therefore were older – 40 plus). They tended to buy more regularly, and in greater quantities (the question of buying practices is discussed further in Chapter 5). Indeed, two referred to buying whole collections as part of their collection-building process. This level of 'holdings' is moving into the realm of accumulation.

Accumulation

> 'There comes a time in every collector's career – sooner more often than later – when he crosses the line between enthusiasm and obsession, between buying records he likes and buying every record possible.' (Stan Denski, in Campbell, 2001: 7)

Discussions of collecting frequently work to distinguish 'accumulation' (and completism) from collecting, stressing discrimination as a defining element of the collecting process. Collecting, as Belk argues, requires a unifying principle (Belk, 2001: 66–7). However, it is also conceded that there is often an element of accumulation involved, and that this characteristic includes elements of compulsion/obsession. This pattern was present among collectors during the 78 era, and remains very much the case with contemporary record collectors:

- 'I collect to listen and gain knowledge from the music. I think that's what defines a collector. One could say I am also a "record accumulator", and I would say that I am probably 70 per cent accumulator, 30 per cent collector.' (John Book)
- 'At times I consider myself a collector (on good days). I also consider myself a hoarder (on bad days).' (Geoff Stahl; see also his profile in Chapter 7).

The tendency to accumulate was reflected in several cases in an unwillingness to part with any items from the collection, even when 'old' formats were no longer played, or, with vinyl, the collector no longer owned a working turntable. Other collectors, however, rejected the accumulator label, and were prepared to sell off 'redundant material'. Quite a few (14/67) actively traded via the internet, or traded in unwanted recordings at second-hand record shops.

Completism

> 'I have a compulsive personality so whenever I got into a music genre, I REALLY got into it and tried to collect as much of the records/music as possible. [But it can be an ongoing process of renewal.] Of course, when I got into a new music

form I usually got rid of most of my older records and only kept my favourites.' (Joel Wing)

The collecting process is both open and closed. The desire to complete a collection is in tension with the fear of doing so, since once this has been achieved the purpose of the enterprise is gone. The consequence is for a 'clear tendency, once a collector has to admit that a particular line has come to its natural term, to start immediately upon another' (Pearce, 1995: 185), or for collections to meander on, without closure. The latter is usually associated with a choice of collectible with no clearly defined limits, a 'set of things' without boundaries (Belk, 2001: 66).

Completism was part of collecting practices during the 78 era, and continues to be identified as characteristic of record collectors (being mentioned by a quarter of my respondents). It can be defined as the need to own all of a particular category, usually one artist's output. This can be regardless of musical quality or artistic merit; for example, a Japanese collector aiming to obtain the whole ECM catalogue, 'independent of his aesthetic judgement' (Hosokawa and Matsuoka, 2004: 155). Such an approach admits the possibility of closure, but this can be indefinitely postponed by a constant extension of the boundaries of the collection. This can occur, for example, by collecting the ongoing output of a living artist, in all its formats and national pressings: 'I have certain favourite artists that I will go to great lengths to purchase everything from, especially when I know that some of their best material can be found [as] B-Sides, extra tracks, only available on side projects, one offs recorded for fanzines etc.' (Michelle Flannery). Or closure can be avoided by simply choosing a goal that is essentially unattainable, given the scope of the subject and the fierce competition for rarer items (for example, 1960s soul singles, and early Jamaican reggae).

Many collectors have a strong interest in particular artists or genres of music, often combining these with a general collection, but taking a more completist approach:

> 'I collect old punk, post-punk and goth records – things usually no longer available (although it looks a lot more impressive owning the original vinyl regardless). I trawl record fairs and second hand stores. I'm especially interested in releases from The Cure. There I'm quite happy to collect bootleg albums, special editions 12 inches ... and I'm always on the hunt for picture sleeve singles. One of my other female friends has a similar devotion to collecting David Bowie stuff. The boyfriend is like this for the Smiths.' (Michelle Wauchope)

Completism is related to an emphasis on the 'hunt' aspect of collecting. As with other collectibles, at its most extreme it can be seen in record collectors selling off a completed collection in order to start a new one. This was a practice commented on by several collectors, in addition to four who had done so themselves. More modest completists are those who attempt to collect all one artist's output, including related literature and memorabilia, the output of a label (for example, Apple), or the work of one producer, an ambition very evident among reggae collectors.

Selectivity, discrimination and cultural capital

Some of my collectors (approximately one third) distanced their own collecting practices from accumulation and completism, instead stressing selectivity and taste as more defining of their collecting. As it had during the 78 era, this valorized collecting as involving discrimination and the acquisition of cultural capital and consequent status, especially within one's peer group. It includes buying only the 'best' or selected examples, or collecting material regarded as more 'on the cutting edge'. Notions of the canon were important here, along with the associated role of the music press (see the discussions in Chapter 4 and Chapter 6). Brennon Wood referred to his emphasis on acquiring 'strong examples of various types of popular music', while Shawn Mawer admitted to 'taking a perverse pleasure of art ownership', and having a need for a representative sample of 'more up to date' music.

The development of discrimination was sometimes seen as a progressive one, often juxtaposed against earlier preoccupations:

> 'At earlier points I would struggle to collect the entire production of my favourite bands, complete with related bands and projects. But very few musicians make exclusively good records, so it was time to empty the garbage and limit oneself to the best, then move on to discover new good music. I know people who carried on as I set out. Now in their 30s, they have 1,000 albums, but only a handful they can listen to. It is no more a question of collecting music for music's sake, it could just as well be stamps or football cards.' (Yngvar Steinbolt)

One aspect of discrimination is the use people make of their collections in relation to self-education and scholarship. As Chapter 1 demonstrated, such an approach was an integral part of 78 collecting. Many of the record collectors I 'talked' with are researching and teaching in popular music studies, so their work is inseparable from their passion. Indeed, it would seem to be a major reason for their choice of academic field. This association can produce an element of rationalization: I need X for my teaching/research, it 'incidentally' also becomes part of the collection. An example of this would be my own recent purchase of the Rhino MC5 compilation on CD, when I had their first two albums on vinyl, but did not have a decent turntable to use these with classes. Similarly, for Keir Keightley, 'I didn't [consider myself a collector] until about five years ago when I realized my research interest in post-war popular music was serving as a perfect cover to buy LPs at outrageous prices … So now I'm a full-fledged collector, and more-or-less proud of it.'

For such collectors, the collection becomes an archive, a resource:

- 'I always think that I will one day write wonderful books on a) record labels, b) soul albums/singles c) reggae singles/albums – drawing on my 30 years of listening to and collecting the stuff.' (Hasse Huss)
- 'I like to hear what I have and use it for a reference library for my interests, research, teaching, performing.' (Craig Morrison)

This dimension of collecting has strong associations with being a connoisseur:

'For instance, I want to be a well-rounded pop listener with a good grasp on pretty much all of the major touchstones. Of course, neither do I want to become out of touch, so I try to keep in touch with new sounds as best I can. In some years I'll buy mostly new music; lately, it's been mostly older stuff.' (Andrew Stafford)

Such views follow the historical tradition of collectors playing a significant role as cultural preservers. Record collectors have left their collections to institutions, to keep the collection intact and provide a publicly available educational resource. This follows the historical practice of book collectors in relation to libraries, and art collectors donating their pictures to galleries. Several commented on this aspect of collecting, with two mentioning quite detailed provisions for donating their several collections (records, music ephemera, books) to educational institutions.

A further cultural capital aspect of collecting is its role for musicians and other musical workers who are frequently keen record collectors. This is the case with many of the collectors featured in Milano's *Vinyl Junkies* (2003); 'The Collector' series in *Record Collector*; and in *Incredibly Strange Music* (Vale and Juno, 1993; 1994). Indie musicians are often keen collectors, since the records provide cultural capital and a resource to draw on for musical inspiration: the old adage about 'bands being only as good as their record collections' (see Bannister, 2006; Fonarow, 2006). This is also evident with DJs, such as Afrika Bambaataa, a fervent collector of vinyl from an early age (Brewster and Broughton, 1999: 217f.). There are prominent examples of record collectors who have founded their own recording companies in order to re-release old/rare material, or become closely involved with reissue labels (see Chapter 3).

Many collectors, including a number of my interviewees, run radio shows, work as DJs or are employed in recording companies and music retail. As with academics, of course, their intense interest in music prompted such career paths. Their work and their 'hobby' are mutually reinforcing; although they may distinguish between the two spheres. As Geoff notes: 'As I also do a radio show, I find that my motivations for buying are often based on music I might play on the show, but not at home. I also play music at home I wouldn't play on the show. It certainly makes for interesting buying patterns' (Geoff Stahl).

Discrimination, cultural preservation and self-education are linked through the conception of collecting as a form of cultural capital. As such, it provides knowledge, intellectual/aesthetic nourishment and resources, and social identity and status. Record collecting often accompanies an interest in details surrounding the music: who performed the song; who wrote it; who produced it; when it was released, and on what label.

> 'As much as collecting may ultimately be about the music, it does also represent a form of collecting knowledge as well. I'd put myself in this category of collectors, since I know my own record buying/collecting is driven by a concern with historicizing music that transcends the specific pleasure I take in many of the albums that I own.' (Steve Waksman)

Similarly, for Liz:

> 'I think it [record collecting] has to do with wanting to have a kind of set of resources. Because I'm writing about music a lot at the moment (both academically and non-academically), I like to have certain "classics" at home. That way it's easy to reference things. If you own or have easy access to a lot of resources on the one topic, then you get to be a bit of a resource yourself.' (Liz Giuffre)

A concern with rarity and economic value

Popular discussion of collecting often focuses on the monetary value of collectibles, and collectors are frequently asked questions such as 'What is the value of your collection?' and/or 'What is the most valuable item (stamp, art work, first edition book) you own?' Speculation in sound recordings is not as evident as in other popular culture collectibles (such as comic books), but it does exist and appears to be increasing – in terms of both quantity and prices. There is an established market, closely associated with second-hand record stores, prestige auctions of music memorabilia (including recordings) and, increasingly, eBay.[7] Both *Record Collector* and *Goldmine* regularly feature stories of the sale of rare and highly priced records, in addition to advertisements with items priced over US$500. This interest can be encouraged by collectors who like to relate how they bought a rare/expensive recording at a bargain basement price (for example Bussard, in Dean, 2001) and accounts of frenzied bidding to a high level which become part of eBay's folklore.[8] Campbell (2001) found that a concern for economic value was a major factor among his 'serious', large-scale collectors (although their 'biggest buzz' was obtaining something of value cheaply). The issue of what is rare, and

---

[7]   See the comments by Ian Shirley, the current editor of the *Rare Record Price Guide*, in his profile in Chapter 7.

[8]   For instance, in February 2002, an obscure Northern Soul single, with a reserve of $6 went for almost US$2,000. (Cody Black, 'You'll Be Sorry', GIG 210); my thanks to Hasse for this example.

how value is constituted are taken up in Chapter 4, in part through a consideration of 'collectable' artists and genres, and recent examples of top selling recordings on eBay.

The tendency to develop specialized collections, including rarer, more exotic or unavailable items, 'provides a chance to excel and distinguish the serious collector from the more general or casual dabbling collectors' (Belk, 2001: 8). Many of my respondents were aware of the economic/rarity value of some recordings, and regarded acquisition of these as part of their collecting: 'I don't think any of us collect solely for rarity, although the albums that are [rare] do get pride of place' (Michelle Wauchope). This is often related to status among a particular group of collectors, specializing in a genre:

> 'The record collectors I know mostly pertain to the metal scene. I would say that most are quite possessive of their collection. Some tend to be obsessed with collecting obscure items and other rarities. Metal collectors pride themselves with such items, it lends status within the scene and amongst other collectors.' (Albert Bell)

Views on monetary value and the importance of rarity were linked to the distinction (drawn earlier) between the use value and the commodity value of recordings. Those holding to this rejected collecting more concerned with the artefact itself rather than its use value. Such rejection was at times passionately eloquent:

> 'Record collectors give people like me a bad name! I'm not obsessive and anal about my records. I buy them to play them for the music inside, and to look longingly at the beautiful covers while I do so. I think the worst kind of collector is someone who sees them as simply parts of a puzzle, pieces to be gathered, tagged, and put in a glass case, rather than music-listening media whose age or rarity is simply an enhancement, rather than an end in itself.' (Keir Keightley)

This attitude was usually linked to an unwillingness to pay what were perceived as inflated prices: 'Others are diggers, like me. Diggers want to find vinyl but for cheap. My limit is $20, although recently I've been going over that quite a lot. Still, the most I've ever spent on one record is $36' (Joel Wing).[9] Joel went on to observe,

> 'Among beat diggers, there are definitely two distinct types. There are the big time collectors and the diggers. Collectors will spend whatever it takes to buy records. There are tons of stories of people spending over $1,000 for a single 45. [And this was in 2002!] A lot of the big time collectors even go through phone books and other sources to find the original artists. The result is that prices for

---

[9]   Beat diggers are interested in the breaks in particular recordings, especially hip hop singles; see collector-oriented hip hop journal *Wax Poetics*, and Chapter 5: 'On the hunt'.

funk records have skyrocketed in the last 8–9 years. One only has to take a look at eBay and type in a few hard to find titles and see how much they're going for.'

While few of my collectors attached much significance to the monetary value of their collections, several had quite valuable items in their collections, including signed editions of recordings, rare releases and scarce recordings they had paid a significant amount for. However, while these collectors follow the market (via auctions, the collector press), I got the distinct impression (subsequently confirmed in two cases) that they will never sell, because these items are regarded as an essential part of their collections. A few mentioned spending levels and amounts paid for scarce items:

> 'I buy from eBay sometimes … A lot of them are 45s at the starting price, typically $3.00, $5.00 or $9.99, but I have been involved in some high bidding for some scarce items too once or twice. The most expensive one was £130.00, I think, but that was obviously an exception.' (Hasse Huss, in 2002; he subsequently sold the item)

Gary Shuker has spent 'around 5 to 6,000 [NZ$] on eBay alone over the past few years'. A concern with value, and more 'serious' levels of spending, are evident among those profiled in *Record Collector* magazine's 'The Collector' series. Responding to a standard question, 'what is it (the collection) worth?' many identify high value items and take pride in owning these. At the same time, however, they frequently distinguish this from their primary love, the use value of the music:

- 'It's worth a lifetime of love for music.' (Ernesto De Pascale; No. 27, *Record Collector*, March 2006)
- 'My collection has nothing to do with value. I react to every mood I experience in my life by putting on a record.' (Kieran Hebden, No. 26, *Record Collector*, February 2006)
- 'Its value has never really interested me – it's always been about the music.' (Graeme Dickenson, No. 43, *Record Collector*, June 2007)
- 'Its worth is equal to the time spent listening and deriving pleasure from it.' (Kat Bjelland, No. 16, *Record Collector*, May 2005).

Collecting and identity

> 'Collecting anything I think is tied to one's notions about personal identity. With collecting, I think the sort of albums people collect on the whole is often a reflection of personal identity.' (Andrew Stafford)

Collecting is a significant part of identity construction, and an important dimension of collectors' lives. Indeed, at its most extreme, it *is* their life. This in part reflects the strong connection between collecting and displaying and memory. 'Repertoires, whether of songs, tales or quilts, are examples of accumulations made over a lifetime. Their powers of evocation derive from the associations that accumulate with them' (Kirshenblatt-Gimblett, 1999: 94; see also Hoskins, 1998). In common with other forms of collecting, record collecting 'is an attempt to preserve both the past and memories of the past' and 'a practice driven by nostalgia' (Montano, 2003: 1). It is a fuller expression of the general tendency for sound recordings to act as prompts to memory, given that they are material artefacts located in time and place, with an ascribed meaning for many listeners (DeNora, 2001: 62). Keith described this in impressive detail:

> 'The CD as object and the music reminds me of where I was (geographically and personally) when I purchased the object. This in turn is influenced by what I was listening to at the time. The song "American Pie", for example, has a deep resonance for me (school days in England), America's "Ventura Highway" (undergraduate days in Canberra), Nirvana's "Smells Like Teen Spirit" (living in a hall of residence studying for my PhD). Similarly, I can go directly to certain CDs in my collection and the CD itself (not the music) will tell a memory story: this one was purchased in Greenwich Village, this one from Berkeley, this one from Ashwoods in Pitt Street, this one from Real Groovy in Auckland, and each has an accompanying narrative related to what I was doing at the time, and why I was in each locale.' (Keith Beattie)

Most record collectors acquired 'the habit' during adolescence. Even if these initial purchases are not equated with 'collecting', they arguably indicate a disposition, which subsequently expands with increased income and opportunity. The subsequent maintenance of 'the habit' is partly reflected in a nostalgic ability to powerfully recall first/early purchases. For several, their interest in music as a collectible began relatively early, during their pre-teens – as with Steve Waksman (see his profile in Chapter 7). Copying, usually from the radio or other audio tapes, is an early method of developing a collection. For the majority, record buying began during adolescence, typically between 12 and 14 years of age. (One respondent also mentions 'stealing quite a few' during this period!) This can be seen as part of the establishment of 'self' during this key formative period of life. The assertion of consumer sovereignty was related to having money (and, increasingly, a disposable income), along with access to a sound system:

- 'I started buying my own records in Junior High School beginning with rock and heavy metal (that was 1982–83). I started building up a serious collection in High School when I got into punk. I would say my collection didn't get into the "huge" size until very recently, 4 or 5 years ago, when I had a job that paid me enough that I could spend some serious dollars.' (Joel Wing)

- 'I got my first record in 1960 aged 13. Would have bought them earlier than that but didn't have a record player until I was given one as a 13th birthday present.' (Tina Janeering)
- 'By 16 I was already in possession of a large amount of audio tapes, and only at a later age I started changing those tapes for the "real" product.' (Steve Mallett)

For Steve, the 'real product' was vinyl records. This view of vinyl as a more authentic sound carrier and cultural artefact was widely held among my sample, and is discussed in Chapter 3).

The clear majority of my collectors could recall with sometimes astonishing and impressive clarity their first purchases. These purchases were all (then) current releases, and were often still part of the collection:

- 'The first recording I bought myself was a mini-LP by a long since forgotten Australian band: Machinations "Pressure Sway", 1984, I think. I can still listen to it. It brings back fond memories of D&D role-playing. It was on sale for something like 50p.' (Yngvar Steinbolt)
- 'Absolutely – Roxy Music, "Siren" – in fact really was after that one song – "Love is the Drug".' (Brennon Wood)
- 'I still have it, my first: the Beachboys Live LP!' (Gary Shuker)

Such vivid recollections are present in other published interviews with collectors, and further indicate the important role of nostalgia and personal memory in collecting. This is also evident in the manner in which collectors can usually distinguish the point at which they began to consider themselves collectors:

- 'I seriously began collecting records when I was about 16.' (Andre Nuchelmans)
- '3 but that was really minor. I didn't buy albums in earnest until 17 and I've been on a rampage since 21.' (Oliver Wang)
- 'First starting buying records at about 14. First started collecting at 19.' (Joe Kellich)

What fosters this progression from the occasional purchaser of records to the status of collector? Various aspects of personal identity formation were often mentioned by my respondents, most notably the desire to turn chaos into order, and the role of nostalgia. Several mentioned Walter Benjamin's characterization of a collector as one who turns chaos into order (Benjamin, 1968). 'I find the world very chaotic, to be philosophical for a moment, and I think collectors are in the business of trying to impose order on little bits of that chaos' (Greg Crossan). Parents or siblings who are record collectors can also be influential on the development of the collector.

The issue of social competence

Social competence is part of personal identity. Related to the view of collectors as obsessive-compulsives is the image of record collectors as socially rather inept individuals, more at ease in their relationship to things than people. Collecting can provide a sense of escapism and a private refuge from both the wider world and the immediate domestic environment, albeit temporarily. In *High Fidelity*, Rob Fleming in times of stress re-catalogues his album collection:

> Is it so wrong wanting to be at home with your record collection? It's not like collecting records is like collecting stamps, or beer mats, or antique thimbles. There's a whole world in here, a nicer, dirtier, more violent, more colourful, sleazier, more dangerous, more loving world than the world I live in. (Hornby, 1995: 73)

While many respondents saw elements of this image in themselves and, more often, in other collectors, there was just as much emphasis on collecting as a pro-social activity:

- 'I have a software version of the file, which is updated more sporadically. Filing and making all sorts of statistic analysis of the collection has been a lot worse (sickly) in earlier days. My wardrobe has, sadly, never been kept to the same standards.' (Yngvar Steinbolt)
- 'I have known many serious record collectors. It is often pretty much the "main event" in their life. Collecting is inherently obsessive and most serious collectors sacrifice spending on primary needs (food, clothing) in pursuit of more records. Usually they are connected to a group or "scene" of serious music makers or other collectors.' (Allen Meek)

Those who regarded collecting as a strongly pro-social activity downplayed the obsessive aspect, and regarded their fellow collectors as generally 'nice people and supportive of other collectors in their areas. Some are very friendly and long term associations develop' (Gary Shuker). 'Through the music I have also been able to forge some of my closest friendships and relationships. This has served to accentuate my bonding with the genre' (Albert Bell). Record collecting, as many respondents observed, provided a way to meet people and develop relationships based on common interests. In several cases, partners shared the interest and collectors would shop together.

Collecting and the life cycle

The collecting process can take on different emphases over time, relating to various combinations of increasing age, changing study/employment, income, the availability of sought-after recordings and domestic responsibilities. 'Over the years and with increased purchasing power my collection increased rapidly and steadily. The collection reflects my musical interests at different points in my life, for example, I have a huge 80s power metal/thrash collection – the genre I was most into in that period' (Albert Bell).

Several collectors related these shifts in collecting patterns to a life cycle, culminating in 'the years of atrophy and senescence, with minor additions to the collection on a fairly haphazard basis and existence by cannibalizing the collection already in existence' (Brennon Wood). Some regarded collecting as a mix of arrested adolescence and clinging on to youth:

> 'Most collectors I know start collecting at the age of 16/17, when they are a huge fan of one artist/ band they want to know and have everything about. Record collectors are the ones that do not stop doing so at the age of 20, but keep on carrying that piece of youth with 'em throughout their lives. Somehow they have been bit by the music virus and can't let go of it. The activity of collecting (buying records) is very adolescent-like. I've seen 40-year-olds being happy as a child because they had finally found that original Iron Butterfly album they couldn't afford when they were young. Just like rock music itself, it is a way of sticking to your youth, and a pleasant escape from the dread of everyday life.' (Steve Mallet)

Conclusion

The *High Fidelity* stereotype is just that; there is no 'typical' record collector. Contemporary record collectors have a shared interest in sound recordings as significant cultural artefacts, with associated notions of discrimination, musical canons and rarity. They also share the dominant characteristics of collectors more generally, albeit with particular inflections of these: the thrill of the chase; obsession, linked to accumulation and completism; at times a preoccupation with rarity and economic value; and a concern for cultural preservation. The last often involves self-education and public/vernacular scholarship, drawing on the collection as a resource. These traits are subsumed into collecting as a significant aspect of social identity, involving the acquisition of cultural capital, overlaid with a patina of nostalgia.

Chapter 3
Formats, collectors and the music industry

The huge range of what is what is collectable is evident from the related literature (the articles, editorial and advertising in the collector magazines; the contents of the guide books and price guides), the organizing of music retail (the categories utilized by record shops, auction houses and eBay) and the music industry creation of collectibles (through promo releases, reissues and boxed sets). It is beyond my scope, and indeed unnecessary, to provide a full account of these.[1] Rather, across this and the following chapter, I consider examples of music collectibles, and the nature of their appeal and collectability. My focus is on sound recording formats, genres and artists, but also included (in Chapter 4) are the collection of chart hits, compilations, bootlegs, music magazines and memorabilia.

This chapter considers the development of successive recording formats, along with the collecting of each, and the role of the recording industry in shaping collecting. The main formats include cylinders, shellac 78s, vinyl (10" and 12" LPs/albums, EPs, 45s, the 10"/12" dance single, and 180g vinyl albums), tape (reel to reel, 8 track cartridges and, primarily, audio cassettes), CDs (albums, singles) and MP3s and other computer downloadable sound files. All represent different forms of music collectible, and historical shifts in the relative status of each format are reflected in record collecting preferences and practices. New formats can take a while to become regarded as collectable, or, indeed, may never be regarded with great favour (as with audiotapes). While new formats may, for most music consumers – and some collectors – supersede the old, this can have the effect of consolidating for some collectors the appeal of the former. Of particular interest is the privileging of vinyl as *the* collectable format, and the relative collectability of audiotapes, CDs and digital music. (The more extensive collector profiles in Chapter 7 further illustrate the general discussion here).

The recording industry has played a central role in the introduction and construction of the relative popularity of formats. Other industry strategies and products are aimed primarily at collectors, both creating and responding to collector demand. Indie and reissue labels have been especially prominent here, with collectors frequently associated with both. Recording industry packaging practices have created a number of collectibles, including picture discs, picture sleeves, boxed sets and 'promos'.

---

[1]   See Thompson (2002), for an excellent overview, along with record price guides and current issues of the magazines *Goldmine* and *Record Collector*.

Formats

I begin with a brief sketch of the evolution of record formats, moving from this to consider the shifting levels of collector interest, and economic and emotional investment in each. Sound recordings are available in a range of formats and, as McCourt observes 'their evolving physical forms have shaped our interactions with them and our perceptions of their value' (McCourt, 2005: 249). There is a clear historical succession of sound recording formats, and the associated development of new playback/listening technologies. Each successive format has less physical presence, while enabling increased music storage.[2] Each new format has seen a greater ease of use, in terms of both the 'recording' itself and the technology required to play it; each also has seen greater potential for 'user programming', the ability of listeners to create their own musical experience. And, as 'recordings shed their mass and/physicality, their visual and tactile aspects are reduced' (McCourt, 2005: 249), a shift that is especially evident in the move from LPs to CDs and the advent of digital music formats.

The 78rpm discs of the gramophone age were restricted to three to four minutes per side, their physical fragility made handling and portability difficult, and the large 'albums' for their storage were bulky and cumbersome.[3] The vinyl LP provided two sides of music, usually around 20–25 minutes each; anything more tended to lead to the needle 'skipping' across the tracks. Vinyl albums and singles required care and attention in their playing, with scratches and wear a common consequence of repeated use. The standard audiotape was the C90 cassette; longer tapes tended to wear much more quickly, and often snagged and broke during use. Compact discs can accommodate up to 78 minutes per disc, while, depending on its gigabyte size, an MP3 player can store up to 10,000 songs in a device smaller than a cigarette packet. With 78s, vinyl records and cassette tapes the listener must physically set them up to play, and physical intervention and effort is required to change the listening order: for example, fast forwarding audiotape or shifting the stylus arm on the record turntable to a different track. In comparison, CDs, MP3 players and systems such as iTunes all allow the listener to determine more easily the sequencing of tracks – the flow – of the listening experience.

The record industry has a vested interest in the introduction of new formats and technologies, utilizing various sales practices and pricing regimes to encourage a new and more profitable catalogue (especially with the introduction of the CD and CD players in the 1980s). Format obsolescence also allows the recording companies

---

[2]   There is now a considerable body of work on the development of recording formats, emphasizing the manner in which technological innovations have impacted on the production and social use of music, including the act of listening itself (see, for instance, Chanan, 1995; Day, 2000; Millard, 1995; Sterne, 2003; and Symes, 2004).

[3]   Illustrating how old formats still have a utility beyond their use as sound artefacts, I have purchased now largely empty ones at thrift shops, to use for storing vinyl LPs in while I am displaying their album covers as 'wall art'.

to recycle their back catalogues, either directly through their own reissues or by licensing rights to independent, reissue-oriented labels. Given that development costs have already been undertaken at the time of the original recording, this is a very profitable aspect of the companies' operations. New markets are created as older consumers upgrade both their hardware and their record collections, most prominently by replacing vinyl albums with CDs in the late 1980s and through the 1990s.

The first major recording/phonograph companies (Columbia, established in 1889; RCA, 1929, incorporating Victor formed earlier, in 1901; and Decca, in 1934 in the United States), were engaged from the inception of the industry in a battle over alternative recording and reproducing technologies. At stake was the all-important market share. Cylinders were replaced by 78s, which dominated from around 1912 to 1952, which were in turn supplanted by vinyl formats during the 1950s Not only was sound quality a consideration, arguably even more important was the amount of music that could be placed on a record, enabling the industry to offer the consumer 'more value for money'.

While the 10" 78rpm shellac disc emerged as the industry standard by the 1930s, experimentation and research continued. In the early post-war years, Columbia developed a long-playing hi-fidelity record using the newly-developed vinyl. In 1948 Columbia released its 12" 33⅓rpm LP. Refusing to establish a common industry standard, RCA responded by developing a 7" vinyl record, with a large hole in the middle, that played at 45rpm. After several years of competition between the two speeds, the companies pooled their talents and agreed to produce in both formats. By 1952, the LP had become the major format for classical music and the 45 the format for single records for popular radio airplay, jukeboxes and retail sales. The 45, the single, provided the main share of the vinyl market in the late 1950s and into the 1960s, along with EP (extended play) releases, but from the late 1960s the LP became increasingly important (Hull, 2004).

Compact cassette audiotape, along with cassette tape players, developed in the mid-1960s, appealed because of their small size and associated portability. Initially a low fidelity medium, steady improvement of the sound, through modifications to magnetic tape and the introduction of the Dolby noise reduction system, enhanced the appeal of cassettes. The transistor radio and the cassette had become associated technologies by the 1970s, with widely popular cheap radio cassette players, and the cassette player incorporated into high-fidelity home stereos. As a portable recording technology, the tape cassette has been used in the production, duplication and dissemination of local music and the creation of new musical styles, most notably punk and rap, thus tending to decentralize control over production and consumption. Until the advent of digital music, the cassette remained the staple format for pirated and bootlegged copies of recordings.

As Thompson notes, by the mid-1970s,

> both the quality and reliability of cassettes vastly improved their performance, ridding the format of its early penchant for jamming, twisting and fluttering. The

Dolby Noise Reduction system was perfected to erase the hiss that plagued early tapes, and, as the 1970s progressed, further innovations in the actual composition of the magnetic tape itself gave the format the aura of quality sound reproduction … from here on, the cassette was unstoppable.[4]

By the end of the 1980s cassettes were outselling other formats three to one. In 1990, Swedish band Roxette's 'Listen to Your Heart' became the first single to reach number one in the United States without being released on vinyl. However, the advent of the CD led to a sharp and ongoing decline in the market share of prerecorded audio cassettes, which had dropped to below 20 per cent in 2002 (Hull, 2004: 225). In Western countries, most mainstream music retailers no longer stock the format, and its production is largely restricted to limited edition copies, made by bands to sell at gigs.

Initially developed by Sony in Japan, and introduced internationally in 1982, the compact disc, the CD, rapidly became established as the main medium for the recording and marketing of popular music. This success was fuelled by ease of use, and (often debated) claims of a clearer, sharper sound along with greater durability and permanence, compared to vinyl. The shift to CDs was a major factor in the exploitation and availability of the back catalogue by the music industry. Indeed, there was a conscious effort by the major record companies systematically to reshape public music consumption by limiting the production of LPs, refusing retailers their option of returning unsold vinyl stock, and artificially inflating the wholesale cost of CDs to guarantee increased profits. Consequently, despite the continued availability of vinyl, as Hayes concluded, 'the vast majority of the record-buying public accepted the industry's claim that CDs provided improved fidelity while requiring less maintenance (as well as less precision when selecting a track)' (Hayes, 2006: 56).

1988 marked a turning point in the music industry. For the first time since its arrival in the market in 1983, compact disc sales surpassed vinyl revenues: vinyl record sales declined 33 per cent, levelling off at 15 per cent of the market, while CDs increased 31 per cent. On April 2, for the first time, all 200 records on the charts were available on CD (Plasketes, 1992: 110). By 1989, CDs had all but eliminated LPs as a viable format, generating US$2.69 billion compared to vinyl sales of US$232 million. The 1980s also saw the CD single gaining a significant market share, and the marked decline of the vinyl single, worldwide sales of which dropped by a third from 550 million in 1980 to 375 million in 1988. The sales of vinyl LPs continued their decline into the 1990s, while CD sales continued to show a significant increase. Globally, unit sales in 1992 were 1.55 billion cassettes, 1.15 billion CDs, 130 million LPs and 330 million singles. Accordingly, writing in that year, Plasketes concluded that the point had been reached where the

---

[4]   Thompson, Dave, 'Cassettes Survive Against All Odds', *Goldmine*, 28 September 2007. This extended the discussion of the format in his book *The Music Lovers Guide* (Thompson 2002).

CD appeared to indicate 'certain death' for the older format. Although he also observed,

> there are many record industry executives and LP sentimentalists who prefer to point to other signs and figures which indicate that vinyl remains valuable; and although forces have combined to squeeze records from the mainstream to the fringe or underground, the subculture movement for the exiled format is a strong one. (Plasketes, 1992: 113–14)

A vinyl revival?

Indeed, pronouncements of the death of the format proved premature, as vinyl began a limited 'comeback' in the mid-1990s, a comeback which continued into the 2000s. In the US market, the number of vinyl albums sold nearly doubled to 2.2 million in 1995, with several major artists choosing to release albums on vinyl before the CD (for example Pearl Jam, Hootie and the Blowfish). This trend gathered momentum at the turn of the millennium, while CD sales declined. Larger retailers, such as Tower Records, began to stock limited edition vinyl albums, such as the White Stripes' *Elephant* (2003), and Outkast's *Speakerboxxx/The Love Below* (2003). According to year-end tallies published in *Billboard*, US CD unit sales dropped from 649,393,000 units in 2001 to 636,485,000 units in 2003, an overall decline of 2 per cent, while formats classified as 'Other' (largely vinyl, but including a small number of DVD audio-albums) rose from 1,292,000 units sold in 2001 to 1,862,000 units sold in 2003, an increase of more than 30 per cent. Vinyl also remained the preferred collector's format (as will be discussed later). Bob Irwin observed that vinyl continued to expand its market, at least among the collectors who love his label, Sundazed, which reissues lost '60s classics on both CD and vinyl. 'In the past two years [2001–02] our vinyl shares have spiked over 35 percent; the romance of holding a 45 or an album is coming back. You can't watch two hours of primetime TV without seeing something like a car commercial, where the needle drops into a groove' (Milano, 2003: 36).

In the past few years, vinyl has continued its revival, although the significance of this is debated and its market share remains tiny. In the United States, vinyl sales increased slightly during 2007, while CD sales were marginally down.[5] In June 2008, *Rolling Stone* featured a piece, 'Vinyl Returns in the Age of MP3', documenting how 'as CD sales continue to decline and MP3s are traded without thought, the left-for-dead LP is making a comeback'.[6] While conceding that vinyl remained a niche market, author David Browne cited Nielsen Sound Scan figures showing that nearly one million LPs were bought in 2007, up from 858,000 in 2006, while CD shipments dropped 17.5 per cent during the same 2006–07 period.

---

[5]   See the Recording Industry Association of America website: www.riaa.com.

[6]   http://www.rollingstone.com/news/story/20947918/vinyl_returns. Accessed 6 June 2008.

According to the Consumer Electronics Association, turntable sales were also up from 275,000 in 2006, with nearly half a million sold in 2007. The vinyl resurgence was attributed to a combination of some artists' preference for the format; the willingness of major retailers (such as Best Buy and Amazon), as well as indie record stores, to stock vinyl versions of many major new releases; and youthful consumers preference for the sound of vinyl, compared to CD and MP3 sound quality.

In the UK in 2006, vinyl sales accounted for around 0.5 per cent of singles and 0.3 per cent of album sales. While such sales levels are minuscule, the vinyl releases can play an important role in fuelling additional sales (of downloads) and generating publicity for live appearances. It is not just established names who have been issued on vinyl: 'in 2007, vinyl releases are regarded as the best way to introduce and build up the credibility of a new name to the record-buying public by both independent and major labels alike' (De Whalley, 2007: 71). Some recent vinyl releases have achieved impressive sales and generated useful publicity. In the United Kingdom in May 2007, a 7" vinyl rerelease of The Kinks' *Waterloo Sunset* (on Sanctuary Records) reached number one on the official *Independent* Top 10 singles chart. The Kinks single was produced in two different vinyl formats, a replica of the original 1967 red Pye-label single; and a four track facsimile of a contemporary French EP. Sanctuary Records used the release to celebrate (and draw attention to) the availability of the complete Kinks catalogue as downloads (De Whalley, 2007: 70). This illustrates the ability of formats to 'live together' in the market, with cross-format production catering for both general music consumers and collector preferences.

The digital download

MP3 is a recorded sound that is technologically encoded to take up much less storage space than it would otherwise, making it practical to transfer (download) high-quality music files over the internet and store them on a computer hard drive: CD-quality tracks downloadable in minutes. Hardly surprisingly, following its inception in the late 1990s, MP3 soon became hugely popular as a way to distribute and access music. Napster software was introduced in 1999, 'designed as a combination search engine, communication portal, and file-sharing software that facilitated the sharing process by granting users access to all other Napster users and the MP3 files they chose to share' (Garofalo, 2003: 31; Garofalo traces the early debates around Napster).

There has been extensive debate around the economic and cultural impact of digital music, with perspectives heavily dependent on whose interests were at stake. For consumers, MP3 enabled access to a great variety of music, much of it easily available and without payment via file-sharing through sites such as Napster and Limewire. It also enables them to compile selectively their own collections of songs by combining various tracks without having to purchase entire albums (or indeed CD singles). MP3 meant that artists could distribute their music to a global audience without the mediation of the established music industry. Digital formats and practices offered a new revenue stream for record companies, especially the dominant majors, but also posed challenges to the maintenance of copyright, and threatened to undermine their historical market dominance.

Beginning around 1999–2000, the mainstream music industry showed increasing alarm at the impact on their market share of Napster et al. and practices such as the downloading of MP3s, and P2P (person to person) file-sharing. Alongside these misgivings, the music industry began to make considerable use of MP3, setting up its own on-line subscription services. Many on-line music retailers offered tracks for download by MP3, hoping these would act as a 'taster' for listeners' purchases. Recording companies recognized the need to utilize the new technology to maintain their market dominance in the new world of online audio music, looking for new concepts in packaging and marketing to retail songs digitally via the internet.

Given that CDs had largely supplanted vinyl records as the main format of choice among music consumers, the digital download made serious inroads into the CD market in the 2000s, with legal downloading taking an increasing share of sales (Hull, 2004: 258–9).

Digital music was made even more attractive by the development of the iPod and its competitors, portable music systems capable of storing huge numbers of songs in digital format. In 2006, a major report showed the shift to on-line music had gained momentum, with it now accounting for around 6 per cent of record company revenues, up from practically zero two years earlier (IFPI, 2006). Nonetheless, the music industry remained concerned that many consumers continued to download music without paying for it.

Formats and collecting

I turn now to the relationship between these trends and record collecting practices. Formats are evidence of historically shifting consumer tastes, and are a particularly significant part of record collecting. As indicated earlier, they provide different recording and listening experiences, in part related to the duration of recordings, along with their changing presentation and materiality. As such, formats have exercised a significant influence on the marketing of particular genres, their associated artists and those collecting them. Changing technologies and their associated formats usually appeal to consumers wanting better sound. Many collectors, especially of vinyl, have very good sound systems and some will even refer to themselves as 'audiophiles'.[7]

---

[7]   The term audiophile, however, is more strictly applied to those spending considerable amounts in search of the perfect sound. Audiophiles are sometimes record collectors (see Milano, 2003), but I am not considering them here, since their emphasis is generally on the technology itself rather than the recording.

There are also those who possess a 'must have' consumerist orientation to new technologies, thereby creating fresh markets as older consumers upgrade both their hardware and their record collections. More significant than the issue of fidelity, among collectors formats are closely linked to notions of nostalgia, aura and authenticity.

As seen in Chapter 1, there is still a constituency of 78 collectors. While it is relatively small, there remains a strong interest in, and buoyant market for,[8] some of these 'vintage' recordings, notably early country, blues and 1950s rock'n'roll, along with the picture discs of that period. I concentrate here on the collecting of the later recording formats, introduced in the above historical sketch. While there continues to be a preference for vinyl, many collect a range of formats, including CDs. A useful distinction here is between collecting a particular format simply because it is the easiest to hand, especially CDs as the dominant industry format, and the acquisition of *collectable* recordings in specific and preferred formats (for example, 12" dance mixes on vinyl). Indeed, some collectors indicated that they do not have a strong preference in terms of format:

- 'I don't have any preference. Cost generally determines which format I'll buy.' (Geoff Stahl)
- 'It doesn't work like this for me. I buy what I can get hold of, but saying this, I won't buy on cassette anymore. I tend to buy CDs for listening and records for the "hardcore" value.' (Michelle Wauchope; using 'hardcore' for those recordings accorded most value among her peers)
- 'CDs and LPs are my preferred formats, and between the two I'm not sure that I have a strong preference.' (Steve Waksman)

The type of music genres collected (and the associated listening experience) influences preference, as do historical shifts in industry standard, and what collectors had grown up with:

- 'Depends on the music. Some music sounds better on vinyl: punk, new wave, others better on CD: techno, classic, noise.' (Yngvar Steinbolt)
- 'In the old days I bought vinyl because that's all there was. When cassettes came in I got lots of those because of the walkman craze. I was slow to make the move to CDs, but now most of my collection is on CD – easy to store, easy to clean, easy to play. But I also have a lot of videos, and live concerts on video, which I love. And lately I'm into MP3s.' (Greg Crossan)

---

[8]   See Ian Shirley's comments in his profile in Chapter 7.

Vinyl collecting

Vinyl is the format most closely associated with record collecting; indeed, the very term 'record' is commonly used for vinyl recordings. This is exemplified in the titles of books like Stanley's *Collecting Vinyl* (2002) and Milano's *Vinyl Junkies* (2003). Vinyl is central in many popular media culture texts that feature record collecting (*High Fidelity*; *Ghost World*), and in those featuring DJs and club culture. Price guides focus primarily on vinyl, (and in some cases exclusively so), and it is vinyl records that attract the majority of the interest and the highest prices at auctions and in set sales. While vinyl offerings are not the dominant format on internet sites such as eBay and Trade Me, they attract more buyer interest and achieve the higher prices.[9] Around half of the 70 collectors I interviewed collected vinyl exclusively. Ian Shirley, editor of the most recent *Rare Record Price Guide*, observes that his own collection includes 3,000 CDs, 'which, for some collectors, doesn't really count.'[10]

The overarching reason for collectors' preference for vinyl can be loosely categorized as 'nostalgia', linked to the perceived aura and authenticity of the format. Vinyl is what many collecting 1960s and '70s groups and genres grew up with, and, as such, is frequently accompanied by positive associations with their adolescence and youth, and a sense of history. This reflects the common tendency for people to retain the greatest affection for the music they enjoyed in their youth, and their continued emotional attachment to it:

> For me it goes back to when I was five years old and started returning any soda bottle I could get my hands on, to get enough change to buy a 45 or an LP. Later on, when I had a job, I remember hitting every record store in a thirty-mile radius, getting those three-for-a-buck LPs. Anything that you heard about when I was a kid I tried to get my hands on. Getting a record was a wonderful thing, and it wasn't just the music, it was the smell of it, the look of the inner sleeve. (Bob Irwin, in Milano, 2003: 40–41; Irwin runs the reissue-oriented Sundazed record label)

Vinyl not only embodies personal history, it also represents the original historical artefact: how the vinyl single, EP or LP was originally recorded, and therefore the form in which it should be listened to. Collectors commonly refer to the look and feel of vinyl and the physicality of the playing and listening experience. A significant part of the appeal of vinyl records is their cover art, primarily with

---

[9]   On Trade Me, on 18 January 2009, there were 383 listings under 'Tapes', 4,967 under 'Vinyl', and 17,750 under 'CDs'. Most interest in the tape and CD categories was for bulk lots, whereas individual sales of 'classic'/collectable vinyl albums attracted considerable interest. Trade Me is a New Zealand website (though with some Australian participation).

[10]   'The Collector. No 60: Ian Shirley', *Record Collector*, November 2008: 8. Although he personally considered them an important part of his collection; see Chapter 7.

LP and EP covers but also with 45 picture sleeves. These various factors are frequently combined in the views of vinyl collectors, but I have separated them out below for the purposes of further discussion.

Nostalgia and generational/historical memory

Historically, vinyl is what those who began collecting in the 1960s and through into the 1980s grew up with. In the early 1990s, Plasketes found considerable evidence of a continued 'vinyl junkie' subculture, despite the impact of the CD and its increased market share. He saw a genre factor at work here, with R&B, folk and blues among genres still holding their own on vinyl. The general profile of this subculture of collectors began with generational distinctions: 'those marked by who grew up listening to music on albums, and have remained loyally devoted throughout the years', largely a male group (Plasketes, 1992: 114). Bob Irwin is an example:

> Vinyl is something we grew up with. You started with singles, and those were like training wheels, then you moved up to albums. If you skip down a generation or two, that feeling will probably vanish. As it is, I think nothing of forking out a couple hundred bucks for a rare LP, but I have a hard time paying more retail for a rare CD. The real emotional experience is the music, but the vinyl is an emotional experience as well. (Bob Irwin, in Milano, 2003: 41)

And their initial encounter with vinyl has often been sustained by younger collectors: 'I LOVE vinyl. It's the first format that I bought music on and have always had a love for the record covers and the feel of vinyl' (Joel Wing).

As most record dealers grew up on vinyl, it remains their preferred format. Interviewed by Tosh, dealer Garry enthused about vinyl, situating it in relation to other genres, and encapsulating the usual reasons mentioned for its superiority as the most collectable format:

> We grew up with records. Other forms of recorded music had their moments … reel-to-reel tapes, 4-tracks, cassettes … but nothing beat vinyl! The 45s and LPs came in cooler packages – picture sleeves, albums with colorful covers and liners with essential information … but most importantly, vinyl delivered the sound! (in Tosh, 2008)

Such views are echoed by many of my collectors who had grown up with vinyl, and began their collections in the 1960s and through the 1970s, before the advent of CDs: 'Vinyl, for sound quality as well as for the sensation of real, life-size covers (and labels). Plus I absolutely hate the plastic cases [of CDs]!' (Hasse Huss).

It is not exclusively older consumers and collectors who prefer vinyl. At the same time, some younger collectors, although born into the age of the CD and the download, prefer the older format. Hayes analysed the (re)emergence of vinyl as an alternative format for music consumption among youth in the digital age, drawing on interviews conducted during research on the affectivity of popular music. He found that only a third of the youth he interviewed were

> … fixated on music from previous eras to the degree that they privileged LPs and turntables over contemporary digitized formats and playback systems overwhelmingly endorsed by their peers. These eight also intermittently purchased new and used CDs and downloaded music files from the Internet, but LPs were their primary music format. (Hayes, 2006: 52)

Several of my younger collectors expressed similar sentiments: 'Having vinyl is something to be proud of!' (Lee Ann Fullington). The reasons for this preference for vinyl were essentially similar to those expressed by older vinyl collectors: the appeal of LP jackets, the physical ownership of original recordings, the more direct engagement in the listening experience (handling records, using the turntable), and the quest for elusive records. For many, vinyl also represented a form of musical cultural capital among their peers, and vinyl collecting could even be an important part of personal relationships.

Authenticity and aura

The preference for vinyl is grounded in it being the original historical artefact, with an associated perceived authenticity as a sound carrier, related to its sound and packaging, and the listening process/experience. Many vinyl collectors take the view that vinyl recordings are how a particular album was originally created, and therefore in a sense represents a more authentic listening experience:

- 'Albums have a kind of historic status – it's not just the sound of *Blonde on Blonde* [Bob Dylan, 1966] or *Sandinista* [The Clash, 1980] that counts, it's the actual object that you have in your hand. Seems to me the digital era lacks this sort of material register.' (Brennon Wood)
- 'I don't wanna listen to Led Zeppelin or the Who on CD because the extra noise on the sound carrier was there originally, and to me it is an essential part of their sound.' (Steve Waksman)
- 'I love vinyl, I am collecting *original* rock and related LPs from the 1960s mostly for my work (teaching, researching).' (Craig Morrison; my emphasis)

For such collectors, vinyl represents a link to the past that is 'immediate and visceral' (Oliver Wang). Paul nicely represents this view:

> The point about vinyl/analogue is that is sounds different to digitally recorded music. I have a large collection of 60s–70s LPs and 45s (as well as 1000-plus CDs). Apart from the sound difference, these are artefacts. They are products of

their time and place. I'm holding and looking at history with original vinyl. I'm not talking nostalgia either, these are documents about our shared cultural past. CD anthologies with good liner notes work in an updated way to the same end. The physicality of vinyl as a format is a key component of its attraction.[11]

Many of Hayes research participants similarly felt that format and authenticity were indelibly tied:

> Although the music preferences of these youth ran the gamut from Elvis to the Sex Pistols, there was a shared understanding that listening to their preferred artists on vinyl somehow constituted an experience more authentic than that offered by CDs. Because most of their favorite artists recorded the bulk of their work prior to the ascension of the CD and decline of the LP, these listeners understood vinyl recordings to be inextricably linked to the original studio session, as close as a music fan could get to the artist's actual performance. (Hayes, 2006: 59)

This aura of the original recording is a major reason for the continued collectability of 1960s artists such as The Beatles, The Who, and The Rolling Stones (see Chapter 4).

In his 'Market Watch' column for *Goldmine*, Robin Platts, documented how UK first pressing LPs of the Stones, especially some of the rarer mono versions and first pressings with various inserts, remained in high demand in 2005. Prices paid included US$3,836 for a mono UK pressing of *Let It Bleed* [1969], listed as in 'stunning condition', complete with the original poster, sticker and inner sleeve, and a promotional booklet that came with only a few copies of the album. 'The common appeal with all the records listed above', Platts thought,

> is getting the chance to experience the Stones as if you were a fan living in Great Britain in the 60s or early 70s. Hearing that glorious first pressing sound, sliding out the record in the original inner sleeve – that's something that no matter how many times the albums get remastered, you just can't get on a CD reissue. (*Goldmine*, July 2005: 16)

Playing and listening

As well as being a material object with historical resonance for many collectors, the physicality of the vinyl recording is a highly significant part of its continued appeal to collectors:

- 'Vinyl is definitely the preferred format. Newtonian physics of a large object that needs to be handled; great packaging, especially with the gatefolds,

---

[11]   Paul Martin, *Record Collector*, May 2007: Letters.

luxurious sensuousness compared with the digitally miniaturized bullet.' (Brennon Wood)

- 'Handling the platters is such a romantic, sacred exercise, as opposed to wrestling with and breaking those stupid, cumbersome jewel boxes.' (Michelle Wauchope)
- 'I just like the feel of the record, being able to see the music in the grooves, and enjoying the cover art and liner notes while listening to the music.' (John Book)

The majority of such comments came from older (40 years plus) collectors, strongly suggesting that a preference for the physical artefact is a function of generational experiences. The majority of contemporary youthful music fans, judging from surveys, cultural commentary and the comments of my students, my teenage children and their friends, do not regard the vinyl album, or even the CD, in the same way: 'CDs are pointless, because it takes more effort to play them, than just downloading them' (Cameron, age 15). For them, the dematerialization of music is a positive development, and their music is acquired primarily in digital form. A research report released in March 2008 claimed that half of all teenagers in the United States bought no compact discs in 2007, accelerating the music industry's painful transition from CDs to digital downloads: 'Going to a store and buying a CD is no longer a rite of passage for many teenagers. But illegally downloading a song might be.'[12] The report, by research firm NPD group, was presented in my local paper under the droll heading 'CDs so yesterday for teenagers'. We may now be experiencing a generational shift in our consumption of music, a waning of affect in relation to the traditional materiality of the sound recording. I will return to the impact of the digital format on collecting later in the chapter.

Packaging

As several of above collectors' comments illustrate, packaging, especially artwork, is part of the appeal of vinyl. Others place even greater emphasis on this:

- 'One major reason [for preferring vinyl] is that the cover and sleeve artwork stands out more than on CD/audio cassette. Secondly, lyric sheets are more readable than the small type on CDs/cassettes.' (Albert Bell)
- 'CDs are more durable and transportable, but other formats often have better or different ARTWORK: this is one of my key reasons for collecting.' (Gary Shuker; an artist – primarily a painter)

While present on the sleeves of 45 singles, as with the distinctive artwork of several punk and indie labels, cover art is primarily associated with albums (and, to a lesser extent, EPs), especially in their vinyl format.

---

[12]　*Dominion Post*, 1 March 2008: C7.

Album covers convey meaning through the semiotic resources they draw on and display, via language, typography, images and layout. They are a form of advertising, alerting consumers to the artist(s) responsible, and thereby sustaining and drawing on an auteur/star image; and they make an artistic statement in relation to the style of music by association with particular iconography, as with the use of apocalyptic imagery in heavy metal, and the fantasy imagery of progressive rock. Album cover liner notes function as a literary and advertising form, while the practice of printing song lyrics on covers often signalled a 'serious' genre and artist. For example, Island's marketing of Bob Marley and the Wailers, with album covers constructing Marley as a star figure and the band as politically authentic style rebels, was important to their commercial success and the mainstreaming of reggae in the 1970s, and their subsequent collectability (Shuker, 2008: 28–30; Steffens and Pierson, 2005).

Part of the original appeal of albums was the development of their covers as an art form, established during the 1950s, but primarily with the strong association of rock culture and the graphic arts in the 1960s. There was a good deal of creative packaging, including supplementary material, in releases during the decade. Prominent examples are the replica tobacco tin of The Small Faces, *Ogden's Nut Gone Flake*, Sony, 1968; and The Who, *Live at Leeds*, MCA, 1970, which included reproductions of concert posters, performance invoices and so forth in a stapled folder cardboard cover. The album covers of The Beatles' recordings were especially notable: 'groundbreaking in their visual and aesthetic properties (and) their innovative and imaginative designs' (Inglis, 2001: 83). They forged a link with the expanding British graphic design industry and the art world, while making explicit the connections between art and pop in the 1960s. The prestigious Grammy Awards began including an award for best album cover, won by The Beatles in 1966 for *Revolver* and again in 1967 for *Sgt. Pepper's Lonely Hearts Club Band*, undoubtedly the most celebrated album cover.

Covers became considered as an art form, with the publication of collected volumes of those that are considered exemplars, along with collections of the work of artists such as Roger Dean, best known for his work with progressive rock band Yes. Particular record companies are associated with a 'house' style of covers, for instance the jazz label Blue Note from the mid-1950s employed a talented graphic artist, Reid Miles, to design most of its album sleeves. The covers represented sophisticated images of fashion, and combined with Miles's personal flair and the pioneering use of typography to signal taste and integrity as a key part of the label's appeal (Marsh and Callingham, 2003, reproduce nearly 400 examples).

A number of graphic artists who have worked on record covers are also record collectors; not unexpectedly, they often have a particular affinity for the artwork associated with the vinyl format:

> It's all about the music, but what makes a collection is the variety of rare picture sleeves. For The Monkees, for instance, I've now got a virtually complete run

of single sleeves for every country from the US to Japan, including places like Italy, France, Germany and so on. (Phil Smee, record sleeve designer)[13]

The album cover continues to be a significant part of the appeal of vinyl, which has been reinforced by the continued publication of volumes documenting album covers and the artists associated with them.[14] Album covers don't just form part of the general appeal for collecting vinyl, some are highly collectable in their own right. This is especially the case with releases by collectable artists where the original album cover has proved controversial, and rapidly been withdrawn and replaced, as with The Beatles 'Butchers' cover (see Thompson, 2002: 17–18).

Singles

Although vinyl collectors tend to concentrate on albums, most will also have some singles.[15] Once again, the appeal of the format is a combination of the music, its restricted availability and the packaging:

- 'I also have [some] 7" singles because the design and the rare b-side element are appealing to me.' (Michelle Flannery)
- '7" EPs are cool. Regular 7"s as well, as long as they come w/ the original photo cover. I also like 10" records (e.g. the Man's Ruin 10" collection is awesome!).' (Mark Vanderdrift)
- 'I've also increasingly gotten into 45s. I used to buy 45s because I just wanted one song off an album instead of the whole thing. I collect them because there's so many of them to find and because there are a lot of artists that only released music on 45s and never put out a whole LP.' (Joel Wing)

With genres such as reggae, rap and early soul, where the 45 was the main form of release, the format will dominate collections. Steve Barrow, the London DJ and co-author of *The Rough Guide to Reggae*, has more than 20,000 7" Jamaican singles in his collection – 'though I haven't counted them in a few years'.[16] John Peel's collection included a huge number of indie/alt 45s; Hasse Husse, a collector of soul and reggae, has 8,500 singles (see his profile in Chapter 7).

---

[13] 'The Collector. No 6: Phil Smee'; *Record Collector*, August 2004: 162.

[14] See M. Ochs, *1000 Rock Covers* (Cologne: 1996). For links to websites featuring album covers: http://tralfaz-archives.com/coverart/coverartlinks.html.

[15] The main vinyl singles format is the 45, although later forms have been significant, notably the EP (especially in the 1960s), and the 10" dance single.

[16] Barrow visited New Zealand in February 2005 for a gig with his Blood and Fire Soundsystem. He was interviewed by Lindsay Davis for Wellington's *Dominion Post* newspaper (4 February 2005).

DJs and vinyl

When I surveyed collectors in 2001–03, vinyl was the clear format of choice for the DJs, essentially due to the limitations of turntablism:

- '[I collect] Vinyl. Primarily because I'm a DJ and am unable to use CDs.' (Joe Kellich)
- 'Vinyl – because of the ability to DJ with them – plus their largeness, the ability to manipulate and mix, the fact that many of the artists I prefer often release vinyl only.' (Matt Glesne)

Furthermore, vinyl was central to a hip-hop aesthetic. As Oliver Wang put it: 'DJs who turn into collectors are always supposed to favor vinyl since that's where hip-hop's sonic origins begin.' Most of the records sought out by DJs, especially through 'digging in the crates' (see Chapter 5), are only available on vinyl. A preference for vinyl did not prevent DJs from also collecting other formats: 'I am getting more into minidisc recordings off the PC – radio shows, MP3s and online mixes. I also buy CDs for old hard-to-find jazz and Latin' (Matt Glesne). More recently, new technologies have lessened the DJs reliance on vinyl, with the ability to copy vinyl records as digital files and play these back at gigs, but the format still retains its cachet of originality and status (Farrugia and Swiss, 2005; and see the profiles of Geoff Stahl and Oliver Wang, in Chapter 7).

Collecting audiotapes[17]

'Without doubt, the cassette is the poor relation of the collecting world. Whereas every other format – even such utter obscurities as Pocket Rockers and 4-Track cartridges – has its die-hard adherents, the cassette remains despised and derided' (Thompson, 2007: 16). In part, this judgement reflects the enduring reputation audiotapes carried over from the more limited durability, sound quality and inferior packaging present during their early development. Certainly, few of the collectors I interviewed placed much emphasis on audiotapes. Several had relied on them for initial collection building, before they could afford vinyl recordings, but later usually replaced them. Although audiotapes were still included in collections in the early 2000s, they subsequently often became discarded, or stored away and largely forgotten: dormant and not listened to.

The original reasons for buying, or copying, tapes were their availability, low cost and compactness, making them easy to transport and access (especially through portable players and car cassette tape players). They were rarely regarded

---

[17] Other tape formats are collected, especially eight tracks featuring quadraphonic sound, but for convenience here I focus on the format's main variant. On 8-track collectors, see the documentary *So Wrong They're Right* (dir. Russ Forster, 1995).

as 'collectable' at this time. The physical characteristics of the format, rather than the music it contained, were the basic appeal. When my own vinyl albums and singles went into storage in late 1973, prior to my going to the United Kingdom on an extended working holiday, I dubbed various 'favourite albums' from my collection onto some 25 C120 audiotapes. While away, when I became bored with these, I used some to dub radio shows, notably Nicky Horn's Rock Show on Radio London (I have retained these, as they represent classic rock radio of the period). In addition, travelling around the UK and Europe a good deal, and not having a turntable, I purchased some new release albums as audio cassettes, and got some bootlegs of live concerts on audiotape from the London street markets. However, I considered few of these as a significant part of my record collection.

Most collectors clearly did not regard audiotapes as 'collectable', in a narrower sense of being different from their vinyl and CD versions. This changed with record company manufacturing practices in the late 1970s, in an effort to enhance their appeal. 'Beginning around 1979, cassette-only bonus tracks came into vogue – one of the best known early examples is the Kinks' 1980 double live album *One For The Road* (Arista 8401), which was issued on tape with the extra song '20th Century Man'. Another interesting practice saw cassettes being utilized to offer 'full length' versions of songs that were edited down for vinyl releases. Cassette copies of Grace Jones's *Warm Leatherette* (UK Island, ICT 9592) are prized for their unique inclusion of virtually a second LP's worth of music (Thompson, 2007: 16, 35; previously, cassettes had simply replicated the contents of their vinyl counterparts).

The advent of the cassette single led to a boom in the cassette's popularity through the 1980s. Malcolm McLaren, former manager of the Sex Pistols, is widely regarded as the father of the format, after his new band Bow Wow Wow issued the *Cassette Pet* single in 1980. Soon virtually every new single release in the UK and the United States was made available on cassette; indeed, some appeared only on cassette, increasing their appeal to collectors. Swedish band Roxette's *Listen to Your Heart* (1990) was the first single to hit number one in the United States without being released as a vinyl 45. As Thompson (2007) documents, many cassette singles now command high prices among fans of individual artists, often as a result of some extremely well-designed, limited-edition packaging or the use of exclusive material.[18] Many 'indie' artists launched their recording careers with cassette-only releases, which were sold at gigs or by mail order, in the late 1990s and through the 1990s; examples include Beck, the Smashing Pumpkins and Marilyn Manson. Such releases are now sought after, especially by completist collectors specializing in the music of particular artists or genres.

As well as at times now being collectable in their own right, audiotapes continue to represent an accessible and relatively cheap form of 'record', as they

[18]   For example, promotional copies of Bow Wow Wow's *Cassette Pet* were issued in a mock-up can of dog food, while several of Frankie Goes To Hollywood's early cassette singles include otherwise unavailable mixes.

frequently appear in thrift stores, and on web auctions, very cheaply indeed. Even the traditional second-hand record shops, focused on vinyl and the CD, have audiotapes for a few dollars each. As do many collectors of contemporary releases, I frequently purchase these when I am interested in the genre or performer, but do not want to purchase their album or CD, which will be at least four times the price.

Older collectable recordings will also sometimes surface on cassette. In 2007, I obtained a number of the *Nuggets* series in my local Salvation Army 'thrift' shop, along with a copy of the relatively scarce Blue Cheer 'Best Of' compilation, *Louder Than God* (Rhino, 1986).[19] I had these garage/punk rock and early proto-metal classics on vinyl, but in poor condition. Sound quality was not a factor here, especially given my view that 'rock' played loud can compensate for a technically inferior recording, and surface noise is an integral part of the genre's appeal. My main motivation was to have access to the music, and to have something to play in the car – admittedly when driving alone, the rest of the family not sharing my arrested garage rock tendencies.

Collecting CDs

Of the 70 collectors I 'interviewed', roughly a quarter collected only CDs. These collectors were almost exclusively a younger group who had grown up with the format, and the material they wanted was largely available on it. They were quite willing to purchase CD reissues of vinyl albums, and were not concerned with having 'the original' artefact. A further quarter of my collecting group included CDs in their collections, along with a range of formats (the remaining half collected vinyl exclusively). Collectors preferring the CD, or at least including CDs as part of their collection, refer to a now standard range of reasons for doing so: their availability, ease of use, the amount of music held, sound quality and durability. Typical comments included:

- 'CDs because I like the quality of the sound.' (Susan Fast)
- 'CD because it's practical and easy to look after.' (Liz Guiffre)
- 'CD for convenience, availability, lack of surface noise and long term condition.' (Warren Green)
- 'CD albums. Simply because this is currently the standard format.' (Motti Regev)
- 'CDs – the easiest format with the best quality.' (Michelle Flannery)

---

[19]   These were the Rhino reissues of the 1980s. Of course, the fact that these were a (NZ) dollar each, made the find even more pleasurable. The role of such searches and chance discoveries is taken up in Chapter 5.

However, even those who preferred the CD format, were not always convinced that CDs had superior sound quality (to vinyl):

- 'CDs, because they're available and moderately indestructible. I probably "prefer" vinyl for the sound.' (Norma Coates)
- 'CD because of its portability and ability to be converted to MP3. However I think vinyl is better for midrange frequency reproduction.' (Warren Green)

And even when vinyl was preferred, this hardly impeded the collection of CDs:

- 'I like CDs if I like what's on it, I'll buy the CD, especially if it's well-collected and notated material.' (Craig Morrison)

By the early 1990s, there was increasing recognition of the CD as a collectable format, especially the promotional CD, but also out of print CDs. In 1996, Neely observed how 'the collectors market has only just began to pick up on many of these', providing the example of the David Bowie compact discs on the RCA label, which were only very briefly available before they were pulled from the market (Bowie, who owned the rights to his masters, had not given permission for RCA to re-release his 1972–82 catalogue). Neely also observed that 'compared to the generally well-regarded reissues on Ryodisc, the RCA's sound pretty bad, so some [collectors] have stayed away' (Neely, 1999: 39).

For collectors with a completist approach, an issue is the desirability of including initial CD releases of recordings which are not of comparable quality to later CD reissues. Of course, an added factor here is the tendency for the later CD reissues to include material not available on the earlier releases. This is especially the case in relation to vinyl albums, with their more restricted running time, in comparison to their CD versions. Prominent examples over the past few years include remastered, repackaged CDs of the original albums by Elvis Costello and The Who. These will include both stereo and mono mixes, live concert versions of the tracks and earlier takes of the original recordings. This has considerable appeal to collectors, even those still committed to vinyl:

> 'I've been investing in some CD remasters lately (The Clash, Hendrix, The Kinks and Lou Reed have all benefited hugely from this after initially poor sound representation on CD; I could barely believe the difference in the Clash's case). Record companies are getting much more creative in their packaging of CDs these days, especially with reissues which cater to collectors, so I'm getting less fussy.' (Andrew Stafford)

Cooper provided one of the first comprehensive guides to collectable compact discs. He identified a number of factors determining CD collectability 'once a disc reaches the threshold of being collectible' (Cooper, 1998: 7). This threshold is reached when a CD moves from simply being a used product, and sold at a fraction of the retail cost, to being in demand: the market determining that it is a valuable commodity – and therefore collectable. The six factors that then come into play are similar to those that apply to vinyl records:

- popularity and/or demand of the artist on the disc;
- availability of the disc;
- uniqueness of the disc;
- history of the disc;
- retail price of the disc;
- age and preservation of the disc; and
- generation and format of music on the disc.

Several of my collectors provided examples of releases that illustrated the interplay of these factors. In my own case I was conscious of the significant differences between CD reissues of bands such as Pink Floyd and Dire Straits in the 1980s, and the original vinyl albums. The emphasis of both groups on sonic experimentation and studio perfectionism made them ideally suited to the digital format of the CD. Their CD releases can be distinguished from the earlier albums in terms of sound quality, track running time and, most important for many collectors, their rarity. Dire Straits' promotional CD of 'Brothers in Arms' became legendary in collecting circles for its scarcity. The collector press contributed to the emergent collector interest in such CD issues, soon providing guidance on the availability of such releases.[20]

Collecting digital music

Digital music has had a major impact on collecting, with the advent of the internet, the music download, hard drives and MP3 players. These collectively provide greater access to a wider range of music, along with expanded knowledge of it and its creators. But along with such opportunities have come shifts in collecting practices, with the digital format arguably undermining the traditional view of 'the record collector' and what is 'collectable'. As mentioned earlier, many of today's teenagers will frequently 'collect' downloads, and not own any physical recordings. What does it mean for record collecting if the musical commodity loses its materiality? There is an emerging body of work on the influence of digital technology on the culture of record collecting and the role of the record (as a physical entity) in it.

Styven regards the primary implication of the abstraction of music in its digital format is a perceived loss of value in the shift away from tangible object to intangible music file: 'Digitization of products leads to an increased abstraction

---

[20]   For example: 'Dire Straits on CD', *Record Collector*, 100, December 1987.

(that) may cause adverse reactions and beliefs that the content is artificial and not authentic' (Styven, 2007). Situating his discussion of digital downloading against Benjamin's classic essay on book collecting, in a provocative essay 'Unpacking Our Hard Drives' Dibbell (2004) suggested that physical ownership is no longer so central to our engagement with music. The popularity of MP3 players adds to the 'computer/techno-geek' thrill of massive storage, despite the initially limited sound quality of MP3s and other file formats.

A compendium of digital files in a hard drive becomes a different kind of collection, while the availability of digital music offers a new reconfiguration and definition of the sound recording as a material artefact. McCourt (2005) sketches a number of crucial shifts resulting from the emergence of digital music technology, with these collectively having paradoxical effects for the sense of 'ownership' of music. He argues that 'Possessing digital files is a more intense and intimate experience than owning physical recordings', an experience that is manifested in three ways:

1. Compacting music allows the consumer to own vast amounts of music in a small area: 'the appeal of digital collecting is predicated in part on the ability to contain huge amounts of data in a small area.'
2. The desire for immediacy, in which the ability to sort and regroup files effortlessly transforms the listening experience: 'as speed itself becomes a fetish, daily life gets a different kind of soundtrack.'
3. The desire to customize, which is 'heightened by the malleability of digital media. Customization via digital software is expedient, efficient, and accomplished at a physical remove. This enables further subjective interaction with the music collection, users are able to assemble unique playlists and are no longer bound by the album, or, to an increasing extent, the song format' (McCourt, 2005).

Such views tend to see a binary opposition between the physical object, with its historically located aura of authenticity, and the intangible dematerialized object; between the analogue sound recording and its digital equivalent. As Kelso contends, however, with the increased acceptance of digitization in the culture of record collecting, this binary may in fact be undermined, and digital music can be considered as being complimentary to analogue. His research suggested:

> the perceptual divide between digital and analogue music may not be as deep as typically thought. Record collecting is typically pro-analogue culture in which the record object is invested with cultural significance, with record collectors assembling collections that consequently contribute to the creation of musical canons. This is countered by the increased ubiquity of the internet as a site of exchange and the digitalization of music. (Kelso, 2007)

Kelso illuminates the influence that the internet and digital technology is having on the culture of record collecting, undermining the traditional opposition between digital and analogue music. Drawing on an opportunity sample, derived from several on-line collecting sites and personal contacts, he considered the actual role of online communities as sites of exchange of information and the actual object of the record. The majority of his respondents indicated frequent conversion of records to digital, giving ease of access in a number of settings as the main reason for this.

'Yes, I transfer some of my (favourite) vinyl albums to my PC ... so I can make CD's or load the iPod ... for daily driving music and road trips.' Preservation of the original was also an important factor. The role of the record collector as a tastemaker and culture broker was reinforced, with collectors 'ripping' to digital to make mixes that they can give to family and friends, enabling their exposure to 'obscure' or just plain 'good' music. As Kelso concluded, to established definitions centred on the practices of the traditional record collector, we can add definitions reflecting the acceptance of the new technology: those of online community member, internet researcher, digitizer and online information trader.

I turn now to the question of how my collectors situate themselves in these practices and the associate debates. When I undertook my initial interviews in 2001–02, a number of collectors were already regarding digital music as part of their collecting:

> 'lately, as mentioned, I'm into MP3s – easy to download, easy to catalogue, unbreakable (though a virus could conceivably wipe out my files, which is why I really need a CD writer so I can store them on a disc instead of the hard drive ...) – and, for the moment, free!' (Greg Crossan)

When I returned to several of them in 2008–09, this was even more pronounced, with several storing their physical recordings on their hard drives and MP3 players, in addition to additional music (see the profiles of Simon Sweetman and Geoff Stahl, in Chapter 7). The increased use of the internet was not just a question of the appeal of the digital format, it also offered a broader market (a point taken up in Chapter 5) 'I agree that buying online doesn't give you the buzz of searching a well stocked shop, but it is a great tool to use for picking up those elusive gems or for selling those items you never thought you would sell in a million years' (Stephen Fox, *Record Collector*, 'Letters', March 2006: 7).

McCourt (2005) claims that the popularity of MP3 files and related formats indicates that access and convenience are increasingly more important than the material artefact and sound quality. While this may hold for many younger music consumers, including some who consider themselves 'record collectors', it is not a view shared by 'traditional' record collectors, who continue to privilege the physical recording, and its associated physical qualities, very seriously. This was illustrated in an instructive exchange in 'The Letters' column of *Record Collector* magazine during 2006.

Stephen Islip considered that the magazine 'takes a very anachronistic view' of record collectors:

> … you seem to be stuck in the past … the most anachronistic section is your *The Collector* section. Each month you feature vinyl train spotter obsessives, who brag about stupid amounts of money they've paid often for unplayable records which they can no longer find in the uncontrollable storage they've had to employ, to keep on top of their subject.

He argued:

> In the next five years most collectors will be collecting via mp3 (or some other forms of electronic file) and they will be organising their 1000s of albums via hard discs attached to PC's or through IPODS. They will have also realised that record collecting economics have been reversed – i.e. like microprocessors, the first model costs 1 million (European pounds), the second copy cost virtually nothing. In other words we will all become 'software collectors'. (*Record Collector*, February 2006: 7)

In response, the editor [Alan Lewis] pointed out that the magazine had been 'covering downloading and other aspects of digital technology for several years' in its column 'OK Computer'. He went on to argue: 'We believe that vinyl and other collectable formats will continue to be appreciated in the download era and may arguably become even more highly valued' (*Record Collector*, February 2006: 7). Other readers passionately came to his support, referring to the fairly standard reasons for collecting vinyl, including the poor sound of downloads:

> I'm afraid that he's [Islip] totally missing the point about record/CD collecting. Most collectors don't just collect vinyl or CDs as an artefact per se, but because they want the music contained in them at the best possible quality, in terms of both recording and reproduction. (That's why they have expensive hi-fis!) Most collectors are audiophiles, and until we get, pardon the pun, equally good audio files in terms of the quality of downloads, few collectors will take them seriously. Downloads are currently the audio equivalent of cassettes, and until they can challenge vinyl and CD for sheer sonic quality, they won't be as desirable as the traditional alternatives. Downloading and iPods in particular, are a triumph of marketing over engineering! (Mark Smith, *Record Collector*, March 2006: 7)

> While many people put their record collection on mp3 for quickness and convenience, it truly kills the art of collecting. I pride myself on my 8,000 LP collection and love having people round to admire it: you could hardly invite someone round to admire your mp3 collection could you? Also, real collectors love the smell of the vinyl, the look of the grooves, the fantastic covers, gatefold sleeves, picture discs, posters, lyric sheets etc.

Mp3s could never compete with the thrill of finding that missing album, or single. (Alan Hare, *Record Collector*, March 2006: 7)

As this exchange suggested, the issue of digital music in relation to record collecting will frequently create controversy. It remains to be seen if the worst fears of observers who see digital replacing analogue recordings will be realized. An indicator of a probable coexistence of the old and the new is the manner in which the record industry continues to produce both formats, as part of its general strategy of marketing to collectors.

The record industry and music collectibles

In my discussion of formats, I have already touched on how the recording industry has played a central role in shaping consumer preferences. Record collectors have been an important target group and constituency for such efforts from both major and independent record labels. During the 78 era, the industry utilized a number of strategies and formats aimed in part at collectors (see Chapter 1). Record companies over the past thirty years or so have produced a range of commodity forms and packaging aimed largely at collectors. These include picture discs, picture sleeves, boxed sets and a wide range of promotional items.[21]

Small record labels have historically served the collectors market, since they were willing to release (or re-release) material in smaller pressings which larger companies considered non-commercial. This practice had long been evident in the jazz and blues fields, and was part of the advent of rock and roll in the 1950s. The cult status of 1960s garage rock is linked to the *Nuggets* and *Pebbles* compilation series, which rescued many recordings from obscurity. In the United States, labels such as Rhino and Sundazed have established their commercial success through catering to a collectors' market with well-packaged compilations and reissues. In the 1970s, the emergence of the new independent labels in the United Kingdom was partly in response to collector and fan interest in punk music. Chiswick owner Ted Caroll ran a record shop specializing in oldies, and saw the music of emerging punk performers as ideal material for his customers: 'I know there wasn't a large market for such groups, but felt sure there would be a small, but large enough collector's market' (cited in Laing, 1985: 10).

Other punk and post-punk oriented labels, such as Rough Trade and Factory Records, also targeted record collectors, with a range of distinctive packaging practices and various release formats. In the 1980s, limited 7" vinyl singles became a standard way to launch new bands, while the limited 12" single remained essential to the DJ and dance market. As the *Rare Record Price Guide* observed (2002 edition: 7): 'there have been a steady stream of instant collectables over

---

[21]   For a fuller discussion of these, see Thompson (2002), and the various price guides (see Chapter 6).

the past decade, either as part of indie-label singles clubs, or as "split" singles, combining two acts from different labels on the same record. All these items are likely to rise in value in the future, and many are already appearing in the *Rare Record Price Guide*.'

Writing in 2007, De Whalley extensively documented how the bulk of reissued vinyl albums remains 'largely driven' by the specialist labels. An example is Beggars Banquet's inclusion of a new White Stripes single as a cover mount with every copy of the iconic UK music magazine *NME*, as a calculated promotional strategy. The label's production manager, Greg Muir explained:

> The NME track is on red vinyl etched with a picture of Meg White and is in a double gatefold sleeve. To complete the package we will be selling a white vinyl *Icky Thump* [the White Stripes new album] with Jack's face on it through regular record shops. We don't necessarily expect that every NME reader will want to complete the set, but we expect all White Stripes fans will do, and lots of collectors too. (De Whalley, 2007: 71)

The repertoire and release strategies of major record companies are usually more focused on the mainstream market, and historically they have at times been slow to recognize the commercial potential of niche/collector markets. This changed with the success of their indie counterparts in the late 1970s and onward, as the majors began extensive reissue programmes, drawing on their often extensive back catalogues, and also began to pay more attention to licensing possibilities. While this was heavily oriented towards CDs, vinyl releases have been prominent, and continue to be featured. For instance, in 2008 Hollywood Records began a two-year reissue programme of the full Queen studio album catalogue on vinyl. To celebrate the sixtieth anniversary of the vinyl album, HMV (UMG) announced the reissue of a series of classic albums, cleverly titled *Back To Black*, remastered in 180g vinyl. Illustrating the increasing combination of formats as a marketing strategy, purchasers also had a download option.

Conclusion

Preferences for particular formats are linked to the age of the record collector and associated notions of nostalgia and popular memory, aura and authenticity. These are primarily related to the 'materiality' of the recording format, and the associated differing playing and listening experiences. Vinyl remains synonymous with contemporary record collecting, but the CD has become collectable, especially among younger collectors. The status of the digital download remains contentious, and is unlikely to replace its predecessors, at least in the view of the traditional collector. As the music industry continues to recognize the advantages of making recordings available in a range of formats, to meet different consumer preferences, the different formats have come to coexist. The record companies have both responded to and shaped collecting through the successive recording formats, along with their 'packaging practices', such as including special album cover art, picture sleeves and promotional items. Collecting preferences are also shaped by considerations of musical value, the subject of Chapter 4.

Chapter 4
Taste, the canon and the collectable

This chapter considers the related issues of taste, cultural capital and the canon, and the question of what is 'collectable'. At one level, you can collect whatever you like, with personal taste in music a basic starting point for individual collectors' decisions as to which genres, artists, periods, labels and so forth to collect. Intersecting with such choices is the key notion of 'collectable', with the collecting process and what is collectable shaped by considerations of demand and availability, condition and cost, aura and authenticity, and rarity and value. Taste and what is collectable are historically contingent, reflecting generational and demographic trends in collecting, and representing varying forms of cultural capital. The complex interaction of these various factors is illustrated here through a consideration of the top ten collectable artists identified by a *Record Collector* poll of its readers in 2000, and a number of the top-selling items on eBay during 2007.

What is collectable can also be informed by a strong sense of discrimination, in part based on views of which artists, recordings and genres have musical/ aesthetic value: a canon. Counter to this, some highly sought-after records may not be considered musically significant (in relation to the dominant canon), but are valorized because of their very scarcity (rarity). Further, there can be an inverse approach to collecting, whereby 'crap records' are valued for their (generally perceived) lack of musical merit, with aspects such as their cover art often valued over the music they contain.

My focus here is on individual genres, artists and records; these are the primary orientation of most record collectors, and the main forms of their collecting. There are also collectable fields which are informed by different organizing principles, and are underpinned by different inflections of taste and collectability. Examples of these, included here, are the collecting of chart number one hits, compilations, bootlegs, memorabilia and music magazines.

Taste

'Taste' refers to our cultural preferences, and is often used in the sense of 'good taste'. Particular cultural texts, activities and practices have acquired a higher status than others, and those who consume such texts are frequently viewed as culturally and aesthetically discerning. Related to this are notions of a canon of cultural texts – the 'best' available – a concept underpinned by a mix of aesthetics and ideology. There are problems posed by the subjectivity of the discourse surrounding taste and the historically shifting nature of what constitutes taste. Further, texts connoting 'good taste' are usually validated by those who are considered to have such taste, a process of self-confirmation. In its contemporary formulations, taste is frequently conflated with the concept of cultural capital (Bourdieu, 1984).

Taste is both constructed and maintained through the efforts of social groups to differentiate and distance themselves from others, and thereby underpin varying social status positions (see, for example, Becker, 1982). Music has traditionally been a crucial dimension of this process, especially the historical privileging of classical music. Music consumption and musical taste are not simply matters of 'personal' preference; they are, in part, socially constructed, serving as a form of symbolic or cultural capital (Frith, 1996; Toynbee, 2000; Clayton, Herbert and Middleton, 2003). Different forms of musical cultural capital are present in particular genres and their associated scenes, as with indie rock (Fonarow, 2006) and dance music (Thornton, 1995). Acquiring popular music cultural capital involves developing a knowledge of selected musical traditions, their history and their associated performers. With this background an individual can knowledgably discuss such details as styles, trends, record companies and the biographies of artists, and even nuances such as record producers and session musicians used on recordings. Acquiring, utilizing and demonstrating such knowledge is an integral part of record collecting. Musical cultural capital does not necessarily have to be part of the generally accepted canon of artists and genres, but can instead function to distance its adherents from that tradition, asserting an oppositional stance. The different forms of cultural capital are present among record collectors; some emphasize the collecting of canonical recordings and others valorize the obscure and the exotic (see the collectors in Vale and Juno, 1993; 1994), although both types of recordings may be included in individual collections.

The scope of the collection

As Geoff observes, decisions on what to collect are, in part, based on restricting the field to what is manageable:

> 'I generally class myself as omnivorous, with certain glaring absences: Jazz, Hip Hop. Not sure why this is the case. I think that it might have something to do with the kind of technical language I would be required to master in order to appear as invested in those genres as I am in others. It's not that I don't like it, it's just a time management strategy.' (Geoff Stahl)

The omnivore is a stock figure in record collecting, as collectors frequently display fairly catholic and wide-ranging tastes, although with a clear preference for particular genres/performers, the main emphases of their 'collecting' interests.

- 'I like obscure indie, rock, and pop but also alt.country and avant garde jazz.' (Michelle Flannery)

- 'Female singer/songwriters, "folky" and alternative, both guitar and piano based. I am also interested in selected male heavy metal bands, and the heavy metal/alternate rock cross, particularly the vocalists (and guitar players when they sing). I do have an interest in 60s music, and "progressive rock" – some mediocre collections here. Oh, also contemporary classical scores too, and some Celtic sounds.' (Catherine Brown)
- 'In the classical repertoire I've collected mainly the Romantics, because that period has been both my passion and my professional livelihood, but I've also collected British composers of (mainly) the 20th century – Vaughan Williams, Britten, Delius, Bax, Elgar, etc. I especially love "pastoral" music and "faery" music. But in the pop world I've been all over the place, from Led Zep and Deep Purple to Sinead O'Connor and the Cocteau Twins.' (Greg Crossan)

The majority of my interviewees collected 'rock', in the broadest meaning of the term, including genres such as heavy metal, blues, soul, reggae and punk/indie/ alternative. Only a handful (3/70) collected classical, or jazz (6) on a large scale. Motti, for example, describes himself as

'basically a "rock" collector, in the widest meaning of the word. From "classic" 60s and 70s artists (including, soul, Motown and funk) through 80s alternative (Cure, Tom Verlaine) to 90s electronica (the Orb, Air). I also have a relatively large section of world rock (NOT necessarily "world music"). In addition, a substantial part of my collection is Israeli music – mostly Israeli rock.' (Motti Regev)

Similar emphases are reflected in other published collector profiles (Campbell, 2001; Milano, 2003; and the series in *Record Collector*). For instance, Joe Geesin collects 'Rock music that I love and grew up with: mostly trad.rock, from late-60s blues to mid-80s metal. I collect the worldwide releases of Cozy Powell and related artists, Nazareth, Samson, The Motors, Foghat and Gillan, UK pressings by Iron Maiden or just remastered CDs from artists such as Kiss and Motorhead.'[1] Along with a preference for the dominant rock styles of the 1960s, reflecting their generational experiences, several collectors had a strong dislike of later genres such as rap and electronic/dance music:

'My main genre preference is what I call mainstream rock, but I also have some likes in music as diverse as blues, heavy metal, folk and some world music. Most of my interests are guitar based. I can't stand jazz, and have absolutely no time for music such as techno, thrash, grunge, rap, hip hop and trance.' (Peter Dawson)

---

[1] 'The Collector, No. 2: Joe Geesin', *Record Collector*, April 2004: 162.

Collecting the work of one recording artist or band is a common approach, which can assume increasing sophistication over time. It is fairly straightforward to acquire the official recorded output of contemporary artists, and collectors will rapidly move past this to seek out overseas pressings, promos and unusual pressings (different mixes, coloured vinyl, picture discs, etc.). This latter stage can become both challenging and expensive, and cultural capital (knowing the artists' work and the market) becomes central to the quest for elusive items. French collector Herve Denoyelle specializes in vinyl Pink Floyd official releases: 'the Pink Floyd 7"s collection is now getting (very) close to 600. I also have approximately 700 to 800 Pink Floyd LPs.'[2] Even an artist with a relatively small back catalogue can generate a fair number of collectable releases. Gary Shuker owned some 80 records by New Zealand's premier singer songwriter Bic Runga, with her dozen or so official recordings collected in every international pressing, as promos, and on compilations.

This is a form of completism, although it certainly does not pre-empt collecting other material, usually in a similar style: 'About one third of my collection consists of the works of two bands/artists: Bob Dylan and the Rolling Stones, of whom I own every official album (some of them twice or more) and lots of unofficial stuff' (Lee Marshall: see his profile in Chapter 7). Other collectors I spoke with have built up extensive collections representing a wide range of artists, including Bauhaus, Magazine, Neil Young, The Who, The Beatles, P.J. Harvey, Madonna and The Cure.

A different approach is that of the 'bricoleur' collector, who consciously combines different styles of records to create a new assembly of recordings. Allen observed that while the records he owned are classified by genre in CD stores,

> 'the way I think about my collection is determinedly about crossing these boundaries. In fact my kind of collecting is an attempt to discern connections and traditions which allow one to think outside the marketing categories. For example, several of my favourite CDs would be found under the Nostalgia category. But if I listen to Marlene Dietrich ("Nostalgia") alongside Lotte Lenya (which would be more likely found in "Classical" under Kurt Weill) and then Dagmar Kraus's versions of Weill songs along with her work in Slapp Happy and Henry Cow (Rock/Pop/Alternative/Progressive) then what? I'm trying to do a kind of cultural history in my listening – which is nevertheless pleasure driven. The tradition might be called "Cabaret", but it turns up in many different genres of popular and classical music.' (Allen Meek)

This exemplifies the manner in which collecting both transforms the status of the individual recording and inflects it with the individual collector's identity, in this case Allen's cultural history of his listening.

---

[2] 'The Collector, No. 61: Herve Denoyelle', *Record Collector*, December 2008: 10.

Collectors explained their preferences in terms of a combination of the nature of the music as sound, especially where it demanded a greater effort/investment in the listening experience, their generational experiences ('the music I grew up with') and discrimination (wanting 'the best').

The sound

Collectors will refer to a wide range of styles and their associated sounds, as informing and guiding their musical tastes. For instance:

> 'In new music, I like indie/alternative with a "power pop" sort of sound, like the Strokes or the New Pornographers, because I'm more on the pop side of the pop/rock continuum, with melody being key. I'm also heavily into "chill out" sounds like Lemon Jelly, because I also like very mood-identifiable music. As well, a lot of chill or "headz" music samples the easy listening/lounge stuff that dominates almost exclusively my used LP purchases: 50s mainstream jazz-pop that's very moody, 60s bossa nova, and late 60s/early 70s "now sound" stuff, in which rock textures are incorporated into Tin Pan Alley-derived productions. Also love new wave into mid-80s "new mainstream" stuff with drum machines, fretless basses, shakahachi samples and vaguely dystopian lyrics. (Keir Keightley)

The lyrics were at times singled out by collectors: 'I like these [Neil Finn and Crowded House, Beth Orton, among others] because of the lyrics mainly – I find them to be beautifully understated. I particularly love Radiohead for that' (Liz Guiffre). For Marc Brennan, 'around the time of Britpop [whose bands he collected] I found the lyrical content much more witty, relevant and playful than their contemporaries.' For many there is an emphasis on music that challenged the listener, and reflected performers 'stretching out'. Susan reflected on her engagement with her collection in these terms:

> 'I will buy from any genre if I've been moved by a good song or album, but my main preference is blues and blues based hard rock, as well as the band U2. Why? I'm still trying to figure this out. The blues because it can be so cathartic, deeply emotional, spiritual – I guess you could describe most of U2's music in those terms as well. Music isn't wallpaper for me – I want to have a mind and body blowing experience when I turn on the stereo. My record collection reflects this.' (Susan Fast)

Other collectors similarly referred to collecting music which moved both mind and body, and possessed qualities such as 'intensity' and musical expertise:

- 'Main loves these days are Atlantic-era soul, especially Aretha, classic Chicago-style blues (Muddy and Howling Wolf) and Pacific hip hop (god bless Che Fu and King Kapisi!). Why these!? Can you really put in words what you experience in music? They all move the body as well as the head, that's for sure.' (Brennon Wood)

- 'I would attribute my passion for the music [Extreme Metal] to a number of reasons – aesthetically, the music is intense and aggressive, playing and listening to it releases intense emotions. Lyrically, it is challenging and tends to address unconventional issues.' (Albert Bell)
- 'I always have loved hip hop and the beats that make it. Music with feeling, attitude, soul, no matter what genre, that makes me say ahhhh is what I like.' (Michael Book)

Views such as these take us back to the primary reason for collecting, identified in Chapters 1 and 2: a love of music.

Generational experiences: nostalgia and popular memory

As with format preferences, the formative influence of adolescence and early adulthood on musical taste, and who and what was collected, are common. Related to this is the role of nostalgia and popular memory in the collecting process, concepts which are central to the general literature on collecting. Baudrillard (1994: 15) saw 'the problematic of temporality' as 'fundamental to the collecting process', posing the question: 'are we speaking merely of nostalgic escapism?' Elsner and Cardinal (1994: 155) regarded collecting as 'a process of nostalgia', with the collected artefact enabling the preservation of the memories associated with it. Muesterberger (1994: 165) considered 'the fundamental motive' for collecting as 'based on the individual's history and essential events, the type and style of selecting and collecting and collecting is effectively guided by the prevailing culture pattern, the mood and values of the time.'

In relation to popular music, nostalgia and popular memory have been systematically explored by research into the social psychology of music (North and Hargreaves, 2007, provide an extensive overview of this), in cultural studies of popular music generally (for instance, Gracyk, 2007: Chapter 7; DeNora, 2001), and in Montano's study of record collecting (2003). As this body of work suggests, the collecting process involves a negotiation of the relationship of the individual and their past. At times, this will take the form of a fairly straightforward identification with the music of one's youth, especially when this is also indentified in canonical terms. Andy Davis, then editor of the *Record Collector*, in 2001 suggested that rock and pop records had become so collectable because 'they are the antiques of the post-war generations. Such artefacts root you in your own history on one level, while on another allow the collector to get that much closer to the artist in whose name those objects were originally created' (Montano, 2003: 9).

Record collectors do frequently demonstrate that nostalgia, in the sense of the influence of their adolescence, is a factor informing their collecting. Tina's main genre is rock'n'roll/rockabilly, 1950–1960: 'I loved it when I first heard it and it still pleases me' (Tina Janeering). For Craig, who grew up on '60s radio,

'I now collect what I like from there: top 40, British Invasion, folk revival, garage, psychedelic, country rock, blues rock, singer-songwriter, some progressive rock' (Craig Morrison). Norma describes herself as 'an old punk rocker from the first go-round (late '70s) and I still love all that stuff' (Norma Coates). Marc collects indie guitar pop, mainly by British artists: 'I guess it is this because my first passionate association with the genre came in my mid teens when I was into the mod moment and bands such as the Jam, Madness, the Specials etc.' (Marc Brennan). This does not mean, however, that tastes remain fixed solely in the soundtrack of the collector's youth. Although Matt Glesne still felt 'grounded in hip-hop, this has declined in the last few years in favour of jazz, funk, soul, rock, latin and dance music.'

As collectors do not limit their collecting to objects issued during their youth, this makes problematic any straightforward association between this period of their lives and their genre and artist preferences. The preference for vinyl among younger collectors who had grown up with the CD and, more recently, the digital download (see Chapter 3) suggest that identification can operate in a more complex fashion. The urge to collect is part of the drive to express individual distinctiveness; as Baudrillard observes: 'It is inevitably *oneself* that one collects' (1994: 12). Identity is a mobile concept, a self-in-process, rather than a fixed entity. Shifts in collecting interests are indicative of changing musical tastes, which in turn are shaped by changes in collectors' lives. I shall return to this central relationship, and its significance for record collecting in the later collector profiles (Chapter 7) and in my conclusion.

Discrimination: record collecting and the musical canon

Nostalgia and personal memory are a powerful influence on collecting tastes, but are inflected by an awareness of what is considered collectable. Art forms are typically discussed in terms of a canon, where works are 'typically presented as peaks of the aesthetic power of the art form in question, as ultimate manifestations of aesthetic perfection, complexity of form and depth of expression which humans are capable of reaching through this art form' (Regev, 2006: Introduction). The canon embraces value, exemplification, authority and a sense of temporal continuity (timelessness). Critics of the concept point to the general social relativism and value judgments embedded in it, and the often associated privileging of Western, white, male and middle-class cultural work.

Notions of a canon are an integral part of popular music discourse – although often implicitly – including everyday conversations among collectors. As Regev notes, 'Canonisation in popular music has gone hand in hand with its very recognition as a legitimate art form' (Regev, 2006: 1). Music critics and the music press are major contributors to the construction of a musical canon. This is initially through choices of *which* artists, genres and releases are even worthy of critical attention, a selection process then reinforced by the use of ratings systems for reviews, annual 'best of' listings, and various 'guidebooks' to key recordings (see Chapter 6). The gendered nature of the musical canon is strongly evident, with the marginalization of women in popular music histories; the privileging of male performers and male-dominated or oriented musical styles/genres in discussions of authorship; and the consequent domination of popular music canons by male performers. The canon is also dominated by Anglo-American performers and recordings, who underpin mainstream accounts of the history of popular music.

General coverage of historical figures, musical trends and recordings are standard content in music magazines, especially those aimed at an older readership, for example *MOJO* and *UNCUT*,[3] and in the main record collecting magazines, *Goldmine* and *Record Collector*. Many of these are rapidly sold out, demonstrating that this is a lucrative market, tapping into and reinforcing popular memory. In addition to their economic value to music publishers, these publications play an important ideological role, contributing to the identification and legitimating of a canon of performers, in the same way as lists of 'greatest albums', which they are closely aligned with. The selection process at work here is an interesting one, indicative of particular views of creativity and authorship. For example, the very title *IMMORTALS: The 100 Greatest Artists of All Time*, displays no lack of ambition and confidence, but the choices of artists from the 1950s excludes Bill Haley, presumably as his image does not conform to a notion of 'rock' authenticity. Interestingly, suggesting a possible circularity at work here, judging from readership polls in the collector press and price realizations for his recordings, Bill Haley is not regarded as a very 'collectable' artist.

There is a canonical approach frequently evident in record collecting, in the aesthetic sense of collectors seeking out 'the best' artists, genres and recordings. This can also be inverted, with a valorization of the obscure, scarce/exotic or just plain 'crap records'. Indications of the relative collectability of particular genres and artists are the coverage given to them in the collector magazines, their status in the various record price guides, the prices generated for them on eBay, their inclusion and sales realizations at auction and their place within dealers' inventory. Collectors are not simply the recipients of this body of advice and guidance, they also play an important role in canon creation through their vernacular scholarship and their involvement in (re-)releasing selected recordings and compilations (a process going back to the 1920s, as indicated in Chapter 1).

An example of this process at work is provided by John Dougan, in his insightful discussion of canonization and blues record collectors in the United States. Dougan describes these collectors as 'musical archaeologists, culture brokers, creators, keepers, and, though their entrepreneurial efforts (influenced by the release of Harry Smith's 1952 compilation *Anthology of American Folk Music*) disseminators of a blues canon' (Dougan, 2006: 42). He sees this role as playing a vital part in the taxonomy of the genre:

---

[3]   In addition, many of these titles have begun publishing special issues and series. Examples here include the *NME Originals*, the *UNCUT Legends*, and the *Rolling Stone* special issues, such as *The 50th Anniversary of Rock: IMMORTALS. The 100 Greatest Artists of All Time* (issue 642, August 2005).

> At its core, canon formation among blues record collectors involves organizing and defending a set of selections made from several possible sets of selections. The resulting 'canon' represents the essence of the tradition, and the connection between the texts and the canon reveals the veiled logic and internal rationale of that tradition. (Dougan, 2006: 45)

An emphasis on the aesthetic qualities of recordings in the collection, rather than the quantity of recordings, turns compulsive accumulation and hoarding into meaningful desire and socially sanctioned consumption: 'The good collector is tasteful and reflective. Accumulation unfolds in a pedagogical, edifying manner. The collection itself – its taxonomic, aesthetic structure – is valued, and any private fixation on single objects is negatively marked as fetishism' (Clifford, 1988: 54).

Collectable artists

The UK-based magazine *Record Collector* provides an instructive example of the manner in which the music press, in conjunction with its readers, construct a collectable canon. A glance through the index to back issues gives a clear picture of the artists most regularly accorded features (often along with discographies, which include indications as to value): The Beatles (and features on each of the group members, particularly Lennon and McCartney), David Bowie, Bob Dylan, The Rolling Stones, Elvis Presley, Led Zeppelin, The Who, Jimi Hendrix, Queen and Pink Floyd have received the greatest coverage. Among more contemporary (in the sense that their careers are largely post 1970) performers to have been featured in recent issues of *Record Collector* are Kate Bush, U2, Genesis, REM, Marc Bolan and T. Rex, Bruce Springsteen and Madonna.

Such coverage is dependent on collector feedback, primarily through the letters to the editor, and other contributions to the magazine, notably the annual readers' poll of the most collectable artists. Collectors send in their Top 10 artists, encouraged by desirable prizes awarded to those closest to the published Top 10. The top ten artists from the 2000 poll, with their position in 1992 for comparison, were:[4]

1. The Beatles (1)
2. Rolling Stones (3)
3. Queen (2)
4. Elvis Presley (7)

---

[4]   *Record Collector*, 248, April 2000: 46ff. The four top artists were in the same order the previous year. In 1992 R.E.M. were ranked 5th, Madonna 6th, and U2 8th; but these did not make the top ten this time. The coverage given in *Goldmine* to artists on the above list suggests they are also very popular with collectors in North America. (For a fuller discussion of both magazines, see Chapter 6.)

5. The Who (n/a)
6. David Bowie (4)
7. Led Zeppelin (13)
8. Bob Dylan (9)
9. Pink Floyd (5)
10. Jimi Hendrix (11)

The obvious point here is the clear privileging of 1960s artists (and the absence of women performers). In addition to those who have died, and groups who have lost key members, most are no longer performing/recording on a regular basis. If anything, by removing them from the public arena (but not, of course, from the ongoing public fixation with celebrity), this consolidates their iconic status. The covers of recent issues of *Record Collector* indicate the on-going importance and collectability of these groups and their members. During 2008, there were cover stories on John Lennon (The Beatles), Brian Jones (The Rolling Stones), David Bowie, (early) Pink Floyd, Jimmy Page (Led Zeppelin). Reflecting this level of interest among collectors, many of the highest price values in price guides and auction sales realizations are for records by these artists.

Of course, there is an element of circularity at work here: value encourages interest and demand, which impacts on value, and so forth. I now want to look further at why these artists remain so popular among record collectors.

Why these artists?

In addition to their being privileged in the collector press, the collectability of these artists is underpinned by the interaction of several additional factors: (i) the strength of their original fan base; (ii) their inclusion in a popular music canon; (iii) their original releases being produced in various formats, and marketed internationally, along with considerable memorabilia; and (iv) their extensive back catalogue, which has enabled on-going repackaging, with boxed sets and anniversary issues.

Lists of collectable artists and groups have clear similarities to the recurring presentation of a 'mainstream' canon of rock and pop recordings, through 'Best Of/Greatest Albums of All Time' lists. Von Appen and Doehring (2006) undertook a meta-analysis of such lists, drawing on 38 rankings made between 1985 and 1989 and 2000–04. The resultant 'top 30' is dominated by rock albums of the 1960s and 1970s, notably those by The Beatles, and there is an absence of women and black artists. The list represents the staple musical repertoire for 'classic rock' radio, which both reflects and reinforces the visibility and value accorded to such performers and albums. Von Appen and Doehring suggest that aesthetic and sociological criteria are important in shaping such lists. The aesthetic places a premium on artistic authenticity, and there is at times a limited relationship between such rankings and sales and chart success. The exclusion of compilation and greatest hits albums from most of the lists included reflected the view that the album must represent a showcase of the work of an artist at a particular point in time. Their discussion of the sociological factors at work here indicates, once again, the role of the music press and industry discourse in shaping taste, along with the cultural capital and social identities of those who voted on the lists.

The same process is at work in the creation of collectability. The early growth of rock and pop record collecting in the 1960s (see my Introduction), reflected the original fan base for genres such as rock'n'roll, doo-wop and rockabilly, and performers such as Elvis Presley. Subsequently, the substantial post-war baby boomer generation represented an even more significant consumer group. As part of the youth culture of the 1960s, they had lived through historical moments such as the impact of The Beatles and Woodstock, and retained an affinity for the music of the period when 'rock culture' emerged. Not all became record collectors, but those who did helped reshape the collecting environment, especially through their demand for the recordings of 1960s artists such as The Beatles, The Rolling Stones and Bob Dylan. At the same time, younger collectors were attracted by the romance of the '60s and its music, sharing the view that it formed a central part of a rock canon (Blake, 1999: Introduction; Hayes, 2006). The development of the album as a holistic and creative artistic statement assisted its subsequent elevation to collectability. Also significant was the role of the music press in canonizing the music of the period between 1964 and 1972 (spanned by The Beatles), and its subsequent exploitation by recording companies with an ongoing stream of reissues, new compilations and boxed sets. In order to illustrate this general process, I now want to briefly consider examples of collectable artists, genres and several records.

The Beatles

Today, The Beatles are clearly *the* most collectable artists, with their popularity among collectors reflected in their records and associated memorabilia fetching many of the highest price realizations at auction in the past 25 years. Yet this has not always been the case. Neely observed (in 1999) that in the 1970s The Beatles did not yet have the collecting cachet they have subsequently acquired, arguing that they were too fresh in the memory of most collectors to yet be collectable.[5] This changed as their original fans began collecting, and as the dominant place of the group in twentieth-century popular music became increasingly recognized.

The Beatles were hugely successful in the commercial music mainstream, and plenty of copies of their main recordings remain available to collectors (although finding copies in mint condition is more difficult). At the same time, there are a large number of variants of these releases, a situation presenting a major challenge to collectors. Their recordings also include unique releases such as the numbered *White Album*, the Butchers cover, and early American recordings on small labels, which sold in very small numbers and are consequently quite rare. The hunt for all

---

[5]   *Goldmine* 25th Anniversary Issue, 1999: 70.

of these has been aided by an increasing number of extensive price guides to The Beatles recordings and memorabilia. Not only are the band the most collectable group, they have the largest body of writing accorded to them of any popular musicians. In addition to the usual biographies (and autobiographies) of the group and its individual members, there are specialist discographies and numerous articles in the music press generally and the collector magazines.[6]

For many collectors, especially older fans of the group, The Beatles are the focus of their collection. For instance, Graeme Dickenson has a large record collection (around 10,000 discs, and about 20,000 CDs), 'a big part of which is my Beatles collection', including about 1,200 Beatles related CDs. Living in Melbourne, he refers to several collectable Australian pressings of Beatles records:

> There are two altered Beatles covers: *Beatles For Sale* has photos of the Australian tour on the front and *With The Beatles* has the rather weird 'floating heads' cover. There are also several unique Beatles best of compilations, e.g. *The Essential Beatles* and several of the EPS have different covers. The covers of Australian pressings were always done on the cheap. You could bet that if it was gatefold in the UK or USA, then it was a single sleeve here.[7]

The Beatles effectively broke up in 1970, but the group are still big business (see Blancey, 2008). There has been a steady flow of 'product', including previously unreleased recordings (for instance, *The BBC Sessions*) and documentary film. This helps maintain interest in the group, along with continued high-profile sales of rare Beatles records and memorabilia.[8]

Genres

Popular music genres have splintered into a myriad of styles since the late 1970s, with each gathering a collecting constituency and greater attention in the collector magazines. Some genres are more collectable than others, and their relative status among collectors changes over time. Record collectors play a role in this (as

---

[6]   This is particularly evident with those commemorating the anniversaries of the Beatles' recordings, as with the 40th anniversary of the release of *Sgt. Pepper*: see for instance the cover stories in *Record Collector*, July 2007 and *MOJO* March 2007.

[7]   'The Collector, No. 43: Graeme Dickenson', *Record Collector*, June 2007. The Beatles toured New Zealand and Australia in 1964. Several New Zealand pressings of their records are also very collectable.

[8]   For example, at Christie's Pop Memorabilia auction in London on 25 May 2006, lot 203, a copy of *A Hard Day's Night*, signed by all four Beatles and with clear provenance, sold for £22,800.

the earlier example of the Blues showed), along with the music press.[9] Critical revaluations of particular genres will encourage their collectability, as will the provision of new discographical information. Once again, such shifts are in part generational: a love for the music the collector grew up with and, later in life, a combination of greater disposable income combined with revisiting 'lost youth'. Younger collectors will be attracted to genres which emerged before they were born, an attraction based on a love of the musical style – often linked to a search for the antecedents of their favoured contemporary performers – and associated cultural capital among their collecting peers, as well as more widely among their peer group.

In the 1970s and into the '80s, auctions and wants lists focused on two types of music: vocal groups [doo-wop] and rockabilly 'to the exclusion of almost anything else' (Neely, 1999). Given that these two genres were largely singles oriented, the earliest price guides for post-1950s, largely post 78 popular music, which appeared in the mid 1970s [see Chapter 6], focused exclusively on 45s. Craig Morrison documents how the revival of rockabilly, which began in England in the mid-1970s and continued into the mid-1980s, 'received its momentum from the interplay of several factors' and 'a combination of the energies of four diverse groups of people' (Morrison 1996: Preface). The first includes dealers, collectors, reissue labels (such as Ace and Charley in England), and 'new labels devoted exclusively or extensively to rockabilly', such as Rollin' Rock in California, which started in 1971. Secondly, 'scholars, reporters, and certain serious fans' who gathered and spread knowledge, fostering the revival through their involvement with specialist radio shows and fanzines, notably *New Kommotion* from England. Thirdly, the audience, who 'sustained the revival by consuming the records, frequenting the discos that featured rockabilly, attending the live shows, and living a rockabilly lifestyle.' Fourthly, the musicians of the revival, who revitalized the original 1950s styles of rockabilly, giving it fresh life. The appeal of rockabilly was the vitality of the music, while interest in it was also 'about connecting to a mental scenery, to a mythical place, where people are imbued with both white and black music traditions, feeling things deeply, and having a down-to-earth life' (Morrison, 1996: Preface).

While 1960s rock and its various genres later supplanted these earlier genres, they have remained highly collectable. More recently, Milano considered that 'most of today's collectors are running after music that's barely two decades old. Punk and rap singles from the '80s have largely replaced vintage jazz and R&B as

---

[9]   *Record Collector* has largely concentrated on rock'n'roll and R&B, especially their British exponents and recordings during the 1960s, British psychedelia, which was given a whole series (issues 231–71) and, broadly, classic rock. Also prominently featured have been soul (especially Motown and Northern Soul), indie bands and labels, and reggae. *Goldmine* exhibits a similar mix of styles, though, reflecting its main market, with greater attention to North American exponents. Its increased coverage in both magazines show indie/alternative music has become more collectable.

the most sought-after items' (Milano, 2003: 19). He cites former *Goldmine* editor Jeff Tamarkin:

> 'Early doo-wop 45s and 78s were the Holy Grail of collecting during the 70's. Now you can barely give that stuff away. Even Elvis seems to be dying as a collectible artist. That's partly because the people who would collect that kind of music are getting older and have different responsibilities. If you're twenty-two and just getting into collecting you're not going to be into that.' (Milano, 2003: 19)

While this judgement of Elvis's collectability was clearly premature at best,[10] newer and younger record collectors have made genres such as rap, hip hop, indie rock and metal as collectable as their historical predecessors. Furthermore, prices for some of these more recent items are starting to reach levels beyond the reach of most collectors. I now want to go beyond artists and genres, to illustrate the convergence of factors determining value, rarity and collectability through selected examples of top-selling items on eBay during 2007.

Value, rarity and collectability

Sales on eBay are tracked in a regular feature of the *Record Collector*, the eBay-O-Meter, with an end-of-year column documenting 'the highest selling records that have changed hands on the auction site in the past twelve months'. The list for 2007 (*RC* 344, Christmas 2007) includes records by U2, The Sex Pistols, Willie Brown, Robert Johnson, King Crimson, Leaf Hound and three albums by The Beatles. Most had earlier been profiled in the column. It is instructive briefly to consider several of these in terms of what they tell us about the rare record collector and market.[11]

---

[10]   The continued collectability of Elvis is based primarily on his role in popularizing rock and roll in the 1950s, his status as a cultural icon, and the role of Graceland in maintaining his legacy. He had a substantial international repertoire, and there is a wide range of 'Elvis memorabilia'. As Elvis collector (and dealer) Bob Solly puts it: 'Elvis' voice and image are still two of the hottest properties on earth' (Solly, 2007). It is the five early Sun singles that are the most collectable of Elvis's recordings: 'Nowadays, Presley's debut single [That's All Right/Blue Moon of Kentucky, Sun, 1954)] can command anything from 2,000–3,000 [British pounds], depending on who is buying and who selling, and the agreement they strike. Is it worth it? In terms of heritage and history, yes' (Solly, 2007).

[11]   The other recordings on the top ten list were: (1) U2, an Australian green vinyl pressing of *All I Want Is You* (£7,500); (2) The Sex Pistols, *God Save The Queen* (£7,205); (3) Willie Brown, *Future Blues* (£5,107): A country blues record, signed by Brown's associate Son House, in London in 1967; and (8) King Crimson, *In The Court of the Crimson King* (£2,460): 'The very first of the original pressings' (*Record Collector*, 344, Christmas 2007).

Reflecting their place as the most collectable artists, The Beatles had three items placed in the top ten. At number four was The Beatles, *With the Beatles* (£4,600), signed by all four Beatles, and by Tony Rivers and Chris Curtis, and at number ten The Beatles, *Beatles '65* (£1,610), an 'autographed' edition of the Beatles' sixth US album. Performers' signatures add value, although their verification can be difficult and there were doubts about their authenticity with the latter.

At number six was an acetate[12] of The Beatles, *Sgt. Pepper's Lonely Hearts Club Band* (£3,600). Although there was a debate around how genuine these recently discovered copies are, the fact that this was sold to raise money for the Rainforest Foundation may have prompted interest regardless of its provenance. 'The acetate is the immediate stage between the (rough) mixed recording on tape and the vinyl records shipped to retailers. The first incarnation of a finished record but one which can still be aborted and not released, remixed or even rerecorded, if found wanting' (Rab, 2007: 81). Acetates may therefore include tracks that do not appear anywhere else, and these 'fragile, handmade, unique records' (Rab, 2007: 81) also provide a fascinating document of 'work in progress'. Acetates of collectable artists will frequently command high prices, as with the Velvet Underground acetate discovered in 2008 in New York.

In fifth place was a Track 7" of John's Children, *Midsummer Night Scene* (£4,500). While John's Children has been very well served by the reissue labels, especially Bam Carouso, it is the rare original releases that are sought by record collectors. Condition was a factor pushing up the price here, as according to its seller the record had only been 'played once, forty years ago'. The strong buyer interest was a combination of the recording as a rarity of early British psychedelia[13] and Marc Bolan's brief membership of the band. Bolan, who went on to form the commercially successful T. Rex, remains one of the most collectable UK artists; in the *Record Collector* readers' 2004 poll of favourite groups, T. Rex was in 5th place; on the 30th anniversary of his death (in 1977), *Record Collector* (October 2007) featured Bolan as their cover artist, and included an article on the acetates of his early work: 'among the rarest and most sought-after items in the world of record collecting' (Rab, 2007: 81). As Shirley observes, for collectors Bolan enjoyed 'the perfect musical trajectory': a stumbling early career, with a number of collectable singles; cult success in the folk rock duo Tyrannosaurus Rex; then mega stardom with T. Rex in the early 1970s (the group had a number of top ten singles, including four British number ones). This was followed by 'a fall

---

[12] Acetates are 'a reference or demo disc usually cut for technical evaluation purposes'; making the cut involves 'making a master disc from which finished records can be pressed; so called because the master tape sounds are transferred to a lacquered disc by a cutting machine which uses a needle to draw the sound patterns into the acetate' (producer George Martin; cited in Rab, 2007: 81).

[13] A genre with a very strong following, indicated by *Record Collector* devoting a lengthy series to 'collectable British psychedelic records' (issues 231–71).

from grace, musical experimentation and an early death followed by resurrection' (Shirley, 2008: 70).

In seventh place was Robert Johnson, *Preaching Blues* (£3,322). This was considered 'an amazing price for a 78 rpm., especially with the B side (Love in Vain) graded at E'. Johnson is regarded as the key transitional figure working within the Mississippi Delta's blues culture, bridging the gap between its rural origins and later urban blues. The 1930s bluesman is an iconic figure, and his small but hugely influential recorded output and early death (in 1938) have accorded him mythical status. The force of this myth, and public and scholarly fascination with it, has led to a spate of books and documentaries on Johnson (Shuker, 2008: 72–4). There continues to be strong interest in his performance style, his recordings and their influence, placing him among the most collectable artists of the 78 era.

At nine was Leaf Hound's album *Grower of Mushroom* (£2,070). This 'hard rocking progressive album',[14] recorded in London in late 1970, was released in the United Kingdom in 1971, in a small pressing ('rumour' suggests only 500 copies). It sold poorly and the group broke up in 1971. In 1994 the album was reissued, gaining Leaf Hound new fans; a new line up of the group formed in 2004, and a new album in 2007 was well-received by both fans and critics. Collectability here is a combination of rarity, the status of the record as a classic in a genre – progressive/hard rock – with a considerable following, and the mystique generated by the original short-lived band. Adding to this status, and reflecting increasing collector demand, mint copies of the original album were selling on eBay for more than double its price in the *Rare Record Price Guide*.

Other collectable fields

I turn now to examples of collectable fields outside of the more common ones of genres and artists: chart singles, compilations, memorabilia, music magazines and bootlegs. These are informed by different organizing principles and are underpinned by different inflections of taste and collectability. In addition to recordings, collectors will nearly always collect various books, magazines and memorabilia related to their main artist and genre interests.

Chart singles

A clear example of a delineated project is the collection of all the singles that have reached number one in an official chart listing. This can be further restricted, and thus made more manageable, through using only one national chart. The collector is able to easily identify the records they need with reference to the chart listings books that have been widely available since the early 1980s, for instance, the series by Joel Whitburn (Whitburn, 1988).

---

[14]   Shirley (2008: 67). The following discussion is based primarily on this account.

In the case of the British charts, the first No. 1 single was Al Martino's 'Here in my Heart', in November 1954. Ray Spiller formed a complete collection of Britain's 999 No. 1 hits until the end of 2004, starting with Martino's and ending his run with the 2004 Band Aid charity song. He had begun collecting the singles in 1995 when Robson and Jerome had a number one hit with 'Unchained Melody': 'I heard it was No. 1 in 1965 as well and I thought it might be a bit of fun to see if I could get all the No. 1s.' By 2000, and having spent £3,500, he had all the originals, as first released on 78, as vinyl 45s and as CD singles. He was then easily able to maintain the collection, which posed less of a challenge, and in December 2004 placed it for sale on online auction site eBay. He admitted his wife was not too impressed with the initial outlay, but she was happier when he turned the collection into a full time business, giving talks to schools and clubs, and doing DJ work for weddings and parties. Having copied the collection on to CDs, he planned to continue this work. 'It will be a real wrench – it'll be like saying goodbye to an old friend.'[15] Yet again, this demonstrates that simply retaining copies of the music does not have the same significance to the collector as possessing the originals, with their associated aura and authenticity.

Stephen Hitchcock, an IT consultant living in Brighton, England, was given a similar collection when he was 12 (he was now in his mid thirties), which had been formed by his grandfather and continued by his father. He kept it up to date, until putting it up for auction in July 2006 at the Abbey Road Studios. Indicative of the changing industry formats was his inclusion of digital download singles.[16]

Compilations

Another example of a bounded field is the collecting of compilations. Historically, such releases were regard as somewhat kitsch, and they became a staple part of the piles of unwanted vinyl albums in thrift shops and at garage sales – indeed, they still feature in these. This fate reflected their absence from musical canons, their perceived status as very much of-the-moment commercial fodder, and their consequent lack of appeal to record collectors. This changed when several collectors started collecting K-Tel records in the 1990s, raising the wider visibility of such compilations. The best-known recent example of their new-found collectable status, is the NOW series.

The series *Now That's What I Call Music!* was started in time for Christmas 1983 in the United Kingdom, and 2005 saw the release of *Now That's What I Call Music! 60*. In addition, there have been two sets of single-year collections, plus a popular *Now Dance* series and other spinoffs, and commercially available collections of music videos from the 1980s. Every regular *Now* volume had two

---

[15]   Press report *Dominion Post* (NZ), 11 December 2004: A14. For Ray's continued activities, and a detailed listing of the British Number One hits see www.number1hits.co.uk.

[16]   *Dominion Post* (NZ) 17 July 2006: A2.

discs with between 30 and 44 songs each, and the first 35 volumes of the UK series were issued on vinyl, with the last vinyl edition coming out on 21 October 1996. This enhanced their collectability, and attracted the interest of collectors in the UK. A version of *Now 4* was issued on CD in December 1984, 'a test run really'. It did not have the same track list as the album, collecting together tracks from Volumes 2, 3 and 4. Indicative of current collector interest in the series, this now fetches in excess of £200.[17]

The UK *Now* recordings have become established as 'collectable', with websites devoted to them, and their appearance on on-line auction sites. Tim Neely recounts his quest to build a collection of them:

> The releases starting from about volume 20 upward, which was issued in November 1991, are pretty hard to find on vinyl, and I've yet to see any of the volumes in the 30s for sale in their LP form. So far I have the first, second and fourth volumes (with *6*, *8*, *9*, *10* and *18* on order), and I'm actually learning some things as I listen. For example, the first volume of *Now That's What I Call Music!* has the edit of Bonnie Tyler's 'Total Eclipse Of The Heart' that has cluttered U.S. airwaves the past few years, rather than the better (and longer) original U.S. edit.[18]

Now was launched in the US in 1998, on Virgin records, as a joint venture of PolyGram, Universal and the EMI Group. The first volume featured 17 hit songs with nothing in common except their recent hit status, much like a glorified K-Tel album. Unlike the K-Tel records of the 1970s, the *Now* CD was sold at regular price in regular music stores and featured full versions of the songs. The release of *Now 1* was accompanied by a multimillion dollar investment of short-form television advertising to promote a roster of major pop acts, and their releases, including top 10 hits from Hanson, Tonic, Backstreet Boys, Janet Jackson and Spice Girls. The debut, and subsequent issues in the series, proved commercially very successful.[19] When *Now 4* debuted at No. 1 in the *Billboard* charts in August 2000, it became the first various-artists compilation not associated with a movie ever to do so. By mid 2005, there had been 18 *Now* volumes released in the United States, plus two Christmas editions, each of which has been certified at least platinum. However, as Neely observed in 2005, while '*Now* is a veritable institution [in the United

---

[17]   Ian Shirley, 'Value Added Facts', *Record Collector*, January 2009: 81.

[18]   Tim Neely, 'Platter Chatter: Now That's What I Call Vinyl!', *Goldmine*, 24 June 2005: 22.

[19]   By 2000, according to SoundScan, the first album in the series had sold 1.8 million copies, with subsequent volumes all reaching the top 10 of *The Billboard* 200. *Now 2*, issued in July 1999, had sold 1.7 million copies; *Now 3*, out in December 1999, had sold 2.3 million; and *Now 4* was just over the 2 million mark.

Kingdom], with its own online discussion forum and collectors' Web sites, that kind of fanaticism has yet to attach itself to the U.S. version.'[20]

Memorabilia

'Memorabilia' refers to 'memorable' things not to be forgotten, regarded as worthy of preservation and collection. There are a large range of collectable music memorabilia: various records, including promotional copies and gold discs, musical instruments, autographs, tour programmes, posters, tour jackets and concert tickets and t-shirts, as well as novelty toys and a whole range of ephemera marketed around major artists like The Beatles (see Doggett and Hodgson, 2003). The motivations for such collecting include investment, cultural preservation, nostalgia and the desire to acquire cultural capital and status through owning top-selling items.

Writing in 1988, Alison Fox, from Phillips auction house in London, claimed that 'Rock and pop memorabilia has become the fastest growing field of collecting' (Fox, 1988: Preface). The first such auction, in London in 1981, included John Lennon's upright Steinway piano. As major auction houses included similar items, this field of collecting gained credibility and respectability, and prices began to rise. In 1988 a John Entwistle (Who bass player) guitar, used on the groups BBC *Top of the Pops* appearances in the early 1970s, fetched £15,000. Audiotapes of very early Rolling Stones and Beatles 'performances' also realized high prices. What set such items apart from mass-produced music memorabilia – though these are also often very collectable – is the attraction of the *aura* of the one-off original. The majority of early interest was in items related to The Beatles and Elvis Presley, but other artists soon attracted attention, especially those from the 1950s and '60s. In the early 1990s, the music press began to document the major prices being paid at the prestige auctions.[21]

The interest from private collectors, the new 'rock museums' (notably the Experience Music Project in Seattle, and the Rock and Roll Hall of Fame in Cleveland) and the Hard Rock Cafe chain has stimulated interest – and prices – in the collecting of popular music memorabilia. Several major auction houses now conduct regular sales, primarily in London and New York (Phillips, Christie's, Bonhams), and the lavishly illustrated catalogues from these have themselves become quite collectable. The collector press has regular columns reporting on these auctions, along with high-profile advertisements for them, while a number of books have documented the increased visibility of the field and its scope (Kay, 1992; Maycock, 1994; Doggett and Hodgson, 2003).

The appeal of memorabilia is based on the romantic aura of musical artefacts, especially when these offer the owner a tangible connection with the original

---

[20]   Tim Neely, 'Platter Chatter', p. 22.

[21]   For instance, *Q* July 1990: 16–17: 'Do I hear 180,000 [pounds]', reporting the sale of a Jimi Hendrix guitar; *Vox*, July 1991: 41: 'Hammer Time. Rock Auction Fever'.

artist. Some objects also have considerable historical significance. Collectors will supplement their recordings with related memorabilia, which at times becomes a significant part of their collection. A profile of Tony Price refers to his 'massive collection of memorabilia', with 'hundreds upon hundreds of objects' throughout his house, including models, badges, mugs and photo albums. Price says how 'buying Elvis Presley's radio which he had before he was famous was an enormous thrill. The radio that he heard the records on which influenced his own music in later life has to be something truly important, right? I got that for 1500 quid at auction.'[22]

An example of the popularity of memorabilia, strongly influenced by demographics, is the collecting of vintage guitars: used guitars which were well-made and have 'come to be recognized among guitar aficionados for their distinctive sound quality, their physical appearance, and for the famous guitarists who have played them' (Bennett and Dawe, 2007; the following account is from their study). The market for vintage guitars is linked to generational demographics, as many people now interested in such vintage instruments are middle-aged baby boomers. Looking at readership data collected in 1999 *Vintage Guitar* magazine, publisher Alan Greenwood observed: 'Boomers are very active in the guitar market. At no time in history have so many people in their 30s, 40s, and 50s been buying guitars.' This reflects the iconic status the guitar attained as the symbol of authenticity in rock music in the 1960s (Bennett and Dawe, 2007: 108).

Bennett and Dawe identify three kinds of buyers for vintage guitars: guitar 'players' – the very small group of professional musicians who can afford them – the 'collector', and the 'player collector'. The collectors are 'non-players who buy vintage guitars just to possess them and perhaps also on the speculative chance that they may appreciate in value'. The vast majority of vintage guitar buyers are player collectors, mainly middle-aged baby boomers, who have the income to indulge their fantasies of being rock and roll stars. As Greenwood put it: 'For the most part, people collect guitars they had, or wished they had, during their teen years, when their musical tastes were formed. We figure that most people don't have the bucks for things like old guitars until their late 30s' (cited in Bennett and Dawe, 2007: 105).

Vintage guitars also illustrate the relative value (and appeal to collectors) of the original musical artefact and a more contemporary replica/reissue copy. There are an increasing number of new guitars created as exact copies of the models or instruments played and popularized by famous guitarists. These replicas can be purchased for considerably less than the vintage originals; for instance a vintage

---

22   'The Collector, No. 4: Tony Price', *Record Collector*, June 2004. Price had been a leading DJ during the 1960s and 1970s, including spending 13 years with Radio Luxembourg; he later founded a record company (DMC), and *Mixmag* magazine. Collectors working in the music industry enjoy many opportunities for acquiring memorabilia. Dick Clark, of *American Bandstand* fame, built up an enormous collection, which was auctioned in 2008.

Fe.nder Stratocruiser can sell for $25,000, while a brand new reissue can be purchased for less than $500.

Music magazines

Music magazines play a significant role in promoting popular music culture, linking consumption to lifestyles. They sell music as an economic commodity while, at the same time, investing it with cultural significance (Shuker, 2008: Chapter 9). Individual copies, or even complete runs of issues, will be acquired as adjuncts to a record collection, serving as valuable reference tools (see Chapter 6). Many have become collectable in their own right. Factors underpinning collectable values are the number of copies of an issue printed, its age, condition and its appeal to particular fan and collector constituencies in the market. Acquiring a full run of a magazine is the challenge for completist collectors. The early music magazines were (and often still are) printed on newsprint, which meant a short shelf life. Magazine dealer Uhre notes that within two years 50 per cent [of a magazine's print run] will be discarded (Bernardy, 2004; the following discussion and quotes are from this article).

In 2004, Uhre talked about *Goldmine*'s collectability and the collectability of music magazines in general: 'The one thing that holds up with *Goldmine* is that there are issues that will always sell. The Beatles, The Rolling Stones ... Neil Diamond.' His best performer had been the Blue Öyster Cult issue (7 June 1996, #414). 'Don't ask me why', said Uhre, speculating that its posting on a fan website spurred sales. He also listed the power-pop issue with The Romantics (5 Jan 1996) as particularly strong. 'A lot of times we'll get stuff that will spike, such as our George Harrison tribute, published shortly after his death and which still sells.'[23]

Not unsurprisingly, it is the earliest issues of *Goldmine* that are the most valuable, with the first five or seven 'nearly impossible' to find, he noted. Uhre said that a British *Goldmine* collector contacts him a couple of times a year hoping to find a #1. 'They aren't out there ... [Founding publisher] Brian Bukantis claims to have a pile up in his attic. It could be a myth. If you can come up with one, they could command a decent price ... Not that there's anything *in* there [there was no editorial content], but it's the idea that it's the first one.'

Collectors who want particular *Goldmine* back issues are collectors of a band or artist searching for more information, especially discographies of their recordings, and cover stories: 'People are always wanting to go back. They want the discographies as much as the covers. All the people who've been in *Goldmine*, with the discographies and all the information that's in there, it's a great piece of modern American history' (Uhre). In 2004, the average price for a back issue of *Goldmine* within the last five to ten years was $10–15, with older ones fetching

---

[23]   C-Bub in Tulsa, Oklahoma, is *Goldmine*'s official back-issue dealer. In 2004, Uhre estimated he had between 8,000 and 10,000 *Goldmines* in his stock of about 80 different music magazines, all the way back to *Goldmine* #10, May 1976.

$25–35. The increased availability of collectibles online had already lowered the price of individual copies of *Goldmine* and other music magazines. The 1960s magazines are worth about $50–60 each nowadays, whereas before the internet they could be $100. In 2008, a search for *Goldmine* found more than 120 current auctions on eBay.

Many collectors refer to purchasing music magazines on a regular basis, with some mentioning the building up of complete runs as part of their collecting (see the profile of Hasse, in Chapter 7). In my own case, I had not considered them as 'a collection' until the past few years, when I realized that my claim that the magazines were a necessary part of my research and teaching activities was functioning as a rationalization for their accumulation – especially since some of the runs I had were not read in their entirety. I had been intermittently purchasing music magazines since the early 1960s, though most were soon discarded (in some cases, 'cut up' for the articles I wanted to retain). Once I began teaching courses on popular media culture, in the late 1980s, I began to acquire representative examples of various types of music magazine: the 'general' publications, those focused on genre, musicians and the industry, and so forth. The nascent 'collection' included some 1980s copies of *Goldmine* and *Record Collector*.

Around 2000, as part of 'research' preparing to teach a course on the history of popular music, with an emphasis on 'rock', I began to systematically acquire runs of what I saw as the key magazines: *Rolling Stone*, *Q*, *UNCUT*, *MOJO* and *CREEM*. I was interested in how these both constructed and reflected musical tastes and trends, and how they contributed to a canon of genres, performers and 'key moments' in music history. The New Zealand dimension of this was the consolidation of a complete run of the main local magazines: *Rip It Up*, *Real Groove* and *New Zealand Musician*. Acquiring a bigger office, and the research into record collecting, led inexorably to the collection of further titles, including *Classic Rock* and *Kerrang!*. I already had a few *Goldmines*, and had been buying the UK-based *Record Collector* since 2001. Obtaining further copies of *Goldmine* proved elusive, and the availability of its articles online lessened the need to do so. I was fortunate to make a bulk purchase of a run of *Record Collector* from the 1990s through the New Zealand website Trade Me.

Since magazine collecting remains a hobby without a price guide, the value of any particular issue is determined by what the market will bear, and it is generally relatively easy and cheap to put together a collection of music magazine titles.

Bootlegs and tape trading

Bootleg recordings and tapes of live concerts[24] are a distinctive form of music collectible, and are frequently associated with a mystique and cultural cachet for collectors and avid fans. They need to be distinguished from other forms

---

[24]   Also of studio recordings which were not originally released.

of unauthorized recordings, such as counterfeit copies of official recordings.[25] 'Unlike pirates and counterfeits, which reproduce and distribute sounds that have already been legitimately released by a record label, the music featured on bootlegs or tapes has *never previously been released* on a legitimate label.' There are important differences between the two forms, and a 'complex and contradictory' relationship exists between them' (Marshall, 2003). Tape trading often occurs with the endorsement of the artists concerned. Bands such as the Grateful Dead (who are usually considered to have initiated the practice), Pearl Jam, Phish and The Dave Matthews Band have permitted their concert audiences to record live concerts and then trade these concert tapes between themselves on condition that no profit is involved. Tape trading, therefore, takes place between individual collectors, on a non-commercial basis. Bootlegging, on the other hand, is a commercial enterprise, with recordings produced on a larger scale than 'one-off' tapes of the same performance. The two activities are linked in that collectors will often dub a bootleg recording on to a tape, which they then use for trading.

Despite being illegally produced and distributed recordings, bootlegs enjoy a rather ambivalent status. Although examples of bootleg recordings go back to cylinder recordings, rock bootlegs made their first appearance in 1969 with Bob Dylan's *Great White Wonder*, a double album originally in a plain white jacket without any printed label or title. (For a comprehensive history of early bootlegs, see Heylin, 1995.) A number of bootleg labels emerged in the United States to meet the demand for such recordings; none of them are still operating, and the vast majority of bootlegs are now produced in Europe. In several cases, bootlegs attain legendary status, occasionally prompting record companies to release an official recording, as with Prince's *Black Album* (WB, 1995), originally recorded in 1987 but not commercially released at that time. Bob Dylan, *The Basement Tapes* (Columbia, 1995; originally the bootleg *Great White Wonder*), and Bruce Springsteen, *Live 1975–1985* (Columbia, 1986), were both released by their record companies in response to the flood of bootlegs of the artists' concert performances. Authenticity is central to the nature and appeal of such concert bootlegs and tapes. These measures of authenticity are 'the same as within the legitimate music industry: an emphasis upon originality over imitation, feeling over reason' (Marshall, 2003: 69). The majority of bootlegs are of rock artists who are exemplars of such authenticity, such as Bob Dylan, The Rolling Stones, Bruce Springsteen and Led Zeppelin.

The collector press was quick to identify bootlegs as collectable. *Record Collector*, for instance, included an article in its second issue (October 1979), and bootlegs are often included in coverage of artists' most collectable recordings. *Hot Wacks*, a press devoted to live music, produced several early bootleg discographies,

---

[25]   The early collector press tended to confuse bootlegs with pirated copies of recordings – reproductions of the original label and recorded performance – but saw them as 'a good way of collecting an otherwise almost unobtainable recording' (Propes, 1973: 10–11). Many collectors have followed his advice since.

and guides to record collecting will include discussions of concert bootlegs and tapes (Thompson, 2002: 31–40). At times bootlegs are semi-condoned: *ICE* magazine refers to bootlegs as 'gray area, live recordings'. Although containing a regular column on such releases, the magazine notes that while bootlegs are readily available in Europe, they 'cannot definitely advise as to their legality in the United States' (*ICE: The CD News Authority*, 'Going Underground'). Some indie and second hand record stores stock bootlegs, and they can be easily found at record fairs and conventions and in street markets.

Most record collectors will own at least a few concert bootlegs, in various formats. Several of the collectors I interviewed were tape traders, operating on a larger scale – a practice which necessitated having a thorough catalogue of one's holdings (see the profile of Lee Marshall in Chapter 7). Of course, such an enterprise also justified the continued maintenance and expansion of the collection, in order to offer an up-to-date and comprehensive selection of concerts.

In Cavicchi's study of Bruce Springsteen fans, 80 per cent indicated that, while they owned all the official releases by Springsteen, 'they nevertheless felt the need to supplement such releases with tapes of unreleased songs and concerts' (Cavicchi, 1998: 74). As they become aware of such live concert 'releases' as a collectable field, some collectors will begin to include these as part of their collection building. Andre Nuchelmanns relates how he 'jumped into the big pool of CD bootlegs' and started collecting them in 2003: 'it is a relatively new phenomenon in the world of record collecting, with a great vast group of traders, collectors and [CD] burners. It's also a very social group of people who do it all to share the music they like.' The *New York Times* devoted an article to the trade in concert bootlegs, citing a number of collectors. Marc Daniel added 1,400 live concert recordings (that were never officially released) to his CD collection during 2002, using the internet to trade for them. He described this mix of acquiring exhilarating music and its questionable legality (trafficking in unauthorized recordings is a violation of federal copyright law) as like 'a coke run without any drugs'.[26] In their descriptions of buying bootlegs, Bruce Springsteen collectors often emphasized 'the illicitness of such an activity', whereas 'tape trading is done far less surreptitiously' (Cavicchi, 1998: 75, 76).

Interviews with bootleg producers and collectors depict the process of taping and trading as a 'contemporary cultural site that reveals divisions and conflicts over the production, consumption and ownership of popular music' (Neumann and Simpson, 1997: 320; see also Marshall, 2005). This involves situating their experiences, practices and musical identity against the dominant modes of commodification and consumption. Collectors of concert bootlegs and tapes, and many of those who make the original recordings of these concerts, argue that they are documenting musical history, especially in the absence of official live

---

[26]   Matthew Mirapaul, 'They Buy All the Albums, but Trade Concert Bootlegs', *New York Times*, 6 January 2003. Shows were traded by mail rather than over the internet as MP3s; this is now changing with improved streaming technology.

recordings; 'for Springsteen fans … buying, collecting and trading unauthorised recordings enables fans to easily and repeatedly experience Springsteen's live performances, where they locate his greatest talent' (Cavicchi, 1998: 77).

Celebrating the approaching fortieth anniversary of the bootleg, Thompson (2008) noted how the mainstream market place holds little interest for bootleggers, who have consistently sought out artists with 'intelligent' followings, and have captured key performers 'at moments of vital transition, moments that would have passed wholly undocumented were it not for the wonder of the boot'.

Conclusion

As with music consumers in general, personal taste in music is the basic starting point for collectors' decisions as to who and what to initially purchase and then more systematically collect. Taste is shaped by nostalgia and personal memory, whereby collecting becomes the negotiation of the relationship of the collector and their past. This process is historically contingent, reflecting demographics and generational trends in collecting, and underpinning collector preferences, especially the continued prominence and collectability of ''60s music'. Different forms of musical cultural capital also come into play here. Many collect canonical artists, styles and recordings, while others valorize the obscure and the exotic. The aura and authenticity of the 'original' recording, especially rare variants of it, are defining features of the items in greatest demand and which consequently will fetch the highest prices.

Chapter 5
Collecting practices

The process of collecting can take on the nature of a ritual. Many collectors refer to the thrill of the chase and finding either a wanted item or something 'interesting'. Frequently it is the search itself that provides gratification, although the anticipation of 'a find' is central to this. Examples of major 'finds', especially if they are cheap and discovered in the most unusual locations, are part of the folklore of collecting. These general observations apply to many forms of collectible; I look at them here in relation to record collecting.

Record collectors constantly refer to both the effort and the pleasure involved in systematically gathering information from other collectors, the music press (see Chapter 6) and now the internet, and then searching for particular recordings. Along with looking for desired items to add to the collection, there is always the chance of simply picking something up that looks interesting, and the spectacular and often valuable find, a holy grail of record collecting, will occur from time to time.[1] Historically, canvassing for records, especially in the southern United States, was central to the record collecting in the 78 era (see Chapter 1). Today, the collector's search will frequently embrace thrift shops, specialist and second-hand record shops, mail order and internet shopping, auctions and record fairs, and mainstream record stores. Preferences for different sites are related to cost, access, the ambience of shops, time and opportunity, and the likely availability of the formats, genres, performers and recordings sought.

There is, at times, an obsessive-compulsive dimension to the process, with a sequence of anticipation, a catharsis with the pleasure of the discovery and purchase of the desired item, followed by a 'let down', and moving on to a fresh hunt. Once items are acquired, they must then be ordered and classified, and stored as part of an on-going process. Private rituals of consumption include (re-) cataloguing the collection; handling, playing and listening to recordings; and reading sleeve notes and admiring album cover art. Then there are the pleasures of displaying and sharing the collection: showing, lending and playing records to others. This dimension of collecting can extend into the public arena. Traditionally this has been though collectors' vernacular scholarship, writing and producing fanzines, magazine articles, books and discographies. Since the advent of the World Wide Web, record collectors have been able to present their collections, and

---

[1] The recent discovery in New York of an unknown early Velvet Underground acetate is the latest to join this narrative.

by extension themselves, through blogs, websites and their participation in on-line groups. These are the aspects of record collecting considered in this chapter.[2]

On the hunt

Hunting metaphors abound in the general literature on collecting, and collectors frequently refer to notions of pleasure and desire in the pursuit of items for their collection. For record collectors, this is a process involving competition, effort (visiting sites of acquisition; the physical act of sorting through 'records') and choice (between desired items – if budget is a consideration), underpinned by a strong element of compulsion. Gary sums up an attitude I frequently heard: 'I collect as a passion and enjoy the auction aspect of internet buying: hunt, chase and ... kill! It is fun to find unusual items and to expand one's collection, and sometimes music tastes' (Gary Shuker). Leibowitz (1980) extends the hunting metaphor in devoting a section of his guidebook to 'stalking the rare record', and discussions of where to obtain records are standard content in the contemporary collector press (see Chapter 6).

Many collectors appear to value the process of gathering music more than the actual possession of it, with an element of compulsion underpinning the search. Lee Marshall refers to it as 'more important than the end result ... it is something that is always on going, *it is always something that you have to do*' (my emphasis). Greg Crossan found the collecting process 'every bit as absorbing as the collection itself – probably more so, because I've been guilty of chasing a particular item for years, then, having finally got it, putting it away in the collection without even listening to it, and promptly becoming obsessed by the next elusive treasure on my list.' This aspect is most evident in the practice of deliberately moving from the creation of one collection to another; the appeal lies in the chase rather than the ownership of the collection itself: 'Collectors [I have known] will act in extreme ways: for example by selling up their entire collection and starting a new one; for example, switching from rock to soul or jazz' (Allen Meek). Here, the hunting ethos is combined with serial collection building and completism.

The search can be one that continues for years. Jonathon Moore (Coldcut; Ninja Tunes), recounts how he once heard Charlie Gillet (on his London Radio show) play 'Down the Road A Piece' by the trombonist Will Bradley. '*I knew I had to have it.* It was like a weird precursor to rock and roll made in 1947. After years I found a 78 for 50p in a junk shop – but I had nothing to play it on. So it remained unheard for another long while, till finally someone sat on it.' Then he found it in a warehouse in Minneapolis, amongst 20,000-odd 7" singles: 'And it still sounded great! It was worth the hunt.'[3]

---

[2]   Such practices are illustrated more fully in relation to individual collectors in the profiles in Chapter 7.

[3]   'Vinyl Frontier', *WORD*, August 2007: 42; my emphasis.

As with 'the find', with which it is often conflated, stories of the intrepid hunter, and the obstacles faced and overcome in the search for records, have become an essential part of the narrative of record collecting. There are many entertaining examples of the hunt landing collectors in strange situations. Dave Szatmary related to Bob Campbell how he drove 'way the hell somewhere in the remote boonies' to check out some interesting looking records the owner had for sale:

> I pulled up in front of this ramshackle place that had these really strange vibes. I almost didn't go in, but *it was for records, so you gotta do it*. [He then followed his host to a room where the records were]. Right away, I spotted some primo rare blues stuff like Skip James and Blind Blake on the pre-Yazoo label. I was really psyched and getting into it when I sensed something behind me. I turned around and there, not three feet away from where I was sitting on the floor, was this 30-foot boa constrictor. I damn near peed my pants. I grabbed the five records I'd had the chance to look at, paid the guy $20, an incredible steal, and high-tailed it out of there with the guy trailing behind, telling me not to worry, he'd just fed the snake four rats. (Campbell, 2001; Szatmary, who had 25,000 records, lived in Seattle)

The willingness to undergo such tribulations indicates the compulsive aspect to the hunt, as do justifications such as 'you gotta do it'.

Broadening one's musical horizons is a further pleasure of the hunt, with the search partly one of hearing or hearing about recordings, styles and artists, then tracking them down. As John Book explains:

> 'There is so much to explore in music, and that's what I enjoy about it. To listen to one record, and be able to branch off in every way possible for more. Hear a conga player on one record, find her playing on hundreds of other records. Hear a favourite song, find various people doing a cover version if it. Like a particular record, hunt down a pressing from various countries. Like a particular style of production, look for other records done by that producer or done in that year.'

There is a mixed feeling about discovering new material. Frequently the acquisition of the desired item will be immediately followed by the creation of a new 'need' and a return to the chase, in an ongoing cycle of desire–success–stasis–renewed desire, a related pattern of repetition:

> 'Is there a greater kick than searching and finding that 7" record w/ the vinyl in mint condition and the original photo cover? Of course, 30 minutes later it's on to the next chase. The collection isn't as complete as you thought. It's disappointing at first, but the hunting season isn't over yet (which is neat!).' (Marc Brennan)

Preparing for shopping trips is a part of the ritualistic nature of many hunts. Andre typifies the approach of many collectors: 'When I visit another town I also always look for second hand record shops or I search for record shops on the internet or in magazines, before I go there' (Andre Nuchelmans). Accounts of such trips become a part of the narratives record collectors construct for themselves and the history of their collecting activities. This is especially the case when international travel is involved, signifying a greater effort and seriousness on the part of the collector. Bob Solly recounts how, in the 1970s, along with other British record collectors he visited the United States (primarily Los Angeles) to search for early rock and roll records (Solly, 2000). More recently, as I show later, Japan has proved an attractive hunting ground for collectors.

A particular form of the hunt is the process of 'digging' through crates, or racks, of records. This has acquired a particular cachet and mystique in record collecting. It is usually linked with DJs'/producers' searches for source material for DJing and sampling, leading to it also being termed 'beat digging', a process involving physically searching though large quantities of records for the ones required.[4] DJ Shadow claims 'there are about 300 must-have funk albums and countless seven-inch singles' ('Vinyl Frontier', 2007). After that, observes Joe Muggs, diggers are in competition to find 'that unique few minutes of music to give them an edge' (Muggs, 2007: 41).

The find and the bargain

'The find' is central to the hunt, with both the anticipation of the possibility of it and its actual realization. Examples of rare finds become part of the body of record collecting folklore. The re-telling of them becomes part of the collectors' narrative of collection building, in a similar manner to those of book and stamp collectors (Basbanes, 2001; Bierman, 1990). The main record collector magazines regularly feature stories of 'finds', especially where these are of high value; for instance, in the *Record Collector* column 'Digging for Gold'.

An example of a find is Strictly Kev's discovery of a lost album by 1960s Californian session band The Dragons. 'I found this surf movie soundtrack *A Sea For Yourself* with the song *It's Food For The Soul* in a London record fair. I grabbed it just because I love musical food puns. I got it home and played it and it was amazing – soulful, funky, kind of naïve, but also subtly out-there – so I started putting it in my DJ sets.' Later, when he decided to include the track on one of his *Listen Again* mix CDs, he researched the tune properly, it led him to The Dragons, three brothers who had been the Beach Boys live back-up band in the mid-to-late '60s and recorded their own material during studio downtime. Dennis Dragon told Kev about another album they had recorded in 1969–70, and sent him the tapes. The record was remastered and released by Ninja Tunes (Muggs, 2007).

---

⁴ See the accounts in the hip hop- and DJing-oriented magazine *Wax Poetics*, also the discussion in Schloss, *Making Beats* (2004) and the documentary film *Scratch*.

Acquiring 'finds' at a bargain price is an additional bonus of the hunt:

> 'collectors will go to all lengths to find a record, no matter what the price. Diggers will put in the effort, but have an added joy in finding records for cheap. There's nothing like the feeling of finding a rare record for $1–$2 that you saw for $40–$50 somewhere else.' (Joel Wing)

Sites of acquisition

Collectors will often go wherever possible to obtain items:

- 'Second hand shops, new shops, flea markets, record fairs, internet, eBay, anywhere you could possibly find records.' (Andre Nuchelmans)
- 'Anywhere and everywhere – roadside markets, second hand shops, especially those specializing in music, chain stores, and more and more the web! Collecting could be better defined as "hunting and collecting". You need to explore all possible sources to build a collection especially if some items sought are up to 20+ years old.' (Gary Shuker)

Where the hunt takes place is related to considerations of time and opportunity, budget, effort and access. There are different pleasures associated with the various hunting sites and practices. For some collectors, there is a clear preference for physical shopping:

- 'I prefer to buy from physical record/CD shops, because I very much enjoy the experience of being in a shop, leafing through rows of albums or CDs.' (Steve Waksman)
- 'If I'm online, it's records I know, and I am actively looking for. Stores can offer so much more surprise, item wise and price wise, so they are always preferred.' (Michael Book)
- 'I much, much prefer buying records in person at a store. It's just the work and thrill of digging through tons of records and finding a few gems that is the basis of record collecting.' (Joel Wing)

This preference is based on a combination of the immediacy of the act of acquisition, and wanting to have the cultural artefact, the record, literally in hand. This is not simply a question of the pleasure of seeing/handling the physical object, but on a more pragmatic level enables a careful inspection of the condition of the recording:

- 'I prefer going into a store as opposed to shopping on the web (although I occasionally do that as well) so that I can pick the CDs up, look at the

covers, etc. and then have what I want right away instead of waiting for it.'
(Susan Fast)
- 'Independent record shops, second hand shops, thrift stores, garage sales.
  Just about anywhere but mail order and the internet. I prefer buying from
  outlets where I can see the record. I'm a little squeamish about buying good
  records unseen.' (Joe Kelich)

Other collectors are just as comfortable with shopping online. In 2002, when I first
discussed this with collectors, it was already evident that the internet was changing
record collecting, with several collectors using it to build their collections:

- 'I just love browsing through on-line catalogues, searching for items and
  so forth. It is much more enjoyable than conventional shopping.' (Albert
  Bell)
- 'I am buying many singles from an internet auction site in the Netherlands,
  because they have a lot of records I would like to own, more than second
  hand shops and they are often cheaper.' (Andre Nuchelmans)

For these collectors, the internet offered greater choice and scope, with its access to
international sites of acquisition, and with less physical effort than visiting 'bricks
and mortar' retail shops. My recent interviews demonstrated that more collectors
are now comfortable with hunting and purchasing records through the internet.
As discussed earlier, in relation to formats (Chapter 3) this may be a generational
shift, not just towards digital music, but also away from the traditional physical
collecting sites. This was evident, to varying degrees, among many younger
collectors (see the profiles of Geoff Stahl, Simon Sweetman and Oliver Wang, in
Chapter 7).

Where to hunt is also a function of the format preferred by the collector, and
the type of music they want. As Steve put it:

> 'Whether I prefer second hand shops or shops catering to more current tastes
> depends on what I'm shopping for – on the right day, I certainly enjoy scanning
> through old vinyl, to come up with odds and ends that in many cases haven't
> been reissued onto CD. But, by the same token, there's so much music one can
> only buy on CD, so by no means do I restrict myself to second-hand shops.'
> (Steve Waksman)

I turn now to the various sites of acquisition, the venues and avenues through
which collectors have historically obtained records. These include mail order and
dealer lists, street markets, thrift shops and suchlike, the music retail shops (chain
store, indie, second hand), record fairs, auctions and the internet, especially eBay.[5]

---

[5]   As the following sketch indicates, the history of music retail remains a neglected
one, and warrants a fuller treatment.

The relative significance of these sites has changed over time, while collectors' preference for, and use of them, varies.

Mail order and lists

Historically, in the absence of specialist shops, fairs and auctions, and before the internet, mail order was an essential part of record collecting. Advertising from collectors and dealers (and these roles frequently overlapped) was a significant part of the early collector press in the 1960s and 1970s. This followed the earlier practices of publications such as *Melody Maker* and *The Gramophone* (see Chapter 1). Mail order provided collectors in England with access to an international market in the 1960s, as Dave McAleer relates: 'I started ordering stuff from Randy's Records in Nashville [USA], run by Randy Wood, who was also the head of Dot Records. They had this incredible list of obscure R&B, country and pop, all at reasonable prices.' In 1960, he started subscribing to *Billboard*, the leading American trade magazine: 'That told me what was coming out in the States, usually long before the records were issued in Britain' (Doggett, 1996b: 41). Today, the space given over to advertisements in magazines such as *Record Collector* and *Goldmine* (see Chapter 6) indicates that mail order – usually through set sales, but also bidding on auctions run through these publications – remain important.

Such shopping at a distance, as later on the internet, serves to structure browsing and buying at the collectors' discretion, avoiding the tendency to impulse buy or 'blow the budget'. It also broadens the geographic scope of the hunt. Collectors living away from the dominant concentrations of record shops, such as London and Los Angeles, and with limited local shopping opportunities, will rely heavily on mail order. Specialist collectors are frequent users of lists, building up relationships with particular dealers over a long period of time; an initially economic arrangement which can be the basis for friendships. Reggae and soul collector Hasse Huss described this aspect of his collecting (in 2002):

> 'I have bought a lot from a friend in England, Adey Pierce (Cotswolds Records). He has a mail-order business selling soul, northern soul, R&B, funk (black music, 1960–80). I get lists regularly (once every month roughly) from Craig Moerer in Portland, Oregon (he carries all kinds of music, although I mostly go for soul). Also I get lists regularly from Reggae Rhythm (Steve Cox) in Manchester (UK), and auction lists from Dub Store (Naoki Ienaga) in Tokyo, and Mill Intl. in Illnau, Switzerland (both great lists for reggae and calypso, although they're only three or four times per year).'

Record clubs offer a mail order service, but their orientation to mainstream releases carries little appeal to collectors. That said, several mentioned to me that their initial music purchases, which led to 'record collecting', were made through such clubs.

Street markets

The rock and pop record collecting market took shape in the United Kingdom in the 1960s, when the first professional dealers began to sell rare rock'n'roll and beat group releases at street markets in London. Drawing on the accounts of collectors, Peter Doggett documents how the Soho market, along with the area's record shops, was at the heart of early record collecting in London during the mid 1960s. As Johnny Rogan observed, 'There was a perverse sense of glamour to shopping in Soho when I was a kid, because of the obvious prostitution and market atmosphere' (Doggett, 1996b: 42–3).

Contemporary street markets remain features of cities such as London, and will generally include several stalls selling tapes, vinyl albums and CDs. These will be a mix of second hand and 'remaindered' record label and retail stock, with condition varying widely. Such markets have also traditionally been places to acquire bootleg recordings. Collectors who move into dealing on a part-time basis through mail order, will sometimes also run a market stall, and they may then move on to setting up a shop, as with reggae specialists Dub Vendor in London (De Koningh and Griffiths, 2003: 218). Many (about a third) collectors I spoke to mentioned visiting and buying records at street markets, especially in their early collecting, although few continued to do so on a regular basis. This reflects the inverse relationship between effort and the reward involved: a great deal of sorting and sifting through records, with very few finds. And as a collector's 'wants list' of records becomes smaller and the records sought rarer, the chances of finding them outside of the more specialized sites of acquisition diminish further.

Thrift shops, garage and car-boot sales

Collectors of all types (of collectible) will make use of several aspects of what has been termed an informal economy of alternative consumption in contemporary societies, consisting of a mix of thrift shops and transitory sites such as garage and car-boot sales (Gregson and Crewe, 2003). As with street markets, these offer the chance of bargains and finds, but involve considerable effort. The willingness to put time and energy – which is physical as well as emotional – into getting to and searching such sites reflects the object of the search. Collectors of exotica will favour thrift stores, deriving enjoyment from the at times seedy ambience of these places, and the sheer amount of vinyl cultural waste to be sifted through (Vale and Juno, 1993; 1994). What is cultural waste to others can be their nirvana. Many styles and artists ignored and unwanted by most collectors, such as easy listening and soundtrack albums from the 1960s, can be very cheaply found at these sites.

Again, while many of my collectors referred to looking occasionally in these, few did so on a regular basis. A personal example of doing so is my own semi-regular ritual of visiting such shops in my suburban shopping centre. This search will take a couple of hours, and 'genuine finds' are scarce. However, it is not motivated by looking for a rarity, though I did once pick up a relatively scarce concert tape by The Jam; it is more about the pleasure of the process, and acquiring 'stuff' I don't own, especially cassette tapes to play in the car. In June 2007, I wandered around the three welfare shops in my local shopping centre: the St John's and Salvation Army shops yielded nothing amongst the usual piles of unwanted classical and easy listening vinyl. I looked through the few audio tapes, and bought two albums by Pearl Jam and one by Soundgarden, as my 'grunge' holdings are thin. If I see a good condition album cover, with appealing art work, I will buy it, regardless of the condition of the vinyl. At the recently opened Catholic Welfare services shop, I bought a mint copy – both cover and album – of The Boomtown Rats, *The Fine Art of Surfacing* (Polygram/Ensign Records, 1979). I'd seen the band in concert around the time of the release of the record, and admired the cover artwork. The hunt ended on a high.

The second hand markets are dominated by cash transactions and represent important alternative consumption sites. Gregson and Crewe (2003) suggest that those who participate in such sites do so in three ways: as buyer, small-time entrepreneur and voyeur: venues such as street markets are places to promenade and to be seen. The recordings sold here are given new meaning having initially been purchased and then discarded by their original owners as no longer of use, a process which recurs as some may be discarded again and recycled once more.

'Record shops'

Before considering the main types of record shops used by collectors, it is useful briefly to situate these against the general development of music retail. As the relative importance of different forms has shifted, along with the availability of particular formats and genres, so has the use collectors make of them. Records were first available through shops already selling sheet music and musical instruments. In the early 1900s, chains of department stores began supplying hit songs, along with sheet music. Later, with the advent of rock'n'roll, smaller, independent and sole proprietor shops (the 'mom and pop' stores in the United States) emerged. By the 1970s, record retailers included independent shops – often specializing in particular genres – used record stores, chain stores and mail order record clubs. The subsequent significance and market share of each of these has reflected the broader consolidation of the music industry, along with shifts in recording formats and distribution technologies. In addition to the impact of the internet and on-line shopping, retailers have had to adapt to changes as mundane as the need for different shelf space to accommodate new formats.

As with the culture industries generally, concentration has been a feature of music retail. By the early 1980s, record retailing was horizontally integrated and monopolistic, and saw the emergence of the large discount retail chains, including the new megastores, such as Tower, Virgin and HMV (part of EMI). The advent of electronic bar coding in the 1990s enabled retail, distribution and production 'to be arranged as an interconnected logistic package', allowing 'music retailers to delineate, construct and monitor the "consumer" of recorded music more intricately than ever before' (Gay and Negus, 1994: 396). A similar process then occurred with the tracking of browsers and purchasers' preferences in on-line shopping through the internet.

Yet this was also something of a high point for the specialist and used record store. As Hayes notes of the United States: 'While many small (largely regional) labels continued to release music on 7" and 12" records throughout the '90s, locating their products was often a difficult task since mainstream retail outlets such as Tower Records and HMV shelved few if any LP releases after deleting previous stock' (Hayes, 2006: 56). This limited vinyl enthusiasts to two main sites of acquisition: a small number of independent retailers who continued to stock vinyl releases, usually limited pressings by small labels, and used record stores.

However, the continued conglomeration and homogenization of music retail outlets during the 1990s led to a decline in the small, idiosyncratic record shop run by a music enthusiast (often a collector). A large proportion of recordings are now sold through general retailers (for example Woolworths – before the company's closure in late 2008 – in the United Kingdom, Walmart in the United States and the Warehouse in New Zealand and Australia), and the music megastores. This concentration influences the range of music available to consumers, and the continued economic viability of remaining smaller retail outlets. While collectors do not generally purchase their recordings primarily from such sources, their market dominance impacts on the outlets traditionally preferred by collectors. The general retailers frequently use music as a loss-leader: reducing their music CD and DVD prices to attract shoppers whom they hope will also purchase other store products with higher profit margins. This situates music as only one component of the general selling of lifestyle consumer goods. In the face of this competition, smaller local music chains have been forced to retrench by consolidating shops and 'downsizing' staff, or have kept operating through niche marketing and their increased use of the internet. The indie and second hand record stores have increasingly struggled, with the impact of the internet and its auction websites, increases in rent for traditional central city areas, especially as these become 'gentrified'/renewed, and the ongoing concentration of music retail generally. I now briefly consider the use collectors make of these main forms of record shops.

The megastores   Often horizontally linked into the record industry, the music megastores (such as Tower, Virgin) are organized around a supermarket model in terms of their use of bar coding, their layout, access and customer service. While they carry recorded music in various formats, they also stock music videos, posters, books and magazines, with inventory tracked using bar coding. Straw refers to the 'abundance and pluralism' of these new record superstores, with their layout showing a 'moralistic concern' for the consumer's comfort, and assuring confidence in the customers' ability to make a choice (Straw, 1997b: 58–9). The megastores publish newsletters; have appearances by artists; sponsor radio shows; may even put out their own records (samplers); and run loyalty programmes with rewards for purchasers.[6] Many collectors will use them for new releases they want immediately (and as cheaply as possible), and when there is a sale:

- 'I have a browse in HMV in Oxford St every 2–3 months, although if I read or hear about a new record [I want] I'll order it straightaway.' (Tina Janering)
- 'I have been doing a lot of shopping lately in JB Hi Fi which has been seriously undercutting competitor's prices and the money talks when you're on a budget.' (Andrew Stafford)

Other collectors are not comfortable with the megastores: 'I don't especially like big mega-stores, though I'll deal with them if I have no options – too glossy, and they never have as good a selection as they seem to promise' (Steve Waksman). For some, there is an ideological aversion to them as rather sterile and soulless, in 'making the record buying experience much more anaemic and mechanical' (Geoff Stahl), they are simply 'too capitalist'.

Indie and second hand   Collectors have a strong preference for specialist outlets, the 'indie' and second hand record shops, due to their ambience and the frequent availability of material outside the commercial mainstream:

- 'I buy new records primarily from an import distribution company here in Chicago (groove distribution), that opens to the public 2 days a week. They get all the newest records that I'm interested in from abroad. Otherwise I get stuff from other DJ oriented record shops, or used shops for my jazz and funk.' (Matt Glesne)
- 'I buy from shops that have significant collections of new vinyl basically whenever I come across them, because there are no such shops in my home town. I like this sort of outlet as they have the latest material.' (Brennon Wood)

Historically, indie or specialist record shops occupy a distinct space within the music market (De Koningh and Griffiths, 2003; Pettit, 2008). In many cases, they contribute significantly to local music scenes by promoting shows, supporting local artists and selling tickets, t-shirts, fanzines and other merchandise not handled by major retailers.

Part of the appeal of such shops is the relationship with the staff, which frequently involves trusting their musical knowledge and recommendations, along with a reciprocal recognition, often hard won, of the collectors' own expertise: 'Acceptance (after 7 years!) as one of the "musically hip" in town' (Norma Coates). Andrew Stafford prefers indie stores 'for their consistent range and variety and

---

[6]   Second hand, indie and specialist record shops will also do much of this, but on a smaller and less frequent scale; for example, Real Groovy in New Zealand.

above all staff who know their stuff. These stores have atmosphere that the others don't (always something new and great playing inside).' He goes on to observe, however, that

> 'On the other hand they can be very intimidating to outsiders – in this regard the High Fidelity stereotype is true. I get a 10 per cent discount at my local for having good taste, but it took years to build up this status in the eyes of the staff! Until I reached my present rarified level of maximum cool, these guys were the personification of standoffish arrogance.'

As Emma Pettit (2008) has documented, independent (and second hand) record shops continue to form a minor but still culturally significant part of record retail. Such shops have been hit by the same trends as their indie counterparts, along with the gentrification and higher rents of their traditional central city locations. They have managed to survive, and in some cases even flourish, by using the internet, by catering to specialist interests, and continuing to stock vinyl. Through their ambience and knowledgeable staff, they retain a loyal collector following:

- 'I also shop at second-hand shops 'cos they have the back catalogue. Most of my records have been bought second hand – it's the cheapest way to fuel the obsession, and these shops have a range of sounds that those mainstreet hole-in-the-wall boutiques lack.' (Brennon Wood)
- 'I never had an unlimited budget, so it was a form of Cheap Thrills (the name of Big Brother and the Holding Company's album, but also of a Montreal used record store). I like the search and chance for unusual items at used stores [and] most of the records I want are old anyway.' (Craig Morrison)
- 'I prefer second hand shops – they are better value and more interesting to browse in. They're also more likely to have unusual records.' (Juliette Taylor)

Collectors have their favourite shops, and will pay regular visits to these. Although DJ Giles Peterson uses a network of dealers around the world, he enjoys his regular trips to the record shops in London:

> As much as I get a million records through the post every week, I still have to go to do the record shops. I suppose I'm a classic Berwick Street/Soho boy, so I go from If Records to Soul Sounds Of The Universe to Vinyl Junkies, Mr Bongos … Its great living in London, going from shop to shop and finding a tune here and there. It's a social thing as well and it's relevant to my line of work. Going record shopping is almost like clubbing, in that you're going around hearing what's up and keeping in touch.[7]

---

[7]   *Record Collector*, 295, March 2004: 52.

Record fairs and conventions

The first record swap meet in the United States was held in The Palms, West Hollywood in the early 1950s, 'in a car park behind a restaurant. It opened at 10am and closed at noon' (Solly, 2000: 59). With an upsurge of interest in rock'n'roll collecting in the early 1970s, the meet expanded into larger premises, with trading stretched over four days, Friday through Monday. Eventually the venue was transferred to a site in Pasadena. In the United Kingdom, where they are more usually called record fairs, 'by the end of the 1970s there were regular events in London and across Britain', with the first international fair held in 1980. (Doggett, 1996b: 53).

By the late 1980s and the unavailability of vinyl in mainstream music retail with the impact of the CD, there was an increasing number of record conventions and fairs internationally. According to Todd Ploharski of Rock 'N' Roland, an Atlanta based record collector organization which sponsored conventions at least six times a year, the vinyl trade, though forced underground, was then stronger than ever:

> The record crowd has always been a devoted passionate bunch of collectors; as intense as any group I've ever been associated with, including the comic book freaks. Within the past few years, attendance at our shows has been phenomenal. Whether its CD anxiety, desperation, the usual obsessive behaviours, or more people unloading their record collections; people have just come out of the woodwork. There seems to be a very special bond, some sense of purpose, among the record collectors, like a little community. (Plasketes, 1992: 116)

More recently though, records that used to be hard to find now turn up frequently on websites like eBay, in mail-order outlets and in auctions. For many collectors, it has become easier to stay at home and look through internet listings than go to conventions. Accordingly, in 2008 David Tosh addressed the question of whether such conventions still had a purpose:

> For me, record cons aren't the place to make my really big scores, but they are where I tend to find elusive items that seem to appeal to a select audience. There's also the thrill of going by a dealer's booth and seeing a special item 'in the flesh' – and most dealers are friendly enough to let you examine whatever it might be up close, with the naked eye. You can't do that on eBay! Most important to me is the human connection – meeting and talking to other music fans, sharing their passion for something you can hold in your hand. (Tosh, 2008: 10)[8]

---

[8]   Tosh was one of the organizers of Rhythmhound 2008 Music and Media Show, 16–18 May, at the renovated Palmer Events Center (formerly the Palmer Auditorium), Austin, Texas.

Social contact remains part of the continued appeal of fairs and conventions in the 2000s. As shown in the advertising and reports in *Goldmine* and *Record Collector*[9] there remains a network of regular fairs in North America, the United Kingdom and Europe, with many now run in several cities by specialist companies. There are also some long-running fairs in New Zealand and Australia, such as the Paramatta, Sydney event. Visits to these remain part of the hunt for many collectors. For some, regular major shows are a social highlight, offering the opportunity to immerse themselves in records, along with fellow enthusiasts, and to make on-going contacts (see Lisa Wheeler's profile in Chapter 7). Once again, the possibility of an elusive find is ever-present.

Auctions

Record auctions will range from those run by individuals and smaller dealers, often in conjunction with retail and mail order business, through to prestige international firms and internet sites such as eBay. Those by major auction houses such as Christie's, Bonhams, Sotheby's and Heritage will generally concentrate on memorabilia and rarer recordings, often with the associated appeal of these having been signed or owned by the artists. Examples of all of these auctions can be seen in the advertising and reports in the collector press. As with auctions of other collectibles, in addition to being conducted at physical sites, record auctions are conducted by mail (and email) and on the internet. In an effort to engage with as broad a purchasing group as possible, they may involve all of these. An example is Nauck's Vintage Records, who hold semi-annual auctions of 10,000+ cylinder and 78 rpm records. These include every genre from 1890 to 1960, 'from opera to rock n roll', and catalogues typically go to 4,000–5,000 collectors and archives in about 50 countries (Bernardy, 2006). Most of my record collectors had bid in auctions, and several had sold as well as bought records and other music collectibles.

The internet and eBay

The web has become a major resource for collectors, providing a knowledge base to draw on and a site for collectibles. Websites, especially those combining the offerings of a large number of dealers, now offer the chance to browse through tens of thousands of collectable records. In addition, there are many rare record and memorabilia auctions on line. The provision of information, with on-line discographies, collector groups and suchlike informs collectors about releases and aids the process of record buying through establishing what is available and comparative shopping.

---

[9]   In his 'Fair Trade' column for *Record Collector*, Ian Peel has covered fairs in the United States and Australia, in addition to numerous ones in the UK. As well as reporting on them, both magazines regularly provide a diary of upcoming shows, along with advertisements for many of them.

In 2002, DJ Joel Wing remarked:

'Years ago the only way you'd find out about these harder to find artists would be through books, college radio stations (where DJs are allowed to play anything they want rather than just top 50, and where you can also find specialized shows of just Hip Hop, Heavy Metal, Dance, etc.), talking to people at record stores and other collectors you might find at stores or at record conventions. Now, with the internet there's tons of sites on the web that can not only give you information about artists, but let you hear their songs through MP3 or real audio.'

Many collectors I talked with in the early 2000s were already web shoppers, and the shift to the internet is even more pronounced today. As Michelle Wauchope noted in 2009:

'I still go "hunting", so my tendency is still the same, it's just changed media format – I go online. I look for bootleg concerts of recordings, video footage of appearances, and other rarities.'

A primary site for record collecting is eBay. Launched in 1995 (as AuctionWeb), eBay is now the world's largest online market: 'a virtual setting where capital, desire and identity converge', allowing 'sellers to design, perform, and sell memorable experiences, thematically linked to goods' (Hillis, Petit and Epley, 2006: 1). As Keir Keightley could observe in 2002: '[I like] eBay because it makes searching so easy and because you can find things in 20 minutes that you've never seen in 20 years of record-store-going.' Record collectors have made increasing use of the site, for selling as well as buying (see the profiles in Chapter 7).

Acquisition: feeding the collection

As acknowledged by many collectors (see Chapters 1 and 2), there is an 'addiction' dimension to collecting, with regular acquisition of new material a significant part of their lives. If not purchasing, this can be through trading, dubbing and downloading practices. In addition, those working in different aspects of the music industry, especially journalists and DJs, frequently receive 'freebies': 'I get a lot of music for free these days [2002], because of my job programming music for an online music company. I also was a Music Director at several radio stations, which puts you in line for lots of free music' (Michelle Flannery; see also the profile of music journalist Simon Sweetman in Chapter 7). Copying (dubbing audiotapes; burning CDs) was a significant part of many of my respondents' collection building: 'Now I don't really purchase records at all … only about a dozen a year. Collection relies mainly on bootlegging tapes off friends!' (Brennon Wood). Given the debates around the impact of copying on the music industry, it is worth adding that this is often done in addition to purchasing records for the collection.

Further, it sometimes acts as an intermediary stage, allowing for trial listening to recordings that may well be purchased later on.

Roughly half of my collectors shopped for records on a very regular basis, and would purchase one to three recordings per week. It was noticeable that nearly all shopping trips resulted in a purchase; collectors found it difficult to enter a record shop (of any type) without obtaining at least one record. Regularity was often related to opportunity and access:

- 'Varies, depending on when I can get to a music store.' (Andrew Njsse)
- 'I currently buy about five to six records twice a week. Within one block in either direction of my apartment there are five independent/dance record and used record shops.' (Geoff Stahl, then [2002] living in Montreal)

The advent of eBay has expanded the opportunities to purchase records, often combined with continued use of physical sites of acquisition: 'Depends on whether there are good eBay auctions running ... probably at least 2 a week, but sometimes none and sometimes 20 in a day.' (Keir Keightley)

Collectors will indulge in what some referred to as 'buying binges' when on holiday or work visits to other countries and cities:

- 'La Fnac [megastore] whenever I'm in France. Fnac is scary. A kick to be somewhere where they've got absolutely everything.' (Yngvar Steinbolt)
- 'Most of my classical albums have come from Christchurch, Wellington, and Auckland – little holiday spending sprees.' (Greg Crossan)
- 'I go to New York City and Boston two to three times a year to see family and friends and spend most of my time buying records. I also go to one foreign country each summer. I've bought records in Paris, London, Japan and Canada.' (Joel Wing)

Once again, the 'find' is an integral part of national and international searches: 'I searched for years for an album called Spacing Out by The Invaders, who are a psychedelic funk band from Barbados. I found it in Japan at a dealers and swapped it for a 7in by the Vern Blair Debate – then found another copy in the next store I visited. I'd been looking for it for ten years, then found two in a day. I just love Japan!'[10] Indeed, Japan is a primary hunting ground for record collectors, who regularly enthuse over the opportunities offered by the numerous record shops there, particularly in Tokyo.[11]

---

[10]   Scratch DJ Cut Chemist, from San Francisco hip hoppers Jurrassic 5; in 'Vinyl Frontier', *WORD*, August 2007: 42.

[11]   For instance, see the comments by Thurston Moore, in Milano (2003). Several of my collectors had visited Japan, in part to search for records there, and two had lived there for short periods.

Collectors' frequency of purchasing is related to being in or out of employment, and their disposal income. This varies at different points in their lives, depending on work, study and family commitments. Liz lamented her inability to buy as often as she might want: 'At the moment [2002] not often enough! Bloody student wages. I tend to buy a few at a time, but not very often.' Redundancy had forced one collector to cut back, and resort primarily to Napster: 'Well, I've just about stopped, because I simply can't afford it now.' At the other extreme, Joel's move to full-time employment in 2001 boosted his record collecting:

> 'There's never a set amount of records I buy a week or month, but the amount of money I spend each month has taken a dramatic increase in the last year [with a full time job]. A year ago I was spending about $400–$500 a month on records. For the last year, I've been spending nearly $900 a month. During this summer I've averaged more than $1,000 a month.' (Joel Wing)

At times, the collector will yield to the temptation to buy 'more than they should', spending more than they have budgeted or can afford; this then requires an effort at subsequent restraint:

> 'On a weekly basis I buy about 3 records, sometimes more, but I have to compensate (for) that the weeks after. But I still go about 3 times a week to a record store or a flea market to look if there is anything. However, when I have already bought more than I ought to, I use higher criteria for the next purchase. *Or I try to.*' (Andre Njsse; my emphasis)

Women collectors tend to have a more careful and budget conscious approach to the economics of record collecting: 'I know my limits. I've passed up many a record … and I've never paid more than I budgeted' (Lisa Wheeler). As might be expected, those with larger collections (5,000 plus) purchase on a very regular basis, and in larger quantities, so spend more.

Bulk buying

One way to expand the collection dramatically is to buy in bulk, including purchasing whole collections.[12] Haase Huss was one of several who had done this:

> '[I bought] three collections (two of reggae, one of soul) in the early '90s They were not very large collections (each reggae collection perhaps had 250 singles, the soul one, maybe 400 singles) but they were lovingly compiled. Only after a few years did I realize that there were also some very scarce items among this

---

[12]   This approach has been facilitated by major websites including categories for bulk lots, and collector magazines reporting on these.

lot. So I was very lucky, with these records I began to realize just how excellent a lot of the stuff released by small cupboard-under-stairs companies was, and that labels and producers, particularly in reggae and soul, are more important than the artist more often than not.'

Bulk buying is, as would be expected, more prevalent with second hand record dealers, and DJs. Earnest documents how Kansas dealer Chad Kassem acquired a 30-ton vinyl LP collection that had been in storage for more than 20 years:

'We went over to this warehouse, and it was all dusty and crammed full of junk. There were pallets of these records stacked three high. I couldn't go through everything, so we went through a couple of boxes and saw a few things, and we made an offer, and we got 'em.' The collector, who died in 1981, had 'often bought multiple copies of records from a variety of genres and left nearly all of them in the plastic, and his family had left the vinyl untouched in a warehouse facility ever since.'[13]

Buying tends to decline with age, increased family commitments, and with the items still sought becoming fewer and more difficult to acquire.

- 'These days I don't buy anywhere near as frequently as I have done in the past. During my 20s and 30s I'd buy at least every fortnight, usually when I was paid. Now I buy much less frequently [though at times the items are expensive ones].' (Peter Dawson)
- 'Not nearly as many as I used to because I walk into a record store and it is hard to find great records I don't already have, but then again one record now could bring me much more satisfaction than 20–30 a few years back.' (Michael Book)

How frequently collectors acquired records, and in what quantity, indicates different levels of investment – emotional as well as physical – in the collection. This is also evident in different attitudes towards selling and trading, and practices such as lending.

Selling and trading

Collection building can also involve selling, trading items for credit, or buying items to sell on. Second hand record shops are constantly purchasing new stock from individual sellers, including whole collections. This is normally a selective

---

13   Brian Earnest, 'Hitting the Mother Lode: Kansas Record Dealer Acquires 30-ton Vinyl Record Collection', *Goldmine*, November 2007: 32.

process, avoiding duplicates and records that are simply not in demand.[14] It can also involve trade, where the seller is given more in the form of a credit for use in the shop, a better price than if they had sold outright. This is obviously a win–win situation, assuming the seller wants to buy other items the shop has – and it gives the collector an excuse to regularly go in to check out the recent additions sections, or to look for particular items.

Trading is a common practice among collectors, but largely for collection building rather than for profit. A number mentioned selling recordings, or trading them, usually to obtain others they wanted. These sales were often of duplicates acquired through gifts or bulk purchases, although they could be of 'unwanted' material. 'Selling on' is also part of the economics of record collecting. I have several times bought a second, duplicate copy if I know it is a bargain and can be profitably traded or resold; several interviewees recounted similar stories. An impressive example of utilizing knowledge to make a quick profit is Garry Warren's purchase, in 2004, of a copy of the brown vinyl version of Iron Maiden's 'Twilight Zone' single. Bought at a Brighton record fair for £75, he subsequently sold it for £1,240.[15]

Selling can include other music collectibles. Ed Montano did not regret selling off his father's collection of Shadows records, but did regret selling some pictures (with copyright) that his father had taken of The Beatles in the 1960s.

> My mum informed me that when they were living in Liverpool in the early 60s, my dad had a friend with a press agency or something, and my dad was into photography, so he got press passes for various musical events. These pictures were taken at the one event I think ... anyway, so sometime in the mid 90s, I sent them down to Christie's auction house in London. The Beatles shots were obviously the selling point, unpublished and we were selling them with copyright. They sold for close to 2000 pounds if I remember correctly. I mention regret because I think now that it would be super cool to have some pictures on the wall in my home of the Beatles that were taken by my dad.[16]

Regret is a recurring motif with such experiences, and is one shared with many collectors of other commodities, notably books and stamps. Some record collectors build in trading or selling as part of their regular collection building, and are comfortable with this. Others, however, relate instances where they have sold with reluctance and a subsequent sense of loss: 'I try to buy when I can afford it, if not I trade – but that hurts!' (Hasse Huss). The difference between those happy to sell or trade, and those who do not, is the degree of attachment they have for their record(s). Those who never sell or trade have an intense personal investment in the

---

[14]   Many top selling chart records are so plentiful, second hands stores will not take them, or, if they do, only at a very low credit for trade.

[15]   *Record Collector*, 294, February 2004: 10.

[16]   Email to author, 12 February 2009; abridged.

collection – at times even when they can't play some recordings (as with retaining vinyl when they no longer having a working turntable). This attitude can change over time, with the realization at some point that there is a limit to how many records the collector needs: this is a defining moment in the life of a collector (Stan Denski, in Campbell, 2001).

The various ways of collection building are linked by the notion of the 'gift', since most of the collection consists of gifts which the collector has given themselves (Pearce, 1995: 369). Indeed, many collectors use the language of gift giving (at times unconsciously?) to describe how they spend money on themselves: 'I got myself a present' or 'I indulged in a little retail therapy'. This helps distance collecting from everyday forms of consumption, such as household shopping, while the gift is also a reward for the effort expended on the hunt.

Managing the collection

Collecting functions as the 'unofficial relocation of objects from the public commercial realm into the domestic environment' (Straw, 1997a: 5). In this process, once items are acquired, they must then be ordered and classified, and stored, in an on-going process. An important aspect of collection management is its display, either privately or in public, and then there is the question of lending from the collection.

Cataloguing

Collectors' approach to cataloguing provides a further index of their commitment to, and emotional engagement with, the collected artefact. It is part of a process of transforming mass produced cultural products into a personal assembly, a construction of the self. I was interested in how meticulous, or not, record collectors were about keeping track of their holdings via some sort of catalogue system. Such practices are one of the pleasures of record collecting, but can be related to issues of obsession. One of the most striking passages in *High Fidelity* is when Rob describes re-cataloguing his collection, through the (fairly common) process of physically reorganizing his records:

> When Laura was here I had the records arranged alphabetically … Tonight, though, I fancy something different, so I try to remember the order I bought them in: that way I hope to write my own autobiography, without having to do anything like pick up a pen. I pull the records off the shelves, put them in piles all over the sitting room floor, look for 'Revolver' and go from there; and when I've finished, *I'm flushed with a sense of self, because this, after all, is who I am*. But what I really like is the feeling of security I get from my new filing system; I have made myself more complicated than I really am. I have a couple of thousand records, and you have to be me – or, at the very least, a doctor of

Flemingology – to know how to find any of them. If I want to play, say, 'Blue'
by Joni Mitchell, I have to remember that I bought it for someone in the autumn
of 1983, and thought better of giving it to her, for reasons I really don't want
to go into. Well, you don't know any of that, so you're knackered, really, aren't
you? You'd have to ask me to dig it out for you, and for some reason I find this
enormously comforting. (Hornby, 1995: 53; my emphasis)

This captures the relationship between cataloguing and the collectors' sense of
identity, and echoes the well-known essay by Walter Benjamin on 'unpacking' his
library of books (Benjamin, 1968).

About half of my collectors simply did not keep a written catalogue. Sometimes
the small size of their collection was mentioned as making it unnecessary, while a
lack of time and the effort required were also cited for not doing so. At times a start
would be made, but not gone on with: 'For the first hundred or so I kept a meticulous
card catalogue and numbered every album; since then I just haven't had the time'
(Greg Crossan). One made a self-mocking reference back to stereotypes: 'I do not
catalogue them. That would be admitting to anal retentiveness. This means I often
can't find what I'm looking for' (Tony Mitchell). Others maintained 'a mental
catalogue': 'The catalogue is forever inscribed in my mind. I know exactly what
two records I'm missing at the moment [in 2002], for instance (Paint Your Wagon
soundtrack and the Mini-Pops LP)' (Geoff Stahl).

Many collectors followed Rob's practice, and organized their collection
on some sort of physical catalogue basis. This generally involved shelving in
alphabetical order and in date of release order, with some distinctions by genre,
without actually having this recorded:

- 'I have them on shelves in my room. They are alphabetized by artist name
  and somewhat separated by genre (hip hop and contemporary R&B on one
  shelf, old soul and jazz another shelf).' (Joe Kelich)
- 'CDs and albums are chronological within alphabet. I do some very
  basic break-out by "meta-genre" (i.e., jazz, classical and rock (which is
  everything else)). I have to keep them organized like this or I would never
  be able to find what I'm looking for.' (Norma Coates)
- 'The collection is the catalogue itself: they are ordered alphabetically and
  sorted by genre, but apart from their physical presentation I do not keep
  track of indexes or something.' (Steven Mallett)

A number (8/70 of those interviewed) had more thorough cataloguing practices,
involving the use of a mix of computer databases along with printed lists. At times,
this was undertaken for insurance purposes, but more to access more easily the
collection and to remind the collector of their personal links to particular records,
their acquisition and economic value. The catalogue could also link in with other
reference sources. In addition to 'rough lists' of his collection, Gary maintains
checklists printed from musicians websites, along with his 'own special collecting

books with bio and visuals plus info about other related items – videos, calendars, magazines, posters, t-shirts, tour programmes, promo displays' (Gary Shuker). Barry had

> 'a list on the computer and also a hard copy for reference stored with the records. For each record I list artist, title, condition, mono/stereo, and value if listed in the collector's guides that I have. I use the hardcopy for updating and emendations until it gets to the point that it has so much handwriting on it that I go back to the computer and enter the new information and then print off a new copy. It's a vicious cycle.' (Barry Grant)

With a neat self mocking aside, Yngvar Steinbolt documents his comprehensive approach:

> 'All records are card filed after two separate systems (*now this starts to sound psychotic*). Bands, artists or composers each have one card, if possible with town and country of origin and period of a band's existence. Below all collected recordings, their format and file numbers are listed. A star behind the file number signifies "original issuing". If I have seen the band live, gigs, time and place will be listed on the back of the card. The other system follows the file numbers. Records are labelled in the order they're bought, separately for LPs, 12" EPs, 7", CD and CD-singles. The year and month of purchase is noted in the file-number list, along with name of band/performer and name of record. It makes it possible to set limits for new purchases, find out what fad I was fooled by at any point in time and, like a diary, date memories triggered by listening to old records.' (my emphasis)

As these comments and practices indicate, for collectors cataloguing is a significant part of constructing a personal musical autobiography.

Storage and use

As with cataloguing, varying practices of collection storage and use reflect different degrees of investment, emotionally and financially, in the collection. The associated reconfiguration of domestic space creates a private haven for the collector: an expression of personal identity and the assertion of cultural power. Some have a slightly apologetic view of their own relatively casual storage/usage, while a few, usually with smaller collections, adopt a 'no fuss' approach:

- 'Just keep them on shelves.' (Juliette Taylor)
- 'Very casually – if there's shelf space, they go on the shelf, if not, on the floor. I do make sure really important LPs get plastic sleeves.' (Keir Keightley)

At times, especially among younger collectors, provision for storage reflected fluid living arrangements, and which parts of the collection were required 'on demand'. Andrew Stafford described his situation (in 2002) as:

'A difficult one, as I'm currently between moves. Less than half of my CDs are in storage. The rest (the ones I either decided initially I couldn't live without, or the ones I've gone scurrying back to the storage facility to retrieve in desperation) are at my temporary abode in boxes, on shelves or scattered around the floor. All my vinyl is stored at home for maintenance purposes, although they're just stacked up against a wall at the moment.'

For those with larger collections, storage can become a problem, and many mentioned having purpose- (or self-) built storage areas/facilities. As Barry Grant's provision indicates, this will involve investing considerable time and money:

'All records are stored in custom made square cubicles that can be stacked in a variety of configurations to fit the particulars of a given space. The cubicles are made of oak so that they can take the weight of the records and of each other as they are stackable. All records are kept in good inner sleeves (I don't have a preference for plastic vs. paper) and in plastic outer sleeves to protect the covers from damage like ring wear.'

Such levels of provision marks another rite of passage in the life of the record collector, a realization of the size and importance of the collection and its right to dedicated space: 'I started with just using those plastic boxes you can find in every supermarket, but as my amount of records grew, the need for something else rose. A year or two ago, I built myself some kind of wooden cabinet with a capacity of up to 500 CDs' (Steven Mallet).

Storage and treatment of the individual recordings themselves could generally be characterized by the word 'careful', and collectors who were also audiophiles describe their handling of records in loving detail:

'Each vinyl LP has its own plastic cover and is always stored vertically. I pick them up very delicately too. Some of them I have treated with permastat spray which reduces surface noise. I have always used a light stylus pressure too – I have a Dual 505 turntable with Ortofon styli. For both vinyl and CDs I put them back in their packaging as soon as I've finished using them. I try not to leave either CDs or vinyl in the player overnight.' (Warren Green)

Having a 'good sound system' was largely a 'given', and collectors referred to a variety of 'record playing' provisions in both their work and private settings.

Lending

I asked collectors if they ever lent records. Behind this question lurked an assumption that record collectors would be reluctant to lend from their collection.[17] This was largely born out, though most were prepared to dub tapes or CDs:

- 'No, but I do burn compilation CDs for friends on a regular basis.' (Grant Mitchell)
- 'Lending is rare in terms of the originals; I am more likely to copy onto a cassette to pass on to others.' (Brennon Wood)

For most collectors, lending is infrequent and only to trusted friends or follow collectors:

- 'No. Well, once in a while. But, only if it's someone who I know is as respectful (read: obsessive) about records as I am.' (Joe Kellich)
- 'Occasionally – to good friends.' (Juliette Taylor)
- 'On rare occasions and only to those who I trust – usually fellow collectors who are friends of mine.' (Oliver Wang)

As the language used here suggests, the reluctance to lend is based on a strong attachment to the collection:

- 'Rarely, and when I do I am somewhat worried about it. Sometimes I will make a copy so I won't have to part with original. I admit that I am emotionally attached.' (Michelle Flannery)
- 'Only when I take them with me and back when I leave, I never leave them anywhere or with anybody when I'm not there.' (Andre Nuchelmans)
- 'Rarely and it is not something I like doing.' (Michael Book)
- 'I have in the past. I would treat each request on its own basis. I have to admit that I get nervous lending my music.' (Keith Beattie)

The treatment of records by some who had borrowed them, along with the occasional failure to return them, were also given as reasons for no longer lending: 'I rarely lend my CDs either as I was always disappointed in the care others took of them. People leave finger marks, scratches and bust the boxes or the teeth which hold the CDs in place' (Michelle Flannery). The failure to return loaned items in the past, was often recalled ironically or sarcastically: 'I do lend records occasionally and can still remember the titles of many that remain overdue 20 years later' (Brennon Wood). And: 'Rarely. I prefer giving gifts' (Tony Mitchell).

---

[17]   This was based on my personal experience. It is also very much the case with many book collectors, see Rabinowitz and Kaplan (1999: 28–34).

On the other hand, several collectors (8/70) did lend more readily, partly out of an enthusiasm to share their tastes/good music, although even then a note of caution was often present:

- 'Absolutely. I'm a musical evangelist. I don't lend so much as foist things on people. I'm less likely to lend vinyl though (and usually don't have to).' (Andrew Stafford)
- 'I lend CDs to trusted people, but note file numbers in any case. Good music must be spread. I only ever lost one record.' (Yngvar Steinbolt)
- 'Yes, as I want other persons to listen to good music too. I do, however, not lend them to everybody, but only to good friends whom I'm sure will take good care of them.' (Steve Waksman)

Accompanying the willingness to lend, there can be an element of establishing musical status, credibility, and cultural capital at work: 'Usually to teenage kids of friends who can't believe that I have stuff by Beck or Sleater-Kinney, etc.' (Norma Coates).

In sum, collectors' attitudes toward lending is closely related to individual levels of emotional attachment to, and identification with, the cultural artefact: the sound recording. Those with a more intense attachment and commitment to the collection prefer to retain their records firmly within their control. Similar attitudes and explanations for them are also present among book collectors.

Display and use

The record collector has traditionally used the domestic space to make a statement about their passion. Smaller collections will take up a prominent space in the lounge or the study (or both!); larger collections will have their own dedicated room. At its most extreme, special provision will be made, such as remodelling a basement, or even building a shed. The collection is a display of conspicuous consumption and cultural capital, and asserts personal identity. As several collectors observed, a wall of shelving – or, better still, a room – filled with vinyl albums or CDs has an impact on visitors, stating 'this is part of who I am'. Storage arrangements will occasionally demand domestic tolerance:

'My collection is the highlight of our living room. CDs and cassettes are stored in pro-logic tower risers (holding around 1 hundred items each). My wife tolerates its notable presence as she is aware of how much music, particularly metal means to me.' (Albert Bell)

Outside of the private space there are a number of avenues for using and displaying the collection. As demonstrated in Chapters 1 and 2, it is common for record collectors to also be working in music related careers, with the collection drawn on as a resource. The obvious example here is the DJ, working in clubs or presenting specialist radio shows. John Peel drew on his extensive record collection for his BBC show, as do DJ collectors Oliver Wang and Geoff Stahl (see their profiles in Chapter 7). Record collectors have started record labels, often to put out material that would otherwise remain unissued, produced compilations and reissues, and contributed sleeve notes and booklets to these.

As was present in the 78 era (Chapter 1), an historically significant form of displaying and sharing knowledge and the collection is through vernacular[18] scholarship: writing for fanzines, music magazines, and the specialist collecting magazines, drawing on the collection for pictorial examples, and displaying musical knowledge/collecting tastes. Much of this will be on a part time basis, although it can move from this to a livelihood, where the collector can turn their hobby into a job. This is typical of journalists who are also collectors, including several who edit and contribute to the collector magazines and guidebooks (for instance, Ian Shirley, the editor of the *Rare Record Price Guide* and contributor of a regular column to *Record Collector*; see his profile in Chapter 7).

The internet has provided another avenue for displaying the collection and the shaping of a sense of community among collectors. Websites devoted to collectors are, as Oliver Wang describes them, 'part shrine, part ego preening'.[19] Collectors have also developed their own specialized websites, as with Lisa Wheeler's on radio compilations (see Chapter 7). Joe Bussard, the stereotypical traditional 78 record collector (Chapter 1), now has a MySpace page and a dealer website, recognizing the value of the internet as a platform of exchange for record collecting. YouTube has an expanding group of collectors/music lovers using digital technology to provide on-line brief 'show and tells' of their prized records, holding up a series of albums and commenting on them. Several show how to go about record collecting, how to maintain and care for the collection, and where to find records. Indicative of the increased importance of this forum, *Record Collector* currently has a column on them. Such practices are playing an important role in helping to shape a new generation of collectors.

Conclusion

The hunt for recordings, and the use and display of the collection, are key record collecting practices. As with other collectibles, the nature and intensity of the collectors' engagement with these and the associated practices, reflect varying levels of personal identification with, and investment in, the collection. Identification with

---

[18]   Vernacular in the sense that the authors are primarily operating outside of 'academia'; that said, the best of this work is certainly 'academic' in rigor and has the added advantage of being accessible to a wider readership.

[19]   For example: http://turntablelab.com/features/record_check/rcmain/rc-main.html and http://www.beatsandbreaks.com/.

the collectible is central to constructing a personal autobiography of the collector; in the case of records, this is primarily a musical biography, which carries with it connotations of taste and cultural capital. Investment operates in several senses: the time, effort and financial resources devoted to acquiring recordings. The display and use of the collection are undertaken in both the public and private spheres. Drawing on one's knowledge of the collectable field is integral to the building and maintenance of the collection. The music press plays a central role in providing such knowledge, and is the subject of the following chapter.

Chapter 6
Record collecting and the music press

The music press is an important part of popular music culture (see Shuker, 2008: Chapter 9), and is a key part of the infrastructure of record collecting. Record collectors are among the readers of the music press in general, but also consume a number of publications aimed more specifically at them. I consider five types of these here. First, the record collecting guidebooks, whose primary purpose is as general reference tools, serving to introduce the process of record collecting and establishing discrimination as a key tenet of this, by identifying which recordings should be collected, a canon. Also discussed here are books that contribute to canon formation, by identifying 'the best of'; while primarily aimed at a general market of music fans, they are extensively used by collectors. Second, there are the record price guides; these pay some attention to process and discrimination, but their dominant concerns are with scarcity, condition and market value. The price guides also function as a form of discography, but this role is more directly undertaken by a third category of publication, specialized discographies. My fourth category are fanzines, especially those produced by and largely for collectors. Finally, there are the specialist collector magazines; while there are a number of these, my focus is on the two main ones: the *Record Collector* and *Goldmine*. As the field of collecting has grown, there has been a proliferation of this literature, along with increased specialization among its titles. This chapter examines the historical development of these publications since 1970, their emphases, and the use made of them by record collectors.

As indicated in Chapter 1, the music press played a significant role in historically shaping the collecting of classical, jazz and blues music during the Gramophone Age. Journals such as *The Gramophone* (UK, 1923–) were central to the creation of classical music collecting, and its attendant emphasis on discrimination, cultural capital and upward social mobility. *Melody Maker* played a similar role for jazz collecting. The development of discography also shaped collecting. The first guides to record collecting appeared in the 1930s, but until the 1970s, they concentrated largely on classical music, with some attention to jazz. Their focus was primarily on collecting as a systematic activity, characterized by the thrill of the hunt, and underpinned by discrimination.

Through the 1950s and into the 1960s, there was little attention to the emerging collecting of 'pop' and 'rock'n'roll' records, although many of the topics covered and much of the advice offered could be applied to these genres. As Bryant's *Collecting Gramophone Records*, published in 1962, claimed: 'Though most of the material has been written with the classical music lover in mind, much of it applies equally to the enthusiast for jazz or "pops" [*sic*]' (Bryant, 1962: 7).

These essentially classical music guides were important departure points for the development of the collecting literature around popular music, as they established models for what such guides should address.

Collecting guides and record guides

Stimulated by the emergence of 'rock culture' in the 1960s, the 1970s saw the first guides aimed at collectors and fans of popular music. Initially these focused on R&B and rock'n'roll, but then extended their scope to include '60s rock and pop recordings. Later, they were followed by volumes on genres such as reggae, hip hop and heavy metal. These covered similar topics to their classical and jazz predecessors, but with rarity and economic value more prominent. They included reference to the handling and storage of records, and identified a number of sites where records could be found (see Chapter 5). As with the guides to classical record collecting, those on popular music also emphasized the role of knowledge in building up a collection.

Steve Propes's two related volumes[1] were among the first to provide systematic guides to the emergent field; published in the United States, they were also available in the UK. They represent an early example of the topics and themes present in the new 'rock' guidebooks. These overlap, but to facilitate discussion can be separated into:

- the legitimation of popular music as a collecting field;
- the scope of the field (artists, labels and genres to be collected);
- discrimination within this (in terms of collectible);
- scarcity, condition and value; and
- information on the field, and where to get records; references, including discographies.

Propes's books constituted a sense of what was collectable, and how the collector should go about building their collection.

He argued that, with 1950s record collecting, there was as yet, 'no universal acceptance and respectability attached to this collecting form'. In providing a guide, he was legitimating the collecting of the non-classical repertoire: 'Here are the ground rules of what records to look for, where to look, prices to pay (especially for rare records) and pitfalls to avoid.' He observed that recordings of the 1950s were usually sold cheaply or discarded by the non-collector and ignored by collectors of other types of sound recordings: 'To the collector specializing in opera or the classics, prewar jazz, blues, gospel, early hillbilly or big band

---

[1]   *Oldies but Goodies: A Guide to 50s Record Collecting* (1973). This project was extended into the 1960s with his expanded volume *Golden Goodies: A Guide to 50s and 60s Rock & Roll Record Collecting* (1975). My quotes are from the first volume.

records, the 1950s 78 or 45 RPM recording is just too new to be taken seriously as a collector's item.' This was changing, with 1950s music 'becoming recognized as an honest and unique art form quite worthy of assuming a collectable status. Consequently, systems of value are being established' (Propes, 1973: 1).

Propes provided discographies of the significant vocal groups and single artists dominating rhythm and blues and rock and roll during the 1950s: 'By giving as full and accurate discographical information as available, the releases of various artists are put into historic and artistic perspective.' This approach distinguished simply accumulating records from a more considered approach to collecting, centred on discrimination. He dedicated his work 'to the collector and to that turn of thought that motivates and nurtures the pursuit of seeking out, acquiring and assembling individual works into a creative whole: a collection'. He justifiably claims his guide to be 'the first systematic attempt to describe and define those elements that constitute a valid [defined in terms of the "significant artists and recordings"] collection of 1950s music. I could not include all recorded works from that era, but I do touch on what I feel are the most significant and influential records' (Propes, 1973: 2).

The comparative rarity of particular 1950s and early 1960s records reflected the reluctance of major and minor companies to press more than a few thousand copies of R&B and rock and roll releases during that period. Sales of that level constituted a fair-sized hit, whereas the number of copies of the typical release was insignificant. Another company practice influencing scarcity was the tendency to soon delete many recordings from their catalogues. While certain performers maintain continuing popularity, such as the Beatles and Elvis,

> for every Beatles issue, Capitol [who released the group's US recordings] has discontinued hundreds of great releases by such artists as T-Bone Walker, the Five Keys and Johnny Otis – records of varying commercial success but almost always of great value in an artistic sense and as a statement of the era. (Propes, 1973: 2)

Propes gives the example of the Five Sharps single 'Stormy Weather': 'No one seems to own a copy of it or a tape of it, and the master was lost in a fire. Not even Jubilee Records owns a copy.' This situation made the record 'the premium item' for most vocal group collectors, especially those favouring the slow romantic ballads of doo-wop (Propes, 1973: 2). Indeed, the record remained among the rarest: the 1999 *Goldmine Price Guide* claimed that only three copies were then known. All were 78s – one of which was cracked – and even that 'would likely sell for US$10,000.'[2]

By the early 1970s, there already existed a common system for the grading of records, introduced by *Record Changer* magazine in the late 1940s, and widely

---

[2]   Neely (1996b [quote taken from 2nd edition, 1999: 184]). All known 45s are counterfeits.

adopted by dealers and collectors in both auction and sales lists.[3] Although some collectors insisted on records in mint condition, Propes considered that 'most are quite satisfied with records in very good condition, though their value is usually less than that of a mint record'. However, such distinctions could easily become hazy: 'Grading, after all, is subjective, depending on the grader's ear, his equipment and other variables, and thus can be a source of controversy and misunderstanding' (Propes, 1973: 4). Condition was to remain a central consideration for collectors.

Value was also determined by demand and scarcity, with the last reflecting different recording formats and record company practices. Some of the rarest 45rpm records were those released in 1950 or earlier. In some cases, the 45 reissue was more valuable than the original 78 release; for example, some of the earlier Oriele recordings.[4] That different pressings and labels were difficult to document, was part of the challenge to collectors. Many smaller record companies in the United States had their records produced by various pressing plants throughout the country. These pressing companies would often redesign the label or the size or type of the print, or otherwise alter its appearance. Such changes make identifying a record in terms of its vintage or chronology a subject of continuing controversy. The smaller companies sold or leased artists or recordings to larger firms, usually to gain wider and more efficient distribution of local hits. The larger labels would then re-release the material. While the re-release is usually more easily found, at times, noted Propes, it is rarer than the more successful original.[5]

Later collecting guidebooks and record guides largely followed the themes and concerns present in Propes. Ian Anderson's *Rock Record Collectors Guide* (1977) is the first example I could locate of a guidebook solely concerned with 1960s 'rock' records. It was soon followed by an increasing number of publications through the 1980s, surveying and identifying collectable releases (for instance: Collis, 1980; Hibbert, 1982; Marsh and Swenson, 1984; Rees, 1985). In addition to general volumes, as the scope of popular music – and the range of what was potentially collectable – continued to expand, more genre or period-specific titles began to be published. In a similar vein were books from music critics, collecting together their magazine reviews, often with value ratings. Early examples are those by *Village Voice* critic Robert Christgau (1982; 1990). During the 1990s, various multi-volume series began to appear, partly in response to the expansion

---

[3]   In brief, this consisted of: Mint; Excellent; Very Good; Good; Fair; Poor; and Bad, with pluses and minuses used to refine these grading values. These were adopted and extended, by *Record Collector* and, with slight modifications, *Goldmine* in the 1980s. Both magazines include their Grading System as a regular part of every issue. The central role of condition in record collecting is discussed in Chapter 4.

[4]   Propes provides a clear summary of the introduction of the 45 by major companies between 1949 and (for most) 1956; and the smaller R&B labels (in the early 1950s). See also my discussion of formats, in Chapter 3.

[5]   For example, the Decca reissue of the Hollywood Flames' material originally on Lucky.

of the range and number of recordings now available. These lengthy compendiums included *The All Music Guide to Rock* (1995), with further volumes on jazz and world music; and *Rock: The Rough Guide* (1996), with additional volumes on world music, classical, jazz and opera (and later ones on punk, reggae and metal). Most recently, some of these have opted for web- rather than paper-based titles (AMG). The latest guides aimed at record collectors, drawn on throughout this study, are those by Dave Thompson (2002) and John Stanley (2002). Finally, the price guides published through the 1990s, and since, included extensive introductions offering general guidance to the collector. I shall have more to say about these later.

Rees sums up what was a fairly typical approach to compiling such guides:

> really it's down to one thing and one thing only. Research, lots of it. I have ploughed through literally millions of pieces of information relating to this book. I go through sales and wants lists in collectors' magazines, as well as articles and interviews searching for crumbs of information that I can include. In addition to this I visit both major and minor record fairs and conventions, as well as many record stores. On my travels the relevant scraps are scribbled down into a tatty notebook and pieced together. You're holding the results. (Rees, 1995: ii)

Here, a few selected early examples from this body of literature must stand for what rapidly became an extensive field. My discussion of these is structured around the set of concerns and practices surrounding record collecting established by Propes: justification and legitimation of the field; its scope; the interrelated role of discrimination; scarcity, condition and value; and the provision of additional information.

The legitimation of record collecting

A substantial (365-page) international directory, published in 1980, showed the field to now be both well established and extensive (Felton, 1980). The various guides published since have needed to provide little in the way of argument that record collecting is a worthwhile pursuit, given its popularity and international scope. As Stanley (2002: 7) put it: 'Record collecting is currently booming because there is now the means to shop globally from your home, to explore the music you once loved, and search out its influences and imitators, foreign pressings, and limited editions.' Along with the challenges of the hunt and personal satisfaction associated with it (see Chapter 2), record collecting continued to be seen to play an important role in cultural preservation. This can serve to rationalize the less lauded aspects of collecting. Leibowitz (1980: 9) refers to 'the obsessive nature of the hard-core collector' but excuses this since 'at heart he is not only a music lover but also an archivist of the first order ... he is literally a keeper of records.'

Scope

The scope of record collecting continues to follow the areas marked out by the early literature, in terms of its emphases on particular genres, artists and formats. As discussed in Chapter 3, the question of formats is central to record collecting. The guides consolidated the field's emphasis on the status of the original recording, especially in vinyl form. Leibowitz, for instance, only includes 33rpm recordings, both 10" inch and 12", since their introduction in 1948, arguing that album cover art and liner notes have 'an historical appeal no reissue can match, represents the closest the collector can get to the actual recording experience' (Leibowitz, 1980: Introduction). Not until the mid 1990s was there fuller recognition of CDs as a collectable format (Cooper, 1993), and, for many collectors, its status remained marginal. While some guides focus exclusively on vinyl (Stanley, 2002), others, such as Thompson (2002), give coverage to a wide range of formats. Albums remain the staple content of most guides, although there are an increasing number of publications on singles (for example Marsh, 1989), including their visual aspects – the record sleeves (see Granata, 2002).

In terms of genre, the early guides were often broad in scope. Leibowitz covers rock'n'roll, jazz and show business recordings, while Anderson's intention was to list 'all the most important records of their type within the boundaries of rock music and its influences and roots. Jazz, blues, reggae, folk and ethnic musics, although they are not covered in depth, are therefore included' (Anderson, 1977: Introduction). His coverage includes sections on the Classic Albums; the Greatest Hits Albums; Compilation Albums; and Humour and Spoken Word, with the first three categories listing artists alphabetically. The inclusion of the humour and spoken word categories indicated the popularity of recordings from comedians such as Bob Newhart and radio programmes such as The Goon Show. Collis's *Rock Primer* offered 'A guide to the history of post-war pop music (and its roots in earlier folk and blues styles) as reflected on record' (Collis, 1980: 7). It dealt with 220 albums in detail, with many more referred to in the text. In addition, 10 of the 11 sections included an appendix of 'essential singles, usually by artists too important to be overlooked who nevertheless did not warrant an album selection, or by otherwise obscure performers who had one great moment of glory'.[6]

Some later guides have attempted broader generic coverage, but this ambition has been constrained by the sheer task involved. By way of illustration, Stanley (2002) includes rock and pop, and subgenres within these, along with uneven sections on jazz, folk music, easy listening (lounge, exotica) and compilations. He also provides more limited treatments of soul, R&B, country, new age and reggae. As Thompson noted at that time, it was already clearly 'impossible to

---

[6]   The sections, written by seven contributors, were; Rock & Roll; Folk & Blues; Rhythm & Blues; Soul; Country; British Beat; California Sun; Dylan and After; Reggae; Punk; and The Seventies. The addition of punk was indicative of the interest the genre was already attracting from fans and collectors.

do justice, in one slim volume, to every musical discipline that can fall under the record-collecting banner' (Thompson, 2002: vii). Accordingly, while writing 'primarily with the rock and pop collector in mind', rather than using genres as an organizing principle his book is organized into three sections: (1) a general introduction to the history of hobby and some of its rules' (including grading, and where to find records); (2) some of 'the individual themes that a collector might choose to pursue', primarily organized around a wide range of forms and formats; presented alphabetically, these include acetates, bootlegs, EPs, export issues, jukebox albums, mono, promos, 78s and transcription discs; and (3) 'an alphabetical directory of 140 American, British, and European record companies, emphasizing each label's history and pinpointing its most collectible artists and releases' (Thompson, 2002: viii). Genres and artists are present throughout his themes.

As previously indicated, popular music guidebooks have become increasingly specialized. To the established range of genres have been added volumes on emergent ones (in terms of collector interest), such as lounge and exotica, and collecting fields such as bootlegs, promotional releases and memorabilia (see Chapter 3).

Discrimination

In Anderson, collectability in terms of musical importance is indicated through the use of a star rating system; three levels are used, with three stars representing 'a masterwork of remarkable quality'. All are included in his Classic Albums listings, consisting of 'those which have come to be regarded as the better work of the artists in question' (Anderson, 1977: Introduction). This approach was adopted and extended by *The Rolling Stone Album Guides*; the first was published in 1979; with a second, greatly expanded version, in 1984. Marsh (1989) provided a comprehensive early appraisal of significant singles, *The Heart of Rock and Soul: The 1001 Greatest Singles Ever Made*. Hibbert's edited volume *The Perfect Collection* (1982), provided a listing of 'The Rock Albums everybody should have and why', assembled from 'the choices of a crack team of music writers and assorted fans whose comments appear beneath each listing'. In some cases, disparate opinions between the various commentators are included.

In addition to rating releases, such guides further exercise discrimination, and shape a canon of artists, genres and recordings, through their very process of inclusion and exclusion. There is a privileging of the album as an integral artistic statement; the place of compilations is at times contentious, but they are usually excluded, albeit often in a separate end section of the guide. Later guides increasingly recognized that for some genres, notably reggae and punk, if a collector could not get the original 45s, a compilation could fill the gap. Indeed, with the efforts of the independent/reissue labels, well-compiled and packaged compilations were increasingly valued and seen as collectable.

Rarity, condition and value

Leibowitz identified a central aspect determining value when he observed, 'The importance of condition with respect of the value of a rare recording cannot be overemphasized.' He claimed that some collectors went so far as to maintain two collections: 'one of mint, unplayed records and one for everyday listening' (Leibowitz, 1980: 36). In his guide, all the listed records are rated as if they are in new or excellent condition (having very rarely been played, and with no defects whatever). Already, as he notes, the status of mint and the preference for it among collectors 'has become legendary'. Formats were a factor here, with stereo issues, introduced into the market in 1958, already usually accorded slightly higher prices than their mono versions. The early stereo issues initially had low sales,[7] and their relative scarcity enhanced their collectability. Mono was largely phased out during 1967–68.

Condition has continued to be the touchstone for collecting guides and collectors. As Stanley observes, 'the headline prices are for absolutely perfect examples – which are very rare.' (Stanley, 2002: 18). The grading systems used by the major guidebooks, and *Goldmine* and *Record Collector*, are widely known and applied, constituting an accepted shorthand for the condition of a recording. That said, grading records remains 'an extraordinarily subjective topic, largely dependent on whether one is buying or selling' (Thompson, 2002: 6). And it is not just the condition of the record itself that is important, but the state of the cover (and inserts and so forth which may have accompanied the recording) may also influence value. Indeed, the standard guides, and descriptions of items for sale, will normally include both; for example, vinyl album X. very good [the state of the record]/fair [the cover].[8]

Further information/knowledge

In addition to identifying and valuing recordings, the early guides, and their later counterparts, generally provide information on finding, caring for and cataloguing the collection. Many also suggest references for further reading: 'intended as a general guide to what is generally available or (in some cases) what is regarded as important' (Anderson, 1977). Included here are a wide range of music magazines, fanzines and the trade press: UK monthly *Music Week*; *Billboard*, *Record World* and *Cashbox*, the American trade weeklies. Felton, for instance, includes a similar list of 'Publications of special interest', claiming that these represent 'only a smattering of literally hundreds of such publications which could have been listed here' (Felton, 1980: 301).

---

[7]   Around 10 per cent of the sales in the late 1950s and early '60s, according to Leibowitz (1980: 36).

[8]   For a helpful discussion of the difficulties of grading records, see Thompson (2002: 6–11).

Later guides continue to stress that 'Your most valuable aide to successful collecting is knowledge' (Stanley, 2002: 10). Indicating the impact of the internet, Stanley's *Collecting Vinyl* includes a list of useful websites, along with a wide range of print publications. A key part of such knowledge is a good grasp of the relative value of recordings, the focus of the price guides.

Price Guides

The late 1970s and early 1980s saw the publication, in both the United Kingdom and the United States, of a number of record collecting price guides. These frequently overlapped with those books, discussed above, providing more general coverage of record collecting. For example, Hill (1981) *The Official Price Guide to Collectible Rock Records*, with some 400 pages of listings, covers 'beginning a record collection, finding what you want, cleaning and storage, condition'. The price guides also cover the relative merits of recordings, primarily albums, although from the perspective of economic value rather than artistic merit.

The first of these appears to have been Jerry Osborne's *Record Collecting Price Guide* (1976), and it was soon followed by others.[9] Shortly after, the two main collecting magazines, *Record Collector* and *Goldmine*, began publishing book-length price guides. The first *Record Collector* guide appeared in 1987, followed by the much more comprehensive *Rare Records Price Guide* in 1992. *Goldmine*'s first such guide was *The Standard Catalogue of American Records*, covering 1956 to 1975, published in 1989. Those collectors specializing in earlier recordings were catered for by *Warman's American Records* (Chuck Miller, 2nd edition, 2004) and Docks's *American Premium Record Guide, 1900–1965* (see Chapter 1). In the United Kingdom, the *Music Master Price Guide for Record Collectors* (Hamlyn, 1991)[10] provided a substantial addition to the price guide marketplace.

By the 1990s, prices had heated up and there was a proliferation of price guides. These both reflected and underpinned the continued growth of an international network of dealers, prestige auctions and collectors, all increasingly linked by the internet since around 2000 (see Chapter 5). The consolidation of the CD as the dominant market format saw the first guides exclusively devoted to collecting them (Cooper, 1998), and its inclusion in guides that had been previously exclusively devoted to vinyl (for instance, *The Rare Record Price Guide*, 6th edition, 2002).

Many of these early guides have continued to be published in increasingly bulky editions: Dock's 6th edition (2001) runs to 592 pages; Osborne's 18th edition (2007) has 768 pages; *The Rare Records Price Guide, 2010* is 1,408 pages

---

[9]   Osborne has continued to produce revised editions of this and other record guides, notably his *Rockin Records*: the 2007 edition, with 1,049 pages, prices over one million records. He is a collector himself.

[10]   Edited by collector and record shop owner, Nick Hamlyn, it had 38,000 entries, spread across 830 pages.

long. Increased length reflected further information about the variety of earlier releases becoming available, and a greater number of listings for these, along with the inclusion of new recordings. Reissues and compilations were now an important part of company catalogues and the collectable repertoire, and their addition further expanded the coverage.

As with the record collecting guidebooks, there are common, interwoven themes and trends here:

- Value is situated as a combination of rarity, condition' and demand.
- Prices fluctuate, but have steadily increased for the rarest items.
- The early guides concentrated on 45rpm records, reflecting the prominence of singles-oriented rock'n'roll, doo-wop and rockabilly as collectable genres.
- The range of what is collectable has steadily increased, with new genres and artists joining established preferences.
- The vinyl album remains the privileged format, and is now arguably the primary focus of most record collecting, but 78s remain collectable, and CDs are now recognized as collectable.
- Later editions feature increasing use of illustrations, now often in colour, reinforcing the visual side of collecting.

With reference to an example of the price guides, and the scope of their coverage, I now want to consider these themes more closely.

The *Goldmine Record Album Price Guide* (Tim Neely, 1999) provided what were now 'standard' sections on grading records; a list of common collecting abbreviations; comments on newer collecting areas such as promotional records; imports. The inclusion of counterfeits shows how creeping values was making the effort of manufacturing them worthwhile, a situation that had long existed with some early recordings of performers such as Elvis Presley (the Sun recordings; see Solly, 2007). The volume also includes, according to its cover: '50 Years of Collectible LPs, 1940s–1990s. Over 40,000 Records Listed and Priced.' At 544 pages and with 100 black and white photographs, this was a substantial volume; yet, as Neely's introduction points out, it was not intended to serve as a complete listing.[11] Indicative of the now dominant concern with condition, added to market value, the guide only included those albums that have a current market value of at least $20 in near mint condition: 'It is meant to serve the need of the collector and dealer who doesn't want to wade through what sports card collectors and dealers would call "commons" (and what some record collectors and dealers would call "junk") to find the material that has some value above the trivial' (Neely, 1999: 4). At the same time, Neely concedes that some titles not listed would go for $20 or more, especially in regard to jazz, soundtracks and various artist [compilations]

---

[11]   He refers readers to *Goldmine's Standard Catalogue of American Records 1950–1975*, published the previous year.

recordings. The restricted scope was also motivated by a desire to expand the generic scope of the book: 'In addition to rock, R&B, and soul, we've got listings for country, pop vocalists, some jazz, and even – for the first time in a Goldmine price guide – selected classical albums' (Neely, 1999: 4).

There is considerable attention to detail:

> All albums are listed individually. When applicable, mono, stereo and quadraphonic versions are listed separately. We also have the most complete listing anywhere of record label variations. In our 'Record Label Identifier' section, we list over 150 different labels and we tell you how to tell a first pressing album from later editions. In addition, we have a 'Reissue Identifier', which will tell you which numbers and prefixes indicate whether your record is a (relatively) worthless reissue or an original, especially in the confusing 1970s and 1980s. All of this, of course, is invaluable information for collectors wanting to ensure they are getting an 'original' recording, as well as providing guidance on the available releases of labels and artists. (Neely, 1999: 4)

Neely initially thought that the rare and not so rare album market had not yet fully recovered from the 'album glut' of the early 1990s, when an unprecedented volume of LPs hit the used record bins as people upgraded to CDs. However, further investigation had suggested that 'prices at the basic layer of record collecting – the neighborhood used record store – are starting to creep upward' (Neely, 1999: 4).[12] In terms of collecting interest and prices, the 'most upward action' was in the blues, Elvis Presley, television-related records and some 1990s alternative acts, such as limited edition releases from the Smashing Pumpkins[13] and Nirvana. The collectability of such performers was largely down to the influx of younger collectors into the market. Having grown up with indie and alternative music in the late 1980s, and grunge through the early 1990s, and with increasing disposable income, some began collecting the music of their youth. The trend had already been picked up on by the *Goldmine Guide to Alternative Records* (1996). Promotional records were a growth area, but as there are too many produced, only selected ones are listed; 'either because they are unique – in other words – the only version of the album is promotional – or because there is a significant, verifiable price difference between the promo and stock copy' (Neely, 1996a: 7).

---

[12]   Neely saw the album market as working in three waves: common, cheap stuff is still common and cheap; the stuff in the middle seems to be creeping upward, probably affected by the upward trend in rare items; and the 'really rare stuff', where 'the listed values seem to be lower than they used to be, the actual selling prices are higher than they were in most cases' (Neely, 1999: 4).

[13]   For example: The Smashing Pumpkins 1994 *Pisces Iscariot*, first edition, a numbered pressing of 2,000 copies that contains a bonus 45 not found in later editions; the 'going rate' is $200 or more.

An interesting and instructive inclusion is 'the $1,000 Club', a feature of the earlier *Goldmine Price Guide to 45 RPM Records*, now carried over to the *Goldmine Record Album Price Guide*: 'We list 255 different albums that, should copies be found in near-mint condition, would fetch $1,000 or more' (Neely, 1999: 4). The highest values items here include 1950s records from Elvis Presley, and Billy Ward and the Dominoes (*The Federal* 10-inch LP); but the majority are 1960s albums from Bob Dylan, The Beatles and The Rolling Stones.

These rare and costly versions have in common a valorization of the 'true' original, even though that is not the dominant version made available to contemporary purchasers. Nearly all of these albums are available in 'regular' versions with, in many cases, the same music on them. An example of this is *Jefferson Airplane Takes Off*, the debut by the San Francisco band, released in 1966. The album did well commercially, and copies remain readily available. In its common form, with 11 tracks (RCA Victor LPM-3584; mono) it is valued at US$25 in mint condition in Neely, with similar values in later guides. However, the 12-track first pressing, with six tracks on the first side, ('Runnin' Round This World' as the sixth song), and the original versions of 'Let Me In' and 'Run Around', is valued (in near mint) condition at $2–4,000 for mono and $4–8,000 for the stereo version. The second pressing of the album, with 'Runnin' Round This World' deleted, but retaining the original versions of 'Let Me In' and 'Run Around', is also highly valued.

Neely notes that a sign of new blood (collectors) entering the field is 'when things that used to be common knowledge aren't so common anymore' (Neely, 1999: 10). An instance of this with a personal resonance is *The Who Live at Leeds* (1970), an album with elaborate and innovative packaging, which I purchased at the time of its release. Today, it is not difficult to find Decca pressings of the original album, though one with all the inserts is a different matter. They were easily mislaid and lost when playing the record, while many purchasers took out the poster [as I did] to decorate the walls of student flats, with obvious consequences. Indeed, individual copies of the poster are themselves quite collectable. Neely was referring to the many owners of the original album who thought they had a reasonably valuable release, but whose copies no longer retained the original 'packaging' that brought them into the higher price range. The album was reissued by MCA in 1973, in a more conventional standard LP cover. In 1995 the original release was expanded to twice its normal size on a CD reissue; early pressings of this came in a 12"x12" box that reproduced all the material included in the original LP, at full size. Of course, none of the later releases have the cachet of the original, which Neely valued at US$40 in 'Near Mint' condition.

Neely's prices were arrived at through market monitoring:

> The more common items reflect a consensus of used record shops and collectors, plus prices in ads and online over the past few months. In some ways, these items are more difficult to get a handle on; they sell without much publicity because of their low value, thus they aren't reported as often. (Neely, 1999: 7)

Rarer items are often the subject of debate and guesswork, as they so rarely come up for public sale: 'A high auction price for a truly rare piece can be the only way such an item's 'worth' can be gauged, no matter what someone says about the value being inflated.' Ultimately, as Neely asserts, 'Records, as with all collectibles, are only worth what someone will pay for them' (Neely, 1999: 7). Such statements are a truism of collecting.

Subsequent price guides show a continuation of several of the trends Neely identified. Ian Shirley, the editor of the latest edition of *The Rare Record Price Guide, 2010*, emphasizes how 'prices for rare records have gone through the roof. Collectors are willing to pay huge sums for rare releases that come to market in Mint condition' (Shirley, 2008: 46). Fluctuating prices for particular genres and performers reflect the conflation of musical fashion, demand and demographic shifts: as the collectors of older genres and 78s pass on, their collections increase the availability of this material. Along with a decreased demand (fewer collecting the artist, genre or format), this can lower prices. As the knowledge of what is available has progressively grown, partly from the discographies produced by collectors themselves (see below), the price guides have been able to expand, and increasingly verify, the information they contain.

Discographies

As shown in Chapter 1, the rise of discography in the 1930s was a key part of the development of record collecting, and has continued to be associated with it. As was the case then, record collectors are frequently the authors of specialized discographies. Often privately published, or produced by small presses in small print runs, such discographies become key references, especially for the advanced collector moving beyond simply the main official releases. In some cases, discographies become collectibles in their own right, selling for reasonable amounts in the second hand market. Felton (1980) includes a lengthy section documenting a wide range of discographies, and production of them has continued apace (there are now extensive bibliographies of discographies). Also significant here are the related volumes of chart listings (see Joel Whitburn's extensive range of Record Research volumes).

Several authors have specialized in producing discographies for the record collector market (for instance M.C. Strong's various rock discographies). A recent example is Patrick Lejeune's *The Bootleg Guide to Disco, Acetates, Funk, Rap and Disco Medleys* (2008). Lejeune ('Disco Patrick') had been collecting these for almost 30 years, and he charts the origins and development of remixes, mashups and extended 12" mixes up until 1986, listing every track from every medley. There are full colour pictures of over 500 record labels, acetates, flyers, magazine covers and early DJ decks.[14]

---

[14] See the comprehensive associated website: www.discopatrick.com.

Fanzines

Music fanzines have a long and honourable place in popular music history (Shuker, 2008: 167–8). In the 1960s and '70s, with only limited coverage of collectable genres such as American R&B in the mainstream music press,[15] it was fanzines that catered to the interests of record collectors. In the United Kingdom, these included rockabilly fanzine *Rock'n'Roll Collector*, *Kommotion*, *Zig Zag* and *Let It Rock* (for a detailed discussion, see Doggett, 1996b: 46–7, 50–51). In the US, titles included *Record Exchanger* (1969–83), *R&B Magazine* (1970–71), *Stormy Weather* (1970–76) and *Bim Bang Boom* (1971–74) (Pruter, 1997). Fanzines continued to be produced, with several titles proving widely influential and achieving iconic status, as with the UK-based *Sniffin' Glue*, which brought punk rock to wider attention in the 1970s, and the US-based *Who Put the Bomp*, edited by Greg Shaw, which played a similar role for garage rock. A common factor in these publications was the involvement of record collectors as editors and contributors.

Such engagement has continued, with the internet providing a new space for the publication of fanzines. The value of contemporary fanzines is recognized by both 'mainstream' music magazines and the record collector magazines giving them regular coverage.

Music magazines and record collecting

Several music magazines have included sections aimed specifically at record collectors, such as *The Record Hunter* insert in *VOX* briefly during the 1990s. In addition to these, there have been special issue magazines and series (*MOJO*: *UNCUT*: *Rolling Stone*), in part aimed at the collector of that style or performer. The general issues of music magazines are also sometimes of interest to collectors, especially in their coverage of back catalogue re-releases and their artist features, which usually include basic discographies.

My focus here is on the dedicated collector magazines, especially the US-based *Goldmine* and the UK-based *Record Collector*. Also worthy of mention is *Discoveries*, founded by Jerry Osborne, the author and publisher of various price guides. First published in January 1988, the magazine was similar in format and content to *Goldmine*, and involved several former Goldmine staff (Pruter, 1997: 31–2). It was eventually purchased by Krause, publishers of *Goldmine*, and absorbed into the older magazine in 2006. In addition, there are more specialist magazines, such as *Wax Poetics*, aimed at hip hop DJs and collectors; *Weird and Strange Music* for exotica collectors; and *Hot Wacks*, for bootleg collectors. The US-based monthly *ICE* lists all current CD releases, and includes recording details on a selection of these, especially key retrospective compilations.

---

[15]   There were a few notable exceptions, such as Norman Jopling's column in the British *Record Mirror*.

When *Goldmine* and *Record Collector* first appeared, in the mid to late 1970s, the 'hobby' of record collecting remained disorganized. There was a general lack of accessible information to guide the collector, especially in relation to discographies of favourite artists, and the prices for recordings. The general guides and price guides discussed earlier in this chapter were not widely available until the 1980s. Fanzines provided some guidance, but were not always easily obtained, and tended to be irregular and at times short-lived. As Peter Doggett later observed of the launch of *Record Collector* in 1979:

> When the magazine was born, record collecting was a small, rather disorganized business, which wasn't making much effort to get new people involved. From the start, RC set out to provide the information that collectors needed, whether they'd been buying and selling records for years, or were just starting to build up a collection. There were two vital things they wanted to know: what records had been released by their favourite artists, and how much were they worth?[16]

Goldmine

Goldmine was first issued in September 1974, by Brian Bukantis of Arena Publishing, who saw a gap in the magazine market. Originally an eight-page advertising tabloid, its early subtitle was 'The Record Collector's Marketplace'; later this became 'For Record Collectors Everywhere' then 'The Collector's Record and Compact Disc Marketplace' (Loescher, 1999). Published roughly every two months, it expanded its market from issue number 12 (no cover date, but published in 1975) with the inclusion of subscribers to the *Record Collector's Journal*, which had ceased publication due to a lack of advertising revenue. For a brief period in 1979, *Goldmine* was published in two parts: editorial, and advertising, but these were merged once more from issue 40 (September 1979). Editorial content in the magazine gradually increased, along with the amount of advertising. During its formative period, *Goldmine* had a strong emphasis on 1950s genres such as doo-wop (Pruter, 1997).

With issue 29, October 1978, Rick Whitesell became editor. In common with nearly all of the early editors and writers for record collecting publications, he was a record collector and music lover. With issue 60, May 1981, Jeff Tamarkin took over as editor, continuing until around 1996, though the role tended to be spread among several staff, especially after *Goldmine* was sold to Krause publications in 1983. Tamarkin was a respected rock journalist and had previously been a *Goldmine* freelance writer; he was also a record collector. Looking back on his editorship, and its relationship to his collecting, he reminisced in 2004:

> It's funny, this collecting thing. Although at one time I owned more than 10,000 records and probably half that many CDs (I have since jettisoned a lot of the

---

[16]   In the *Rare Record Price Guide 2002* (2002: 14).

vinyl), I never considered myself a collector. I was more of an accumulator. When people described record collecting as a 'hobby', I always winced. To me it was not a hobby like collecting coins or Star Trek memorabilia. To me it was a lifestyle, a passion. I did not seek out records because they were rare or valuable ... all I ever cared about was the music. My job as editor of Goldmine introduced me to so much of it, in every genre, from every period. Goldmine to me has always been about the quest, and for three decades it has helped countless thousands satisfy their own quests, whatever they might be. (Tamarkin, 2004: 18)

A colour cover was introduced in 1983, and the magazine became a two-weekly one in 1984. By 1987, circulation had topped 20,000, with 11,000 subscribers (the remaining copies were sold through record shops). By the mid 1990s, circulation had reached 35,000, with the length of issues consistently around 200 pages. Some issues sold more due to the appeal/collectability of particular artists featured, as with the Tori Amos cover issue (368, in 1994). In the late 1980s, *Goldmine* expanded its operations to included price guides, which remain a substantial part of magazine publisher Krause's catalogue. Another initiative was a directory of independent labels; the first, in 1988, was simply a section of the magazine, but from 1992 it came as a pull out directory (issue 315, 21 August 1992).

Its 25th anniversary issue (501, 8 October 1999) indicates the scope of *Goldmine* around that time. Edited by Greg Loescher, the large A4 format and 184-page magazine covered an impressive range of editorial content and advertising. Now regular columns were 'Please Mr. Postman' (letters to the editor), 'Grapevine' (a news digest), Record Show listings, a Store Directory, New Releases, and Reissues. Advertising makes up the bulk of the content, with a range of categories. Unit space advertisements are the most extensive; these are supplied camera ready, and often reduced to fit the available space. The resulting small print, often hand annotated, makes perusal difficult but a ritualistic part of the effort put into the reader/collector's search. Also substantial (13 pages in this issue) is the Collectors' Showcase section, boxed advertisements that are typeset by *Goldmine*. Craig Wenner's feature article for the issue (pp. 14–20; 28), on Stevie Wonder, is typical of the in-depth, research-based treatment accorded cover artists. Tim Neely, the magazine's Research Director (and Price Guide editor), supplies a discography of Wonder's US releases (pp. 30, 32). By this point, the magazine has a website.

Goldmine is currently published by Krause, based in Iola, Wisconsin, a leading publisher of leisure, hobby and collector periodicals and books. Edited by Peter Lindblad, the magazine has continued with much the same mix of columns, features and advertising material. It covers 'collectible records, CDs, and music memorabilia covering rock & roll, blues, country, folk, and jazz' (see its website: www.goldminemag.com, which provides an introduction to the magazine's coverage and associated activities). Most recently (early 2009) *Goldmine* has launched an online radio station. It remains the dominant North American record collecting publication, and its claim to be 'the world's largest marketplace for collectible records' is challenged only by the UK-based *Record Collector*.[17]

Record Collector

Record Collector was first published in 1979. The editor, Johnny Dean, had previously been republishing issues of *The Beatles Book*, the group's fanclub magazine, which was originally issued in the late 1960s and early 1970s. Original copies of this fanzine were now highly collectable, and the reissues had wide appeal, given the increasing fascination with the now defunct iconic band. The reissues were now to be published along with the new magazine. The first issue of *Record Collector*, September 1979, proclaims in capitals on its cover: 'CONTAINING AN ORIGINAL COLLECTORS COPY OF THE 41ST ISSUE OF THE BEATLES FAN CLUB MAGAZINE', (with the cover of the earlier fanzine reproduced as part of the cover of the new publication).

In his first editorial, Dean explains:

> The reason that I have launched the RECORD COLLECTOR is that for some time it has been obvious from your letters and personal adverts that many of you have a deep interest in collecting the records and memorabilia of other important artists and groups as well as the Beatles ... So I decided that we should extend our editorial coverage to include ALL our readers' interests in the fascinating world of rare record, books, magazines, posters, etc.

The first issue included a general overview, 'Collecting Rare Records' (by David Hughes), an article on Stu Sutcliffe, a feature on Elvis Presley's recordings, and a list ('the first ever') of Top 50 Rare Records. An enthusiastic response led to an expanded section of small ads, and a charge for their insert (they had originally been free) from the second issue; this included an article on bootlegs (Adrian Sole), and the first of a series on rare Tamla Motown records, with a collector's price guide.

By early 1980, Dean was foreshadowing a shift towards 'a lot more in-depth information and special articles of interest to serious record collectors, plus an ever expanding Rare Records Chart and comprehensive discographies' (issue 6, February 1980). The magazine now dropped the accompanying Beatles Book (from issue 7, March 1980) which was again sold separately, and RC (*Record Collector*) steadily expanded in length and scope, by 2000 averaging around 200 pages. Production values have remained high, with colour introduced along with a higher quality of paper. RC also moved into publishing price guides; its first, in 1987, was 'a slim volume which was designed as a quick and easy reference

---

[17]   Clearly, it is difficult to validate such claims, which depend on how frequency of publication, length, sales and so forth are compared.

source to records by around 2,000 important artists.[18] This was followed by various editions of *The Rare Record Price Guide* and two specialist collecting books: rock'n'roll, and psychedelic records.

In issue 253 (September 2000), then editor Andy Davis defined the regular reader of RC as an ardent fan of one or more particular artist of genre. The readers were also substantially funding their passion. Statistics based on a survey of members, published in 2006, showed the average RC reader owns 2,144 vinyl records, and 1,046 CDs. Twenty two per cent spent over £350 on vinyl and £250 on CDs in the last year; while 31 per cent of readers spent over £500 on CDs in the past year.[19] The slight edge to spending on vinyl suggests the continued privileging of it as *the* collectable format, although it may also have been the result of the higher prices usually paid for vinyl records, even in their re-release versions (especially on 180g vinyl).

As its cover subtitle claims, *Record Collector* is *Serious About Music*.[20] The magazine continues to profile a wide range of performers, often accompanied by detailed discographies, with values.[21] Its regular features include columns providing both information and reports on record fairs ('Fair Trade'), record shops, gigs, formats, eBay prices, internet sites of interest, fanzines, a series 'The Collector', music news, genre categories, auctions, a 'most wanted' column on rare items, often memorabilia, that have come onto the market, a 'not forgotten' section of obituaries, and 'value added facts', in which Ian Shirley, the current editor of the *Rare Record Price Guide*, 'answers your questions'. There are extensive reviews sections on albums, DVDs, books and live music. The advertising includes record label releases, music fairs, music storage systems, record shops, auctions and memorabilia. There is also the smaller format 'Record Listings: Set Sales & Auctions; Records Wanted', and, not unexpectedly, subscription offers. RC has a website, and subscribers are given exclusive website access. This is an impressive body of information and commentary.

Record Collector, like *Goldmine*, has characteristically had record collectors as its editors and feature writers. Alan Lewis, who has had extensive experience in the music press, has been the editor since 2003. He reflects on his own collecting, in part situating it in relation to the magazine's readers:

---

[18]   *Rare Record Price Guide 2002* (2002: 14).

[19]   *Record Collector*, 322, April 2006. The data was used to target advertisers: 'don't miss out on this unique high spending audience'.

[20]   The following overview refers to the November 2008 issue (number 355), which is representative of RC over the past few years. In the interests of 'full disclosure' I should admit that it is one of several music magazines I always purchase.

[21]   Its index, a useful resource given most back issues are still to be found, indicates who has received the most attention / are regarded as most collectable, a view reinforced by regular surveys of readers' views.

I began buying records in 1958 at the age of 13, just standard chart pop, but through listening to Radio Luxembourg I quickly realised that I preferred the US originals to UK cover versions. From there I developed an instinctive preference for black vocal groups and artists eg The Drifters, Shirelles, the Spector-era girl groups ... and then of course with the arrival of black pop/soul labels like Motown, Atlantic, Chess etc the floodgates opened and I was spending every penny on 'R&B' as soul was called at first. For a while I tried to buy literally every release on those labels, but of course that soon became impossible because of sheer volume. Also I was never an obsessive collector in the sense that some of our readers are, ie 'completists' who have to have every track by every artist or every release on a particular label ... for me I had to really like the music. It was never just an item to own. That's still my attitude today, and although my tastes have broadened to include most genres, including classical and even contemporary 'serious' music, my first and greatest love is still 60s Soul. (Alan Lewis, editor: email to author, February 2009)

Record Collector continues to dominate the UK collector market, and has a considerable presence internationally. Sales remain stable at around 30,000, with about a quarter of these sold overseas, mainly in the English-speaking countries; a slight decline in bookstall sales in the United Kingdom in recent years has been offset by a growth in subscriptions (Alan Lewis; email to author, February 2009).

Rock books

The final type of music press publication I want to consider here are the various publications under the broad label of 'rock books'. These provide valuable reference tools for popular music collectors, and some have become collectibles in their own right. One category of these, of course, are the reference books already discussed: the various record collecting and price guides. To these can be added music histories, collected interviews, popular (auto)biographies, histories and genre studies, and volumes compiling statistical data related to record sales and hits charts.

Taylor's extensive, annotated bibliography covering writing on popular music since 1955 revealed a considerable body of literature, which increased dramatically during the early 1980s (Taylor, 1985). Subsequently published bibliographic guides showed rapid growth continued during the following decade (see Krebs, 1997). More recently, the review columns of music magazines and leading popular music academic journals reveal a steady stream of titles. Many are from specialist publishers of popular music titles, notably Da Capo, Omnibus and Backbeat. In June 2006, the British *Observer* weekend magazine included an article on the 'fifty best music books'; a further 50 could have been comfortably added. Initial attempts to profile this body of work included guides by Hanel, Taylor and Doggett. Hanel's volume, *The Essential Guide to Rock Books* (1983) was published by

Omnibus Press, then establishing itself as a specialist in the field of popular music books. It described a thousand English and American rock books, many of them already rare (for example the Lester Bangs biography of Blondie). The list included biographies of major artists along with less well-known performers, as well as chart books, encyclopaedias, photographic books about 'rock' and books of album cover art. As with later such overviews, Hanel's was indicative of current popularity; it includes, for example, five books on Adam and the Ants, a British new pop band then enjoying considerable UK chart success. Taylor, a librarian in the UK, undertook a similar project, with his book-length bibliography, and a contribution to the *British Book News* (November 1986: 623–5) providing a more selective, critically annotated 'Top Fifty'. Taylor's summary of the field is apposite: 'The variety of these publications is matched by the variation in the quality of their writing, accuracy and scholarship, which means one must approach them with a degree of discrimination and care' (Taylor, 1985: 1). Some 25 years on, this judgment still stands.

Doggett provided a selective but comprehensive overview in a substantial feature for *Record Collector*, and his inclusion of values brought 'rock books' into the area of the music/record related collectible (Doggett, 1997). Starting from the premise that 'rock books have never been documented with the same thoroughness that we expect from record buffs', he traces the literature 'from its roots in the Hollywood star-making industry, through the golden era of the 60s underground, to its role today as an arm of music merchandising' (Doggett, 1997: 35). Doggett identified a number of subcategories: rock books before The Beatles; pop annuals; autobiographies, often ghost written; the rock biography; rock critics' collected writings; and rock histories. His account traces the gradual sophistication of the literature, albeit with quick cash-ins still very evident. Following their popularity among record collectors – and a wider public – The Beatles and Bob Dylan had come to dominate the music book market.

There has been surprisingly little in the way of further guides to this extensive body of work. Certainly not all of these publications are useful, let alone collectable, and many have a very short shelf life. However, the level of interest in key collectable titles on sites such as eBay and Trade Me (New Zealand), and the prices asked by dealers (see ABE Books, the main online book selling site), suggest a continued active market for them, especially where they have been issued in very small print runs.[22]

Having sketched these print publications that are, to varying degrees, aimed at record collectors, I turn now to the use made of them by collectors. It is self evident that collectors will draw on such sources, and even actively collect them, but the extent to which they do so varies.

---

[22]   For example, the pioneering volumes written and edited by Vernon Joynson; the latest, *Fuzz, Acid and Flowers Revisited* (Borderline Productions, 2008), had a limited hardback printing of only 750 copies.

Record collectors and the music press

Collectors draw on a variety of print sources for information in the hunt for records: books, music magazines, the free street press, fanzines, newsletters and newspapers. Most collectors I talked with had quite extensive holdings of music books, including record/collecting guides, biographies and discographies.[23] Along with magazines, these form an adjunct to the record collection and contributed to collection building:

- 'Magazines, and in general the written word (on the web, in record guides and reviews etc.) is an important source of information and opinion that affects my purchase of records.' (Motti Regev)
- 'These [books] give me the history, the context, the discography, because I like to "know" about the music I listen to. I like musical history the same way I like literary history.' (Greg Crossan)
- 'It all has to do with the love of music. If you love music, you want to see the groups live that actually create it. You want to read about your groups and genres. You can also learn about new records to find through magazines. I really think collecting is as much about finding knowledge as owning the records.' (Joel Wing)

Collectors will often buy magazines that have features on their favourite artists:

'It's all part of a band or artist record! I keep those pretty well catalogued actually, even though I don't catalogue recordings. Also, I find myself buying special issues such as "the Rolling Stone greatest albums of all time" type of thing. Again, that's so I can learn more, particularly about artists I've heard of, but don't know well. These are good references for when I go into second hand shops.' (Liz Guiffre)

Obviously, preferred magazine titles reflected collectors' genre preferences.

Heavy metal collector Albert Bell included *Terrorizer Magazine*, *Metal Hammer* and *Classic Rock*, among his reading, and bought extreme metal fanzines from time to time. Punk collector Michelle Wauchope had a subscription to the Australian Goth fanzine *Dark Angel*, and also occasionally, for specific articles: *NME*, *Melody Maker* (while it was in print), *Q*, *Rolling Stone* and *Zillo*, as well as smaller fanzines. 'I've got some copies of magazines from 1982 called "Punk Lives!" which I'm quite pleased to own.'

In addition to buying occasional titles, collectors who were particularly avid readers of the music press will have several magazine subscriptions. Catherine

---

[23] A few of my collectors (8/70) tended largely to reject the music press as a reference tool. Their reasons for this included a preference for alternative sources of information, related to a negative view of 'rock journalism' and perceived reviewer bias.

Brown subscribed to *Rolling Stone* and *Q*, and also bought *Guitar World/School*, *Kerrang!* and *Spin* 'when they're interesting'. Michelle Flannery subscribed to *Mojo*, *Wire*, *No Depression* and '[I also] pick up some fanzines'. This aspect of collecting could extend to purchasing back issues of magazines, a form of completism: 'I buy *Mojo* magazine every month and have been hunting down back issues I've missed on the online trader eBay' (Andrew Stafford).

Collectors who wrote on music saw reading music magazines and record collecting as interrelated: 'The whole gaze of the music journalist so often is like the collector's. There is nothing like a good library of music magazines when you try to make a living from writing about music' (Hasse Huss). Music journalists and editors will have large reference libraries; for instance, Colin Larkin, the editor of *The Encyclopedia of Popular Music* (now in its fourth edition) sees his complete runs of magazines such as *ZigZag* and *Beatles Monthly* as very much part of his 'record' collection.[24] Of course, the justification that such material is required for research purposes also provides a rationalization for collecting.

In 2002, the internet was already an important source of information:

- 'Occasionally I buy an issue of *Mojo*. Instead of magazines I often surf the web to the *AMG* site or to magazine sites (*NME*, *Rolling Stone* etc.).' (Motti Regev)
- 'I upload metal webzines when I have time and I am also subscribed to various email newsletters such as "Hair of the Wolf", which includes quality album reviews and other interesting stuff.' (Albert Bell)

More recently, as several of the profiles in Chapter 7 indicate, collectors have made increasing recourse to web-based sources.

Collectors will move on to the more specialized collector magazines as their interests and informational needs become more specialized, and their hunt for records is cast ever wider. Those who regularly read or subscribed to *Goldmine* or *Record Collector*, and publications such as *Wax Poetics*, had larger collections and had been collecting longer.

Conclusion

In the world of the collector, knowledge is power. The general record collecting guides, along with the price guides, play an essential part in providing this knowledge. Contributing to this process are discographies, fanzines and, most importantly, the dedicated record collector magazines. For most collectors the music press, including the collector-oriented sector of it, is a significant part of their collecting. It is part of their broader love of music, serving to reinforce and expand tastes, and at times influence purchases.

---

24   He was the featured collector in the *Record Collector*, 314.

Chapter 7
Collector profiles

I have drawn extensively on the views of collectors throughout this study. Their comments have been informative, perceptive and, frequently, entertaining. However, in 'cut and pasting' the views of individual collectors across the various chapters and topics covered, rarely is a sense of the 'complete' collector – the individual voice – allowed to emerge. Accordingly, this last chapter includes a series of collector profiles. Most are of collectors with whom I have had on-going contact over the past eight or nine years, in some cases, even longer. This time frame, with the opportunity to reflect back on earlier collecting compared to their current practices, demonstrates the shifting physical and emotional investments made by collectors in the hobby, as their musical interests and life circumstances change. (I shall have more to say about this in my conclusion.) I have chosen the ten collectors' profiles to represent a range of collecting interests, ages and geographic locations. In most cases, the emphasis is on what is collected and why; other aspects of their collecting practices have generally been utilized in the appropriate earlier chapters.

The ten collectors are:

Peter Dawson (Australia)
Lee Ann Fullington (United Kingdom; United States)
Hasse Huss (Sweden)
Lee Marshall (United Kingdom)
Ian Shirley (United Kingdom)
Geoff Stahl (Canada; now living in New Zealand).
Simon Sweetman (New Zealand)
Steve Waksman (United States)
Oliver Wang (United States)
Lisa Wheeler (United States)

Peter Dawson

Peter Dawson is an Australian collector. His records, books and DVDs take up a good deal of space in the high-rise apartment (and its basement garage) in Sydney where he lives with his wife Debbie and son Marshall. Peter has been a cameraman for the Australian Broadcasting Corporation for 36 years. As well as being a record collector, Peter is a keen photographer. Now in his early fifties, Peter has been collecting since he was 15, though he acquired his first record, a Beatles EP, as a gift when he was nine. Growing up as a teenager in the late 1960s, his collecting preferences are primarily in mainstream rock bands of that period, with a special love for Jimi Hendrix.[1] In addition to records, Peter has a large collection of music books, primarily biographies. One of his most prized is a signed copy of George Harrison's *I Me Mine* (Genesis Books), a leather bound edition, limited to 2,000 copies.

Peter has painstakingly rebuilt his collection since a robbery in 1997 saw the loss of many prized records, including rare editions of The Rolling Stones albums *Sticky Fingers* and *Their Satanic Majesties Request*. In 2001, when we first discussed his collecting, he had 'about 700 CDs, 100 LPs, 200 45s and approx. 50 assorted cassettes, some pre-recorded, but mostly my own compilation tapes'. His subsequent collecting concentrated on CDs – he now has around a thousand – along with concert DVDs. Much of his older format recordings have been sold off through eBay.

While his collection is not large, it is a strongly focused one. Additions to it are usually the result of a process of research, drawing on the music press and the internet, and then purchasing from specialist record shops, both physical and on-line, and through websites such as eBay. There are also some serendipitous finds. Over a number of years, Peter has shared stories of his collecting, illustrating the varied ways in which a collection can be built up. A few of these follow.

> 'For quite a few years I worked with a Pommie [English] sound operator, at the ABC, who had worked at the BBC during the '60s and early '70s. Once he realized how much I like rock music of that era, he told me that he had a copy, on reel-to-reel tape, of the master tape of Cream's farewell performance, from the Royal Albert Hall, in November 1968. During my time in Outside Broadcasts (1985–92) I was fortunate enough to hear a bit ("White Room") one day when he brought it in to see if the recording was still OK. I knew straight away what it was because it was a version of "White Room" that I'd never heard before. George [not his real name] took a redundancy from the ABC about a decade ago, but he still puts in an appearance occasionally as a freelancer, when we're short-staffed. On Monday night he came over to me at tea break, and told me how he, and one of the other sound operators from work, had only recently finished editing it and another solo Clapton concert, from "The Old Grey Whistle Test" in 1977, and had burnt a CD from each tape. The next words from my lips were: "Are you approachable, George?" To which he replied: "I'll give you a copy of each, Peter, on the proviso that it doesn't go any further than you OK?" I gave him my word, and then we set about working out a payment that he'd be happy with. So, I now have in my hot little hands a copy of the aforementioned CDs, for which I paid one bottle of "Wild Turkey" bourbon. How's that? "$40. That's expensive!" Debbie exclaimed in the bottle shop. I then replied: "Jesus Christ, I'd be prepared to give him a case of the bloody stuff for these 2 CDs"'

---

[1]   Peter and Debbie's son, Marshall, is named after Jimi (James Marshall) Hendrix.

In 2005, after he made over $2,200 selling his old motorcycle brochures on eBay, Peter had a small buying spree:

'I bought the sound and vision set (CD and DVD) for Hendrix's performance at the Isle Of Wight concert a few years ago, when it was first released. Then I saw this guy in Canada who was selling a "Winterland" 6 disc set that is as rare as rocking horse shit. All the other "Winterland" sets I've seen for sale, have a concert at the Civic Theatre in Chicago on them. This one doesn't, so I had to spend up big to get it. I told the seller that it was costing me a fortune, due to the exchange rate, and they had better be worth it. He assures me I won't be disappointed.' [He wasn't.]

And the lucky vinyl find, (even when he can't play that format):

'I had an extremely successful visit to Glen Baker's "Time Warp" [a well-known Sydney record shop] yesterday. I found a mint copy of "Ghost Writer", which didn't have a price on it. When I asked how much they wanted for it, the reply was "$1"! Then I looked under Y and found two albums by Stomu Yamashta, "Go" ($3) and the music from "The Red Buddah Theatre" ($10). I still can't believe my luck. All I have to do now is get them transferred to tape, as I don't have a turntable anymore.'

Peter later acquired a scarce copy of 'Ghost Writer' on CD from the UK. When Raven Records undertook a compilation of Garland Jeffrey's material in 2002, and needed the best available copies of his original recordings, Peter lent them his CD. In return he got his name on the credits and 10 CDs from Raven's catalogue: 'Raven Records are just about to release their Garland Jeffrey's compilation CD, with my name on the credits (boast, boast). Ian McFarlance, the guy who originally contacted me about borrowing my copy of "Ghost Writer", sent me a couple of copies earlier in the week.'[2]

Illustrating the tendency for collectors not to share with their partners details of their spending on the collection, especially if the item purchased is expensive:

'I've been doing a bit of clandestine buying in the past few weeks, and thought you might like to know what I've purchased. My copy of "In the West"[3] arrived a fortnight ago, and now has pride of place in my collection. At $124 it's the single most expensive CD I've ever bought, and am ever likely to buy.'

---

[2] Garland Jeffreys, *Wild in the Streets (Best of 1977–1983)*, Raven, RVCD, 2002. Raven is a leading reissue and compilation label, based in Australia: www.ravenrecords. com.au.

[3] Jimi Hendrix died in 1970. Reflecting strong fan and collector interest, there has been a continued stream of official releases, compilations and bootlegs of his work; see Glebbeek and Noble (1996).

And the acquisition of previously unreleased material:

> 'The American chain store Borders have opened a couple of stores in Sydney,
> and I was having a look around their Pitt Street store a few weeks ago, when
> I came across a very interesting Beach Boys compilation called "Hawthorne,
> CA". Now I must confess that the Beach Boys have never been my favourite
> band, and some of their songs, like "Barbara Ann" I can't bloody stand, but this
> album really appealed to me because it's a double CD of previously unreleased
> material like rehearsals, promo spots and even commentary from various band
> members.'

The pleasure of another find [my emphasis]:

> 'Have you heard of Single Gun Theory? I finally found a copy of their "Like
> Stars in My Hands" album, second hand, for $20, at Utopia. I was at Red Eye
> Records last weekend and couldn't quite believe my luck. Prior to the robbery in
> 1997, one of my most cherished LPs was the first Master's Apprentices album,
> which I can still remember buying for $3.50, in about 1970, from Woolworths
> Cowra. I never believed I'd ever see it again, in any way, shape or form, but
> a small local label called Ascension has released the entire early Master's
> catalogue (1965–68) on the one disc, which includes all the tracks from that first
> album plus numerous other goodies. *There is a god after all.*'

Peter has been quick to utilize new technologies to expand and catalogue his
collection, getting a new computer and the technology to burn CDs and DVDs
and buying and selling on the internet. Over recent years, ABC has been almost
constantly 'restructuring' and cutting staff; with cameramen now largely being
replaced by automated systems, Peter faces the possibility of redundancy. Amongst
all this turmoil, Peter's record collection, along with his family, provide him with
emotional support.

Lee Ann Fullington

Lee Ann Fullington is currently living and working as a library professional at
UCLA in Los Angeles. She grew up in New Jersey, and worked in 'a very reputable'
independent record shop in Princeton, NJ, part-time as an undergraduate and then
went full-time for two years after she graduated. Lee then studied in the United
Kingdom, where she completed an MPhil thesis on the role and significance of
independent record shops in popular music culture.[4] Lee has eclectic musical
tastes, with an ongoing interest in indie rock, Americana and 'alternative' (for lack

---

[4]   *Counter Culture: The Role and Significance of Independent Record Shops in
Popular Music Culture*, Institute for Popular Music Studies, Liverpool University.

of a better qualifier). She still remains devoted to The Smiths and Morrissey and has a continued attachment to vinyl.

In 2002, Lee was keen to distance herself from a particular conception of the 'record collector':

> 'I do not consider myself a record collector in the, if I may call it this, classic sense of the term. A record collector seems to collect vinyl LPs/singles for the sake of collecting something rare that has to do with music, or collects pressings by certain bands or performers or genres. I do not see records as a collection such as a collection of stamps or coins. I love music and I like to buy what I can to have the music itself. Although if I had a choice between an original and a repressing with some sort of not so original graphic, I would rather have the original. I am not a record collector in the purest sense of the term, but I do have preferences for format, issue, etc.'

In 2009, looking back at this earlier view:

> 'My attitudes towards sound carriers have changed. I do consider my record collection a "collection", they really are artefacts and I have an emotional connection to them. Not only is the music important, but the story that goes with buying the record itself, whether it was just a nice day out with my boyfriend or something I picked up at a random shop in Birkenhead when I was doing my research. Or even something from my record shop staff days that I found when I was pricing records and was pleasantly surprised when I put it on the turntable!'

When did you first begin buying/collecting records?

'My mom bought me my first 45 by my request when I was about five. But I began buying my own music very consciously at about 12/13, when I began getting involved in alternative rock/hardcore.'

How many records do you own?

In 2002 Lee had 'anywhere between 700 to 1,000 recordings in all formats', though 'I haven't counted lately and most of my stuff is in America while I am studying in the UK.' (In 2009) 'I probably actually "own" less recordings just because I've been offloading my CDs and using digital formats, but my vinyl collection keeps growing, especially now that my boyfriend and I live together and have merged our record collections.'

What are your preferred formats?

'While I was an undergraduate I started working at the Princeton Record Exchange and developed a taste for vinyl there. I was exposed to so much music between the people I worked with and the customers, that not only did my CD "collection" balloon up, but I began collecting vinyl. I don't consider having CDs "collecting" in the sense that I would consider buying vinyl and keeping it as a "collection". Sure I have lots of CDs, but I don't really have any pride in having them.'

'Having vinyl though is something to be proud of! My boyfriend is also a vinyl person, so we go record shopping together now. I've uploaded all of my CDs to my computer and have joined the iPod generation. I have no emotional connection to my CDs; except for any special issue ones. I still [2009] have an attachment to my vinyl versions though and I do not intend to part with them. If I buy new music now, I try to buy the vinyl but will have the digital version for my iPod. I've been going back and buying vinyl versions of albums I've loved that I only had the CD of. Now, I don't mind a reissue of older indie stuff like Songs: Ohia etc. It just sounds so good on vinyl and handling the record is much more involved than pushing play on the iPod. I suppose I could do this with CDs too, but they just don't have the resonance for me that the vinyl does.'

'I prefer vinyl for rock, jazz and punk recordings because they just sound better, more full. Hip hop stuff you basically can only get on vinyl and again the bass just has so much more bottom. Electronica I buy on CD if it's a full length for these recordings tend to really flow track to track so it's kind of a pain to get up and flip the LP over when you are in that groove! But if it's an electroncia single, vinyl. I prefer vinyl for the most part, even though it's hard to lug back and forth between the US and UK. I love the way the records sound, I love the big sleeves, the whole feel of records, thumbing through them. So much more tactile than CD.'

What are your main genre/performer preferences?

'I love electronic (warp label type stuff, Kraftwerk, etc.) a bit of hip hop, esp. abstract hip hop like the Push Button Objects, Hieroglyphics vein hip hop. But the other half of my stuff is guitar orientated rock/punk/mental/country stuff including the Stooges, Black Sabbath, Royal Trux, Jane's Addiction, Mogwai, Johnny Cash. All these musics just get me going, I love the textures and sounds and feels of these somewhat disparate musics.' (in 2002)

'As I've gotten a little older my tastes have crystallized more on the rock end of the spectrum. I rarely listen to electronic music these days and have very little interest in new electronic/electro. I still have a soft spot for hip hop though.

But overall, I'm a sucker for the guitar and I've been digging backwards for music I somehow missed the first time around, things like Nick Cave and the Bad Seeds, anything Jason Molina and Will Oldham have done, and filling in the gaps from things I THOUGHT I had bought when I worked in the shop, but confused the memory of hearing the records all the time with actually owning them!' (in 2009)

Do you attend live concerts?

'Yes, but as I live in Liverpool not much electronica or hip hop comes here and it's not quite feasible to go to London or Manchester (money, places to stay, etc.) so I wind up going to indie rock gigs a few times a month to get out and enjoy music.' (in 2002)

'I still love going to live shows, but it's pretty much limited to things that are guitar-based. If Morrissey is coming around, I'll be at as many of those shows as possible! Part of the reason I moved to Los Angeles was to be closer to gig spaces to catch bands that are just beginning to find their audience – places like The Echo, Spaceland, and even the Music Box and the Wiltern for more established bands.' (in 2009)

What use do you make of the music press?

'I tend to read online electronica magazines like *Absorb* and I will pick up *NME* once in awhile. *Wire* is good for the electronica stuff too. Skateboarding magazines also tend to have good reviews of music, not written by rock critics/ experts, so they are often a better indicator of music I may like as they aren't conflated or pompous.' (in 2002)

'These days, with the explosion of blog-style music magazines, like *Prefix*[5] (which I write for), *STereogum*, *The Daily Swarm* and *Idolator* just to name a few, I get most of my information about music that way. Sadly, the print format for good music magazines is going the way of vinyl … and online magazines are the easier and less expensive way to go.' (in 2009)

Lee remains a confirmed vinyl lover: 'Give me a turntable and a needle, a beer and a couch to curl up on, and I'm home.'

---

[5] http://www.prefixmag.com.

Hasse Huss

Hasse Huss is a Swedish music journalist and academic, and a long-time collector of reggae and soul records. In his mid fifties, he lives in Stockholm with his wife and three children (aged 9, 12 and 16), and an extensive record collection. Hasse exemplifies the merging of a love of music with record collecting, music journalism and academic research. A keen concert goer, during the 1960s he saw Hendrix (six times) and Dylan (five or six times, including the Stockholm stop on the legendary 1966 tour), among others. Concerts attended in recent years include Leonard Cohen, Bryan Ferry, James Taylor, Brian Wilson and Smokey Robinson: 'All excellent, except Smokey which was simply too wonderful for words!'

His PhD study on the Jamaican phenomenon of toasting (or DJing), has provided him with the opportunity and rationale to visit Jamaica on several occasions, along with trips to the United States and Japan. A more recent project, resulting in a co-written book forthcoming in 2009, concentrates on popular music and gender. Hasse's chapter discusses the music everyone loves to hate, or in some cases used to love to hate: Abba, Italo Disco, Céline Dion. He is also a successful songwriter, working with Mikael Rickfors;[6] Hasse's song-writing financed the first years of his academic studies. These days, his collecting is financed chiefly by selling and trading records.

At what age did you begin buying records?

'I was ten, in the summer of 1962.'

Do you recall your first purchase?

> 'I recall it very well. The first one was The Marvelettes "Please Mr Postman" – it blew my mind completely. Another one I recall buying – this would be around six months later, Christmas 1962 – was Little Eva "The Loco-Motion". I think they both sound absolutely incredible to this day!'

> 'The first album I bought was one by Chubby Checker, *For Twisters Only*. I'm not sure I liked it so much though I did like his "Let's Twist Again" but that was not on the album. As a rather curious aside, when my father bought me my first record player, one of those great Bakelite or plastic things with the speaker in the cover, the record shop threw in one single for free, Merrill Moore "Red Light"/"Bartender's Blues". That's one I didn't like a lot initially, but as I only had a handful of records at the time, I played it a lot. Many years later I read about him in Nick Tosches' *Unsung Heroes of Rock 'n' Roll* – Moore was

---

[6]   Their compositions have been recorded by, among others, Cindy Lauper ('Yeah Yeah'), Santana, Jim Capaldi, Richie Havens ('Daughter of the Night') and Percy Sledge ('Blue Night', 'Shining Through The Rain').

one of the (unsung) founding fathers of rockabilly – and pulled it out again. It sounded great. I later found a great compilation of his stuff. I actually remember thinking, it's funny, I could just as easily have become a rockabilly or a country and western fan (and collector) had that one record hit me a bit stronger than it did in the early days. Of course after The Beatles and Motown (and Dylan) hit Sweden (*circa* 1963, 1964) there was no turning back. But I always loved soul (only it wasn't called soul then, of course, it was just good music on the radio). In 1963, 1964 I bought Martha and the Vandellas "Heat Wave" and The Impressions "It's All Right", along with The Beatles "A Hard Day's Night" and Bobby Vee "The Night Has a Thousand Eyes" – there simply was no problem in mixing styles like that.'

How did your collecting develop from that point?

'With regard to the reggae collectors (and I guess collectors of many black musics or music styles), one thing that strikes me is that DJs' record collections are also their tools of the trade as it were. The question is, are you a DJ first, or a collector? You could easily work as a DJ for quite some time, buying records to play in bars and clubs (and building up a substantial collection in the process), without even thinking of yourself as a "collector". (And then you will meet up with a collector proper and the sparks will start to fly …) In a way, this is how I came to have such a lot of 45s, I worked as a Club DJ for many years in the '70s, mostly before the days of 12-inches and disco-mixes; it was the trusted 7-inch 45 that carried the swing.'

'Reading about rare records and then trying to track them down is not something I did until the late 1980s. Buying three collections (two of reggae, one of soul) in the early 1990s also steered me in this particular direction. They were not very large collections (each reggae collection perhaps had 250 singles, the soul one, maybe 400 singles) but they were lovingly compiled. Only after a few years did I realize that there were also some very scarce items among this lot. So I was very lucky with these records, I began to realize just how excellent a lot of the stuff released by small cupboard-under-stairs companies was, and that labels and producers, particularly in reggae and soul, are more important than the artist more often than not.'

'Some collectors go for different or rare pressings of well known artists like The Beatles or Madonna. This is a kind of collecting that does not interest me. I like to collect the original vinyl (a lot of the stuff I collect simply isn't available in any other shape or form). I certainly have no problem with a good compilation album – or compilation CDs such as the soul collections on the Ace/Kent label and Numero's Eccentric Soul series, particularly if they come annotated.'

How many records do you own, and what are your preferred formats?

In 2002, Hasse's collection included 8,500 singles;[7] 3,500 vinyl albums; and 75 CDs.

In 2009, he observed that he had 'traded and sold quite a bit in recent years. I'd say my present holdings are around 8,500 singles 3,500 vinyl albums and 500 CDs. Most of whatever rock I had has gone. I've held on to Bob Dylan, Laura Nyro, John Martyn.'

Hasse does not maintain a catalogue of the collection.

> 'My preferred format is vinyl. Generally speaking though, if it's old soul and reggae, I try to go for the originals (if I can afford them, that is); if it's new releases (or pop or rock), I'm happy with a CD. I find I do need some sort of a physical disc; I've yet to download anything myself (other than clips from YouTube) though I have friends who buy a lot through iTunes. I recently (2009) bought one (!) tune as a download.'

How often do you currently purchase records and what are your preferred sources?

> 'These days it's mostly eBay, both for old vinyl and CDs. One of the world's finest record shops, Pet Sounds, is in Stockholm so I get some things there. I've known the owner, Stefan Jacobsson since the 1970s. The average, once a week, still holds, roughly. Most of the things I am interested in – currently, '60s soul singles and girl groups, later '60s rock steady and 1970s reggae – are simply not available outside specialist outlets (and on eBay).'

> '[In 2009] the situation is slightly different. Seems I'm not the only one who's fond of these genres, and there are some fantastic compilations available. At the same time, I've begun to appreciate the CD format. Having said that, there's still a lot of great music not available on CD. There are a few labels I collect; both American and Jamaican, and I will try to pick up an original when one comes along, if I can afford it. I always seem to make the excuse that these purchases are for research purposes; sometimes they are, sometimes that's stretching it a little.'

---

[7]   With reggae, the single is elevated to a more significant space in collecting. This reflects the historical nature of the production process in Jamaica, with an emphasis on the rapid turnover of records, and keeping costs down. Accordingly, many reggae artists and labels primarily put out singles, although subsequent compilations are also very important to collectors. Soul, especially from the 1960s, presents a similar situation.

What are your genre and artist preferences?

'I still [2008] collect soul and reggae 45s. The interest in soul is about the same (strong) but reggae perhaps has gone down a little. This past year I've listened a lot to yé-yé, i.e. French pop from the 1960s. France Gall, Francoise [Françoise] Hardy, the lovely Sylvie Vartan and Brigitte Bardot (and a host of unknowns). The common denominator here often is Serge Gainsbourg, in the producer's chair and as a songwriter. I do have one or two original EPs but I don't collect them in that format, it's all on CD. Some are very nicely presented, in digi-paks with booklets.'

'My interest in French music has grown. I love the fantastic Mylène Farmer. I also like Barbara Carlotti and the productions of Bertrand Burgalat (Valérie Lemercier's 1995 album *chante* is a particular favourite.) As my daughters listen to Rihanna, Pink, Christina Aguilera and Beyoncé, I discover new favourites all the time. I like Girls Aloud, Little Jackie and Lady Ga Ga. All great pop in 2009 is made by female artists, interestingly enough. Little Boots is fantastic. I like '80s and '90s pop, like Human League, Kylie Minogue, Saint Etienne. I find it increasingly hard to listen to "rock".'

'If I were to make a genre and artist preference list today it would probably look like this.

1. Pet Shop Boys; 2. Brill Building, girl groups, Brian Wilson, Burt Bacharach/ Hal David; 3. French pop, yé-yé; 4. Recent French stuff, Mylène Farmer, Barbara Carlotti, Christophe Willem; 5. Rocksteady; 6. Northern Soul (Motown, Chicago Soul); 7. '70s soul bordering on disco, early Gamble & Huff for instance; 8. Early Jamaican dancehall (early '80s); 9. Early digital reggae (late '80s); 10. House.'

Music magazines

Hasse is an avid reader of music magazines, observing that there is 'nothing like a good library of music magazines when you try to make a loving from writing about music, but surely it's a rationalization (not to mention justification) for collecting as well!' In 2001 Hasse still purchased *MOJO* (monthly); *Echoes* (a British black music monthly that was a weekly in the '80s and '90s); *The Beat* (US bi-monthly).

'I probably read the *New Musical Express* more or less every week between 1964 and 1991, then I lost interest. I've also most likely read most issues of *Black Music* – an excellent British monthly – between 1973, when it started, through to the mid 1980s when it deteriorated in my view. I used to get some soul fanzines, mostly British ones, and *Soul Survivor* (out of Toronto, Canada).

Never read *Blues & Soul* in its heyday, but bought around 150 back issues in London a few years ago. Paid rather too much for them I thought at the time, but now I'm happy I did – very happy, in fact!'

In 2009: 'I stopped reading *Echoes* a couple of years ago. These days I still read *Mojo*, *Uncut* and *Record Collector* but more selectively. I buy some but not all issues of *Wax Poetics*.'

'Reading music mags and record collecting are tightly knit, I think, not least because the gaze of the music journalist so often is like the collector's. Tracing (tracking?) careers, listing early incarnations of a band – to every Beatles there's a Quarrymen, to every soul hit there is a handful of forgotten obscurities. Providing discographies. Some mags more than others obviously, but it's part of a general approach in many ways I think. Ordering and collecting go hand in hand. It's interesting to note Record Collector's facelift in this light. The colour format and the wider interests (now there's Motown, reggae and Sylvie Vartain as well as British psychedelia in there, makes a more attractive mix surely.'

Lee Marshall

Lee Marshall is an academic[8] and record collector, with a focus on Bob Dylan and The Rolling Stones, including concert bootleg recordings, on CD. These intersect through his research into bootlegs,[9] and a recent book on Bob Dylan.

When we first discussed Lee's collecting (in 2002), he was reluctant to identify himself as a collector, a status he associated with

'… someone who is more concerned about the artefact itself, rather than the use value of the object (i.e. the actual music it contains); a can't see the wood from the trees situation. I see this so much with bootleg collectors who are just obsessed about getting a recording of every concert, which makes it impossible to listen to a show more than once if you collect Dylan. I felt myself going down that path and have retreated quite a lot. I'm not sure if it is possible to collect many bootlegs without suffering from that kind of madness.'

More recently (in 2009), he still considered himself 'a music collector rather than a record collector', although conceding that 'the materiality [of the sound recording] does have some significance [for me].' The development of Lee's collection and collecting practices illustrate the changing narrative of the collection, and the

---

[8]   For Lee's academic profile, and publications, see http://www.bristol.ac.uk/sociology/staff/leemarshall.html.

[9]   See Chapter 4.

social identity of the collector as life circumstances and musical tastes change. Particular attention is paid here to the current status of his bootleg collecting.

At what age did you begin buying records?

> 'The first time I actually chose a record to buy (although someone else paid) was in 1979, aged 6. I was always interested in music. I guess I consciously began to buy records about age 13/14. I got into The Stones, and then Dylan, at 15/16, and began buying bootlegs at about 17/18 (although I realized later that I had unwittingly bought a couple of bootlegs earlier than that). By the time I was at university, I was buying a lot of bootlegs, and I started tape-trading about that time too. The tape-trading really intensified when I was in my early twenties – perhaps 22.'

How many records do you own, and what are your preferred formats?

In 2002, Lee estimated he had

> 'around 1,500 CDs/CD-Rs of which: 700 Bob Dylan; 350 Rolling Stones; 450 everyone else. [Along with] 800 cassettes, of which: 650 Bob Dylan; 100 Rolling Stones; 50 everyone else. Since getting a CD burner in Oct '98, I have spent a lot of time replacing shows I had on tape with CD-R versions. My tape collection peaked at about 1,500 and has been shrinking as the CD-R collection grows. I also have about 25 vinyl, all Dylan and Stones. I don't own a turntable but could never throw away anything by either artist (perhaps that does make me a record collector).'

In 2009, he thought that 'I now have 2,000–2,300 CD/CD-Rs – 1,000 Dylan; 450 Stones; 1,000 everyone else (very roughly).' But, since he now rarely played them: 'I threw away all my tapes! I took them to the dump. The second immediately after tipping them over the edge was a heart-stopping one; a sudden panic that I had done the wrong thing. I hadn't though. But I still have the vinyl.'

How do you treat/provide for their storage and use?

Initially Lee used custom tape storage boxes for cassettes and 'doctored bookcases' to store CDs. These have now been replaced by custom made shelves for CDs, with discs placed in alphabetical or date order. However:

> 'I recently began worrying about running out of shelf space (as an academic, I have a battle between CDs and books for storage space). I have started removing some concert recordings from jewel cases and using little plastic wallets. However sad it may seem, this was a difficult decision. I like having a wall of CDs, and I like people coming to the house and seeing my wall of CDs. Partly it

might be a form of intellectual snobbery – "this is how much I know about this thing" – but mainly it is because those discs are a big part of who I am. Music means a great deal to me, and that wall of CDs offers an image of just how much it means. When people see it, they recognize just how into music I am. Shrinking it, by replacing jewel cases with wallets, means that the materiality of the collection does not adequately reflect its significance to me. For this reason, I am a long way from just storing my CDs on a computer server (the other possibility I considered).'

Do you keep a catalogue of them?

In 2002, Lee had a catalogue of 'all Stones and Dylan stuff on Microsoft Excel which records a) date of recording b) place of recording c) length d) sound quality (subjective rating) and, where relevant, e) title of bootleg. This is out of necessity. I have a fairly good knowledge of what I own Dylan wise, but dates and places can easily get muddled; and, in order to trade, traders need lists to send to each other.' (Lee's list of CDs, like those of many other traders, was then online.) This database was still maintained in 2009, 'for my own records, and if I ever start trading again.'

How often do you currently purchase records?

In 2002, Lee said

> 'I very rarely buy official CDs now; my main source of acquisitions comes from trading (for bootlegs) and copying friends' CDs (for official releases). I dislike buying new CDs from major record shops because of my ambivalence toward the mainstream industry. I will, of course, automatically buy official releases by those artists of whom I collect bootlegs and I occasionally buy records from more obscure artists who my friends don't already have. I probably have two CD buying trips a year, when I'll pick up about 8 CDs.'

In 2009, Lee observed,

> 'My trading and, therefore, my purchasing of official releases, have changed very much over the last few years. For a variety of personal, social and technological reasons, I am probably not as invested in bootlegs as I once was. Firstly, as I have mentioned before, when you get to a certain level of bootleg collecting, it becomes an all-or-nothing activity. The scale of collecting needed to make sure you a) know what is available and b) have the trading resources to be able to trade for it, mean that you do lots of legwork for the elusive catch. In the end, that became a little tiring – I don't need 70 shows from each year! I have more music to listen to than I need, and if something is really important, I'll still find out about it.'

'Secondly, the nature of trading has changed. For me, all of my "trading" is now done online, at specific bootleg torrent sites. This changes your attitude to trading as it becomes less about personal contact (no parcels through the mail, no letters saying a quick hello …), which I think lessens the investment that you have with it. It also means that every Dylan show is available online for me to download should I choose (which is another reason to resist completism! But it also diminishes the sense of work, and therefore achievement, that you used to get when you finally obtain a show you really wanted.) On the plus side, it has enabled me to download LOTS of bootlegs from other artists (The Specials, for example), which I wouldn't have had access to through conventional trading.'

'Another reason for my lessening focus on bootlegs is that, professionally, I needed to become more aware of more music – for teaching and research. More time for other – legitimate – music means less time for bootlegs. That said, to anyone from the outside, I'm still very invested in bootlegs. I've just listened to 7 CDs' worth of outtakes from Infidels; that may tell you something. With downloading/torrenting, I probably get 8–10 new bootlegs a month, along with 3 or 4 bootleg DVDs. But that is alongside 8–10 legitimate releases.'

'My purchasing of official music has of course been impacted by all of the above factors. I purchase a lot more official material now. Four things have really helped me in this regard: (1) P2P software. If I now read or hear about something that's interesting, I download, listen and buy (or not buy). The ease of sampling has led me to find lots of new music that I would not have bothered chasing up in the past; (2) copyright expiration of '40s and '50s recordings, has resulted in lots of very good, and very cheap reissues. I have stacks of blues, R&B, country CDs that I haven't played yet (and I now find these more helpful to me, in understanding Dylan/Stones/etc., than listening to 70 concerts from 2008); 3) the price of CDs has declined significantly, so I now don't mind taking a chance on a CD that looks interesting; 4) online record shops. There is one bricks-and-mortar record shop in Bristol that I occasionally drop into. It has great bargains and I'll go and buy 10–20 CDs in one go. With the exceptions of trips to that store, my purchasing is very targeted. I no longer browse record shops, either online or offline. I find the process tiresome; I know of most of the things I want and have bought them. I don't find new artists by accident; even if I did find something, I would want to check online that this is the best/most complete version to buy before actually buying it. So, most of my purchasing is at online stores, knowing what I want and finding it immediately.'

What are your main genre/performer preferences?

In 2002, Lee favoured

> 'individuals rather than genres, specifically Dylan, Stones, Waits. If I was being
> specific I would say blues music and those directly influenced by blues musicians
> (i.e. not those influenced by the Stones or Dylan). But then I like things outside
> of that, too. The defining factor, I think, is that they all contain guitars.'

In 2009:

> 'My tastes are pretty much still the same, though there is perhaps more of an
> alt-country influence. I don't think my tastes have changed dramatically, but I
> do think I find things I like in a lot more places now. I've started going to small
> festivals a lot and things like MySpace enable you to keep track of smaller-level
> artists that you find there. That is the part of music consumption I get most
> pleasure from at the moment. And I've been getting into lots of '40s and '50s
> stuff as well. Aside from the ever-present Dylan and Stones, my main interests
> seem to be a) music made 50 years ago and b) music made now on small labels.
> I don't find a lot of new stuff in between.'

Ian Shirley

Ian Shirley is an English music journalist and an avid record collector. He is the
editor of the *Rare Record Price Guide 2010*; contributes a regular column to *Record
Collector*, 'Value Added Facts', in which he answers readers' questions; and was
No. 60 in the collector series in the *Record Collector*.[10] His early collecting interests
(mid 1970s to early 1980s) included punk, new wave, electronic pop and 'more
experimental stuff', and he 'got into jazz in the mid-80s': 'I've got everything
Miles Davis ever recorded on vinyl and CD. Musically my collection ranges from
Johnny Ray via British jazz to trip hop.' Ian estimates his collection includes in
excess of 4,000 vinyl albums and 5,000 singles, 3,000 CDs and 2,000 78s.

Ian has written articles on a wide range of collectable records, artists and
genres, most recently on British Jazz Collectables (*Record* Collector, 347, March
2008. 'Part 2: The Modernists'), the 'Top Thirty Beatles Collectables' pressed in
the United Kingdom (*Goldmine*, 21 November 2008), and the 200 rarest United
Kingdom albums (*Record Collector*, 355, November 2008). His books include an

---

[10]   *Record Collector*, 355, November 2008: 8–9. The quotes in this preamble are
drawn from this profile.

illustrated history of music and comics,[11] studies of Bauhaus and The Residents,[12] and two science fiction novels, *Shadowplay* and *Heavy Mental*.[13]

In short, Ian is a leading authority on record collecting. In March 2009, he responded (by email) to a number of questions I put to him on trends in record collecting. My initial intention was to edit these into the relevant chapters here, but they clearly warranted keeping together.

> Roy: In your Record Collector profile, you mention that 'to some collectors CDs don't count.' I'd agree that vinyl is 'privileged' by the majority of collectors, though a fair number of my interviewees only collected CDs, and several had most of the 'collection' on their hard drives and iPods, and owned few physical recordings. Is 'traditional' vinyl record collecting going to disappear with the baby boomer generation?

> Ian: I don't think that CDs don't count. I have a massive collection of CDs that are a vital part of my record collection. The CD boom of the 90s 'refreshed' the approach to collecting music especially when original albums were augmented with bonus material. The length of a CD – around 70 minutes – was also perfect for compiling – in some cases – the entire work of a band. Thus one album and a handful of singles could fit on one CD along with excellent liner notes. 2 CDs would compile 2 albums or contain a wealth of unreleased or bonus albums. Thus you can get a huge chunk of rare singles for a great price and in some cases a CD can become rare as it was only issued once and contains everything that band did in one easy format. Whenever I write about music I always reach for my CDs to listen to music. Also some of the box sets are astounding from Miles Davis to Magma. The amount of mainstream and obscure music that was released is phenomenal. It is all about the music and those people who burn their CD collections and get rid of them are MAD!

> The trend towards owning music on hard drive is natural but disturbing. This has nothing to do with my taste for vinyl or CDs but the fact is that with downloading people are becoming indiscriminate. When you buy something you are 'investing' and therefore will take the time to listen to it. I have friends who use free download sites and just siphon up huge tracts of artists' material. The entire Kraftwerk back catalogue or the entire works of Duke Ellington; but they don't listen to it. They just have it like a trophy and these digital collections are simply archives that are in many cases not touched by their owners.

---

[11] *Can Rock'n'Roll Save the World: An Illustrated History of Music and Comics*, SAF Publishing, 2005. This includes a fascinating, detailed interview with cartoonist and 78 collector Robert Crumb.

[12] *Meet The Residents: America's Most Eccentric Band*, SAF Publishing, 2001; *Dark Entries: Bauhaus and Beyond*, SAF Publishing, 2001.

[13] See *Record Collector*, 351, July 2008: 101.

Of course, the other side of the coin is that many people download and play the music all the time. I personally don't see the music in my hard drive or iPod as a 'collection' it is just music that I have put in a storage system that is easy to play when I work or am on the move. My 'collection' remains my shellac, vinyl and CDs. I always imagine a scenario where a computer crashes or the hard drive is wiped clean and then your collection is no longer there! My daughter will disagree as she is 15 and only bought about two CDs in her life – for her a 'digital only' collection is normal.

Roy: Is 78 collecting on the way out, as you suggest in your recent Value Added column?[14]

Ian: Record collecting will be with us as long as there is a man on the earth. The desire to collect, acquire and catalogue and collect is inherent. There is something satisfying about buying and playing a record – rare or otherwise. Although the current young generation have less collectors the fact that new and established bands still release records on vinyl – from Radiohead to the Kings of Leon – shows that there is a market and need. Also with vinyl you are buying something that looks and sounds fantastic and serves as an 'ultimate' artistic package – especially an LP. Great cover art, and the luscious vinyl inside – aahh. Just looking at records you can't afford or own is thrilling in itself. Looking at your own collection is great and playing a record that might be 50 or 40 years old just brings that artist back to life whether it is Lavern Baker or Jimi Hendrix.

78 rpm is certainly in decline as the generation that collected it are moving up to the Heavens (or their wives would say going off to Hell). A lot of vinyl collectors have no interest in 78rpm music as they just do not collect the format. As for 78s, the interest lies in rare rock and roll or hillbilly music or those wonderful '60s pressings of Indian Beatles 78 rpm records. I have over 2,000 78 rpm records acquired in the last few years. Played on a proper 78 rpm hand wound system they sound great. But interest is in decline although some of the most important music as released on 78 – Charlie Parker, Duke Ellington, Louis Armstrong and Elvis Presley!

Roy: I am intrigued by the continually rising prices paid for some items (I have looked at auctions and eBay), and the consequent shifts in the Price Guides. In your *RC* November 2008 article on the 200 Rarest UK albums, you note that 'Collectors are willing to pay huge sums for rare releases that come to market in mint condition.' The answers may be self-evident, but what do you see as behind the trend? (I hope it is not a South Seas Bubble, Dutch tulips kind of thing!) My sense is that in some cases this is for investment purposes, rather than actually wanting the music for itself (especially given it is often available

---

[14]   *Record Collector*, 347, December 2007.

as 'standard' releases; e.g. The Beatles *White Album*). I own quite a few of the albums listed, having begun purchasing records in the mid-late 1960s, even a few of the desirable pressings listed, but of course many of these are in far from mint condition.

Ian: There are some people who do buy rare records as an investment and simply salt them away in order to preserve their value. I always find it strange that the ultimate in record collection is a mint record. This means unplayed. As a music lover it seems sad that we hunger for records that someone bought but never played. I have many mint records but many that are not mint. If I buy a record in mint I will probably play it unless I already have it and then I store it. But people pay a lot of money for great music and what is a highly sought after record. There may have only been 1,000 of an album or single pressed and to get one in mint condition after 30–40 years is well worth the investment. Collectors love music and thus will have an 'emotional' investment in paying a high price for something they want. I have paid a lot of money for records over the years. Money well spent.

As for South Sea Bubble you must understand that prior to Broadband people could only buy rare records at record fairs or face to face in dealers shops. Now if I have – say – a rare mint copy of a psychedelic single for sale I can put it on the internet and bidders from all over the world will be able to look at it and make bids. Thus this helps drive up the price especially if a record is really rare. Even in this current economic downturn if a rare record comes on the internet there are going to be collectors who are going to go all out to buy it. I know people who have sold records from their collections to buy cars and even property.

On his writing

I got sick of reading reviews and articles by people who did not have a clue what they were talking about. I have a history degree and take a lot of time and care when writing articles, reviews or books. Thus I like to bring my skills to bear on what I write. Sometimes I make mistakes as a writer and people might not agree with my opinions but the passion is there always.

Geoff Stahl

Geoff Stahl is a Canadian academic, record collector and DJ. After living in Montreal in the 1980s and 1990s, followed by periods in Berlin and Helsinki, he is now resident in New Zealand, teaching in Media Studies at Victoria University of Wellington.[15] His main interests are in popular music, especially music scenes, and new media technologies.

For Geoff, music collecting and listening is a social activity and taste gauge. He has some hesitation about calling himself a collector, a label he associates with completism and an emphasis on economic value. He is interested, rather, in 'music that others don't have, [such as] rare exotica', but which is not necessarily 'collectable' in terms of economic value: 'I have a lot of records, but I don't have a lot of one particular genre; I'm not a completist in that sense.' As a discussion of his collecting interests amply demonstrates, Geoff is a musical omnivore: 'There is a world of fascinating sounds; I just want to be exposed to them, and share them.'

Geoff began collecting at age 12, and, like most collectors I talked with, can clearly recall his early purchases:

'Blondie's *Parallel Lines* was my first LP.'

'Split Enz's "I Got You" was my first 7 inch.'

'Peter Schilling's "Major Tom" was my first 12 inch.'

'ABC's *Look of Love* was my first cassette, which came with my first Walkman.'

'My first CD was Van Morrison's *Astral Weeks*.'

Building the collection

In 2001, Geoff had approximately 11,000 records:

> 'When I first dove into collecting, I initially took advantage of a specific historical situation in Montreal, when warehouses were selling vinyl, including one that sold it by weight. Because I was doing radio at the time, late night radio, I had a lot of freedom and wasn't constrained by genre. I bought a lot of terrible records that I'd never listen to at home, but I would play on the radio.'

Later, living in and visiting other cities [Berlin, Wellington] exposed Geoff to other vinyl sources, and he further expanded his collection. Nor was he restricting himself to vinyl: 'If it's a song I'm looking for, it doesn't matter what format it is. I'll go into a record store and look through all the racks.'

By 2008 Geoff estimated he had about 15 to 16,000 records, with half the collection stored back in Canada. 'It's been about five years since I had my full collection with me, and I don't miss most of it.' He considers, 'I am still collecting and scavenging, but I've become more discriminating over the past few years. I feel I am less of a hoarder these days.' However, he admits having never sold

---

[15]   I met Geoff when he was researching New Zealand indie music (especially Flying Nun records), and visited New Zealand in 1994. In the following years, we met at several academic conferences, and shared a couple of record store trawls when I was in Montreal. The account here is based on an email interview in September 2001, subsequent discussions, in person and by email, and a face to face interview in January 2009.

any record: 'Except once when I was 18, for financial reasons. I sold a whole lot of Depeche Mode records; you spend the next 15 to 20 years regretting it.' The majority of Geoff's collection has been acquired fairly cheaply: 'The most I have paid for a record is NZ$150 for a French "cosmic disco" 7 inch single, "Action Minet", by Morris Action from CDNLP – it is great for the dance floor.'

Geoff does not do 'the thrift shop thing' so much today. 'As I'm getting older, I'm less inclined to kneel down and dig through some crates. It's not as pleasurable in the same way anymore.' He now obtains most of his vinyl online: 'I use a couple of on-line shops, [notably CDNLP in France], which have more of the music I am interested in: slightly rarer and off the beaten path. In addition to ripping vinyl, I pay for digital downloads, though I don't like the compression rate from iTunes. I am a bit of a fetishist when it comes to sound quality.' One of Geoff's main reasons for travel is to find new sources [of records]: 'Whenever I travel, I want to find a record store. In a city like Berlin, I'm always hitting record shops, there seems to be two or three on every block. I feel I can stock up when I'm there.'

Cruising blogs

The internet is proving a fertile ground for Geoff's collecting:

> 'I've been keeping up with the various eulogies through a number of blogs that have cropped in the wake of OiNK's demise. It's fascinating to watch the mad and often shameless scramble to find new sources for music. As it's Monday and I've started my weekly ritual, a glimpse into the start of my week: I love the thought of waking up and starting the day by cruising blogs looking for new/ old songs and LPs. I certainly appreciate bloggers' efforts to lovingly annotate each upload, often with the kind of connoisseurship and expertise that makes me envious. That I can hear just about anything from any era on the global jukebox that is blogspot makes my week. What appeals to me the most about this is that, on the one hand, I can explore, in painstaking detail, a particular genre and/or band/artist, which stands as an affirmation and rounding out of my tastes, and, on the other, I've never found myself listening to so much music that falls outside my standard repertoire.'

> 'I probably download about twenty albums/singles/EPs/12-inches a week. Most of these are out of print CDs or vinyl rips, with the occasional new LP thrown in. I listen to each of these, and will often, eventually, just keep the cuts I like, if only to keep the hard drive space free. This is certainly more than I was buying pre-digital download. Three external hard drives chock-a-block with music now.'

The music

Geoff's collecting has been dictated by his various guises as a radio show host and as a DJ.

'Part of this, and this is where I can be a bit pretentious about my musical tastes, is what I am interested in is music that others don't necessarily have, or music that I think people want to hear. So I look for the rare, I look for the exotic. I look not necessarily for the collectable, but that something that is a little bit different, off the beaten path. Now, it may be stuff that DJs are playing in other parts of the world, but if I am playing it down here [Wellington, New Zealand], it is often music that nobody has ever heard before.'

The clubs where he DJs take him 'because my tastes are eclectic, I don't play the usual things.'

In terms of musical styles, Geoff describes himself as 'a bit of a dilettante, dabbling in a whole lot of genres'; most recently synth pop, French rai, and Italo disco. 'I don't consider myself an expert on any one genre, although there are certain genres that I feel much more comfortable with, and I know a lot about. I don't go deep into a genre, the same way a lot of other collectors might.' While Geoff still considers himself omnivorous, there are constraints: 'I feel like I have kind of missed the boat with some genres such as reggae, though I like ska. I'd need to know more of the history, and I want to avoid becoming a clichéd white guy. It's just not me.' As indicated above, internet blogs have become his primary means of finding new music, '[they are] where specialists can assert their particular interests, for example Tropicala – Brazilian music from the 1960s – garage rock, and so on.'

'I'm still gathering, hoarding, collecting, scouring for new music all the time. I constantly want to hear interesting sounds. It's one of the primary ways I relate to the world and other people.'

Simon Sweetman

Simon Sweetman is a freelance writer/reviewer, living in Wellington, New Zealand. He covers music for a wide range of local publications, contributes to a TV show (Good Morning on TV1) and has a blog (on stuff.co.nz). To support his freelance writing, Simon has worked in music and book retail, and taught in popular music courses at Victoria University of Wellington. In addition to recordings, Simon is an avid consumer/collector of music DVDs and the music press, which form a significant adjunct to his collecting: 'for me, it's mostly about "knowledge" and keeping up to date.'

When I first discussed this project with him, in 2005, Simon was reluctant to term himself a collector, a status he saw as embracing preoccupations with collection size and completism, along with 'anorak' and 'trainspotting' stereotypes. He later (in November 2008) elaborated on this stance:

'I used to consider myself a collector, particularly when I was buying a lot of material and becoming very particular in "collecting sets" – i.e. complete discographies for certain canonical artists. I never worked too hard to get b-sides and bootlegs but I would want to own all the original albums by, say, Neil Young, Bob Dylan, Leonard Cohen, Bruce Springsteen; I consider myself a reviewer. Sure I have a collection, but I have lost my completist approach.'

Gradually, however, there was an acceptance that: 'I am a bit of a collector. I always organize my CDs; I always make sure they are in order and I feel happy doing that. So in that sense it probably is accurate pertaining to me. But I have pruned my collection somewhat' (2008). And Simon continues to emphasize the use value of his collection, distancing himself from simply acquiring the material artefact, the sound recording:

'As far as collectors and the collecting process – I never really understood the need to have something that you don't plan to listen to. To me it's about accessibility and reference; I have things because I WANT to listen to them or I want TO BE ABLE to listen to them, for reference, if/when I need to. Again, now I'm more towards the reviewing angle than the collecting/listener angle. But there's major crossover there obviously.'

When did you begin buying records?

'I remember actively listening to music at about age six. I would ask questions about The Beatles. I bought my first tapes in 1987 – I was 11. I purchased U2 *The Joshua Tree* and Midnight Oil's *Diesel and Dust*. After that, I saved pocket money and basically bought a tape a week. [I mowed my aunt's lawns for $10 and she also gave me a blank tape, that I would dub.] I didn't start buying CDs until 1994. Quite late, because I had amassed about 500 original tapes and didn't want to changeover. We didn't have a CD player until the early 1990s, when my dad won one in a competition, and insisted that I start changing to buying CDs. I did, slowly replacing a lot of the tapes. I don't have any tapes now – I gave the last of them away about a year ago. They seemed completely redundant.'

How many records do you own, and what are your preferred formats?

'Hmmm? I can't be much of a collector if I don't know the exact answer?! Um, I have a full 160gig iPod, so that has about 2,500 albums on it. I also have a full 80gig iPod (though there's some double-up there). I own about 3,000 CDs, but this has dropped from about 5,500 (about five years ago). I also have about 1,300 vinyl LPs. And I have about 200 music and movie DVDs.'

'I buy CDs and DVDs. And about every couple of months I like to buy a brand new sealed vinyl or a reissued vinyl. I'm slowly assembling a bit of a time-capsule I guess? Most recently I bought Guns'N'Roses' *Appetite For Destruction* on sealed vinyl with the original artwork that was banned from the tape/CD when it came out. Now, I know I said that I buy things to listen to rather than save, but here I'm buying something I already have on MP3 and/or CD – so I'm saving them up for the future. I have a few things like this: White Stripes, Wilco, Ryan Adams, The Prodigy … and so on …'

Do you keep a catalogue of the collection?

'I just have two [MS] Word documents, again simple alphabetical, for CDs and DVDs. I started one for vinyl, but it was too hard to maintain. I think a [MS] Word document is enough for me. I don't mark things off or make lists when I loan stuff, I can tell by looking at the shelves what is missing. And I just adjust the Word doc when I sell stuff, get new stuff, or discover CDs lost or damaged and in need of binning.'

How do you treat/provide for their storage and use?

'I have all my CDs in a wall-unit space that was built by my father. My original CDs though are kept in alphabetical order, then within an artist it will be chronological by release date. I have all of my CDs together apart from classical – I have separated those out (about 200 CDs) in to their own collection and again they're alphabetical by composer. The vinyl are not in any order, but that's because they're in storage and not at my house. I don't currently have a turntable. Everything stays in its cover, case or sleeve, apart from that I would not say I was too anal with the collecting.'

How often do you currently purchase records?

'I would receive up to 30 CDs a week for free; for reviewing. So weeks and weeks can go by without me buying anything. I am trying not to buy CDs at all, basically. But about every two months I will do a "big shop" and buy about half a dozen CDs and half a dozen DVDs – and catch up on the new stuff that I have not been automatically sent. And complete old sets, and pick up old favourites. And every now and then buy an impulse record.'

Where do you buy from, and why these sources?

'I mostly buy from Real Groovy and Slowboat in Wellington. I know the staff; I often trade for credit and buy using that. The things I'm looking for now are not mainstream so I know I've more chance of buying there. I have bought from The CD Store and Borders and still do, sometimes. I basically walk in to any store that has a SALE sign flashing – because I'm always after a bargain and that idea that I might find whatever it is I never realized I was looking for is something that still sucks me in every time. I figure I can access anything these days online, or being sent a comp, or going to the library, or borrowing from friends' collections or computers. The real interest in buying new CDs for me now is in getting something different.'

What are your main genre/performer preferences?

'Pretty much anything within reason – but I go on splurges buying jazz. And country. And I have a lot of rock and indie-rock based stuff. I sometimes go out to specifically buy classical (a genre I only started warming to about 2 years ago). And in terms of collecting, I'm now looking to get "final" elusive albums from people like Paul Simon and bootleg and rare items for Bob Dylan, Tom Waits, Springsteen, Lou Reed ... that sort of thing – so classic rock stuff basically. And pure pop (1950s–1980s).'

Do you attend live concerts?

'Yeah, almost every week. Of course that's because I review; but I was always a big concert person, going to all the big-name gigs when I was a student, whatever ones I could pay for. I had seen hundreds of gigs before I ever started getting comps to review. I still pay to go see gigs if it's not being reviewed [by me] and I really want to see it. And I like to buy CDs at gigs, if an artist is selling something independent – a rarity, EP/live show/bootleg that you might not find in a store.'

I understand that you have a collection of music DVDs?

'I do watch music DVDs – I love watching docos of any kind; genre, band, time-period, etc. and selected live concerts. I'm not much interested in collections of video/promo-clips, unless it's part of an artist history. I had a HUGE collection of music DVDs – hundreds – from working in music retail. I got rid of a lot of them, because I simply ran out of room and have been on a programme that I like to call "downscaling my ephemera". I have replaced that with buying music books of course, so I'm worse off in many ways. I still get sent a lot of music DVDs to watch/review and I make a habit of trying ALL of them, even the very terrible. It's all knowledge/reference and all ideas for writing. But I keep very few of them. Having said that, I'm now going out and buying "definitive" music films on DVD (*Spinal Tap*, *Blues Brothers*, *Wayne's World*, etc.). And selected box-set doco/anthologies and classic concerts (Talking Heads *Stop Making Sense*, etc.).'

As a music journalist you obviously follow the music press?

'I used to purchase a lot [of music magazines], but having just been in book retail I was able to read a lot of them for free. I still regularly (i.e. most months) buy *Mojo* and *Uncut*. They are the staples for me. I will occasionally buy *Rolling*

Stone and *Q* (about three times a year now only) and *Word, Record Collector, Jazztimes* and *Modern Drummer* sporadically. A lot of reading is done online now at blog posts and websites. *Pitchfork, Metacritic, Stuff*

Simon can be contacted through his blog: www.stuff.co.nz/blogs/blogonthe tracks.

Steve Waksman

Steve Waksman is an academic[16] and a record collector. These two activities are strongly related, as Steve draws on his record collection as a research resource, while his shifting research interests will stimulate additions to the collection. Complementing Steve's record collecting are a passionate commitment to live music, and his strong interest in the music press and the role of music critics in establishing taste and the musical canon.

When we first discussed his record collecting,[17] Steve was keen to distance his personal collecting practices from a perceived stereotype:

> 'Yes [I consider myself a record collector], in a manner of speaking – in the sense that I purchase music regularly, that I keep what I purchase rather than discard, and that I make some effort to organize the music that I have (by performer and year of release). Not in the sense that I am especially concerned about the size of my collection, or that I pursue specific artefacts intensively and am willing to pay a lot of money for them.' (2001)

Later (2008), he recalled:

> 'I remember being reticent about the term collector. I'm less so now, partly because I think the amount of stuff I have is more worthy of the title, but also because I think I act a bit more like a collector than I used to, to the extent that I have at times put a good amount of effort into locating certain recordings. I still don't go after high-value items and I still care a lot less about having a particular issue of a certain recording than just having the music, but there are times when I much prefer to buy something on vinyl than on CD, and I still very much prefer both formats over the forms of digital audio that one listens to on

---

[16]   Steve is currently Associate Professor of Music and American Studies at Smith College, in Massachusetts, having joined the faculty in 2001. For his academic profile, see www.smith.edu/music/faculty_waksman.php.

[17]   We first met at an academic conference in Turku in 2001. I then interviewed Steve by email in November 2001, and we had intermittent contact over the next few years. In 2008–09, he 'updated' developments in his collecting for me, through several exchanges of e-mail.

an iPod or through one's computer (I don't own an iPod, but I do have a good bit of music downloaded on my computer, some of it things I use in class, some of it recordings I've been able to locate online that I've never found in any other format).'

For Steve, this was 'an interesting time for me to put down some thoughts about how my record collecting has developed in the last several years': he now had all the collection in one place for the first time, had made special provision for its storage, catalogued the collection, and arranged better shelving. Steve's musical tastes are eclectic, but with a preference for guitar-based hard rock and metal, and jazz.

When did you start buying and collecting records?

'I became more invested in record owning and record buying somewhere around the ages of seven and eight, and that was when my tastes started to shift from the "kid's stuff" I'd listened to earlier to rock. My parents bought a reissue of Beatles songs (*Beatles Rock 'n' Roll Music*) when I was seven, and I basically appropriated it and made it my own. About a year later, I actually made what I would call my first really conscious musical purchase, using money I'd made from selling some of my childhood toys at a family garage sale *(talk about a rite of passage)*. The album I bought was *Kiss Alive*.' (my emphasis)

How large is your collection and what are your preferred formats?

In late 2001, Steve roughly estimated his collection at 1,200–1,300 in all formats: 'I don't keep an exact count.' At this point, more than half were LPs, 'but the CD portion of my collection is catching up. A few cassettes, but those are decidedly less preferred by me as a format.' In 2009, having now been catalogued, his collection had 'grown quite a bit', and consisted of 949 vinyl records, and 1,059 CDs; making a total of 2008. This did not include any cassettes,

'... which I have pretty much stopped listening to and am replacing all that I can in other formats, or any albums that are owned solely in digital form. I divide my catalogue into vinyl and CDs, [see below] rather than grouping it all together. Within each format division, the catalogue is arranged alphabetically by performer and then each performer's recordings are in roughly chronological order. This is the same way that I have the stuff shelved in physical form.'

For Steve,

'LPs are still far more satisfying as actual objects, and I very much value my vinyl collection for its material qualities (album cover art and liner notes that aren't miniaturized). I like CDs mainly because they store more music, because so many quality reissues are available on CD, and because they're in a sense easier to listen to. On this last point, sound quality is less my concern than that the running time of a CD means not having to get up and switch in the middle. Of course, there are times when an album side worth of listening is just right, so the length of CDs isn't always a blessing (it's often a curse in terms of its effects on the programming of contemporary new releases).'

The collection reunited

'I just [2009] achieved something of a milestone in my music-owning life. My parents are getting ready to move out of the house I grew up in after living there for over 40 years, and in the process I had to clear out all of my possessions that had been left there and ship them back from their house in California to my home in Massachusetts (that's a distance of about 3,000 miles). As a result, I shipped about 350 records that had been left there, and now for the first time in my adult life my entire record collection is all in one place. So, I've been spending the past couple weeks getting reacquainted with a number of albums that I hadn't listened to for a good while.'

Addressing the problem of storage

'To prepare for this new stock of records, I had shopped for some new shelving to house my records. This was another little milestone. I had always kept my records in some pretty basic shelves – I had a couple of cheap but sturdy wooden shelves that I had bought, and a couple of old wine crates left over from many years ago when my dad owned a liquor store. They were functional but were very spread out across my living room, and my girlfriend, with whom I share a house, had become less than thrilled with the amount of room they took up. Knowing that I was going to be increasing the size of my home collection pretty significantly gave me cause to upgrade, and I found some great shelves at a local furniture store that were not bargain basement cheap but are strong, sturdy, nicely designed and have the further virtue of being significantly more vertical than horizontal (two shelf units, each about 7 feet tall, with room for six shelves of records each).'

The catalogue

'The other major change that's occurred in the last several years is that, about two years ago, I decided that I needed to catalogue all of my music collection. I did this partly because I seemed to be buying a lot more stuff than I had in the past (due to research, but also due to having more disposable income), but more so because I was finding that it was hard for me to keep track of some of my recordings because of how split up it was. So, the catalogue became a way for me to be sure that I know what I have, and having it written down makes it easier for me to be confident in knowing that just because something is out of sight [at work, or lent out] that doesn't mean it's gone.'

What are your preferred genres and artists, and why these?

'One [of my preferences] is loud rock music. When I was younger, this was mostly of the heavy metal variety, but over time I've gotten more into the brand of "hard rock" (for lack of a better term) that to my mind bridges the gap between clearly or not so clearly defined categories like punk or metal: The MC5, The Stooges, The New York Dolls, Monster Magnet and Motorhead. My musical first loves were things like Kiss, Ted Nugent, Led Zeppelin, Aerosmith. I've added a lot of diverse listening pleasures onto that stuff, but that style – 1970s hard rock and metal – still in many ways forms the core of my musical dispositions.'

'Why these genres? Well, I think between them they address a lot of my core values and principles about what music should be and how it should sound. I don't especially like music that's easy to digest. I like music that's thoughtful, but I also like music that's physical, visceral, and over time I've come more and more to see that relatively straightforward musical forms like hard rock and funk give the most room for the more intangible aspects of music (groove, feel, sound) to take control.'

Having the catalogue, meant that Steve was able to compile 'a list of artists by whom I own the most records, most CDs, and then most overall. They're an odd mix of genuine favourite artists of mine with artists on whom I've done significant research and have collected more of their recordings than I would have otherwise.' (I have conflated Steve's lists here).

Top Artists overall: Ornette Coleman (15); Jimi Hendrix (13); Led Zeppelin (12); Chet Atkins (11); Miles Davis (11); Black Sabbath (10); Kiss (10); John Coltrane (10); Van Halen (10); Pink Floyd (9); David Bowie (9); The Who (9); Grand Funk Railroad (9); Judas Priest (9); Ted Nugent (9); Motorhead (9); Rolling Stones (9); and Frank Zappa (9). His other vinyl holdings included Pink Floyd (9); The Beatles (8); King Crimson (8); Yes (8); Aerosmith (7); Jeff Beck (7); Blue Oyster Cult (7); and Rush (7). The artists primarily on CD included those purchased as part of Steve's recent research into conflict and crossover in heavy metal and punk:[18] The Stooges (6); The Runaways (6); Black Sabbath (5); Black Flag (5); Melvins (5); Motorhead (5); Slayer (5); and Soundgarden (5).

---

[18]   Steve Waksman, *This Ain't the Summer of Love, Conflict and Crossover in Heavy Metal and Punk*, University of California Press, 2009.

The music press

In 2002, Steve described in some detail how music magazines and books had influenced his record collecting:

> 'I make a lot of decisions about what to buy based on reading about a given band. Yet I'd have to say that I've done a lot more buying based on published, book-length record guides than I have based on weekly or monthly music publications. I own two editions of the *Rolling Stone Record Guide*, Robert Christgau's guide to the 1980s, Chuck Eddy's *Stairway to Hell* (on heavy metal), Martin Popoff's *Collector's Guide to Heavy Metal*, and *The Trouser Press Guide to the '90s*.'

Music magazines were also important to Steve, especially *Guitar Player* and *Mojo*:

> '*Guitar Player* because it caters to the guitar geek in me (certainly one of the fundamental aspects of my interest in music), and because it has tended to be very open about covering a wide range of styles and genres, thus feeding into my own rather eclectic tastes. *Mojo* because they have such good journalists, for the most part, who do a lot of historical research on the bands they cover.'

In 2009, Steve reflected on the influence of this and subsequent publications on his jazz collecting:

> 'I came to my interest in jazz artists like Ornette Coleman, Miles Davis and John Coltrane the way I came to so many of my musical interests, through reading. The original edition of the *Rolling Stone Record Guide* had a great section of jazz reviews in the back, almost all of which were written by a Boston-based critic named Bob Blumenthal (who now seems to write liner notes for every Blue Note reissue that comes on the market). If I remember correctly, his review of Ornette Coleman's *Free Jazz* compared it to the Sex Pistols; my curiosity was piqued and soon I began a long-standing interest in the more experimental wing of jazz. My interest in Coltrane and Miles pretty much followed a similar trajectory.'

> 'My record buying/collecting is driven by a concern with historicizing music that transcends the specific pleasure I take in many of the albums that I own.'

Steve's blog is at: http://themetalpunkcontinuum.blogspot.com/.

Oliver Wang

Oliver Wang is an academic, journalist, DJ and record collector. He has been writing on pop music, culture and politics since 1994, and, more recently, on Asian American cinema. A DJ since 1993, he hosts a weekly Latin/soul party in Echo Park. Oliver has a PhD in Ethnic Studies from UC Berkeley, completed while living in the Bay Area, and is currently an Assistant Professor of Sociology at CSU-Long Beach, living in LA.[19] Oliver compares collecting records to sharing secrets: 'You're selective about who you talk about them with but when you do, there's a thrill involved in having the power to share. If knowledge is power, records are knowledge in this context.'

In 2002, Oliver admitted that he was

'… always a little wary to self-identify [as a record collector] as such to others. I suppose it's because there's an image of collectors – as obsessive eccentrics – that I don't want to cultivate myself as (though I'm probably both). I'm also a DJ and it's easier to just say I'm a disc jockey and have that explain why I own so many damn records.'

More recently (2009), he was more comfortable with the label:

'In other words, I'm admitting to be an obsessive eccentric. Especially in such an intense digital age, the desire to still collect records (as opposed to collecting songs or albums, regardless of medium) clearly suggests a particular relationship to the physical object that, for me at least, is still important. I know several top-tier collectors who have been digitizing and then liquidating parts of their collection; for them, the physical object is less important than the music itself. I respect that attitude but I've yet to come around to it myself.'

The following integrates email interviews and follow up discussion from 2002 and 2009, showing the continued growth of Oliver's collection, shifts in his musical tastes and changes in his preferred sites of acquisition.

When did you begin buying records?

'[Age] 13 but that was really minor. I didn't buy albums in earnest until 17 and I've been on a rampage since 21. The first recording purchased was Art of Noise's "Invisible Silence".'

---

[19] For fuller biographical details, with links to Oliver's activities, including several blogs, see www.o-dub.com/about.html.

How many records do you own?

In 2002 Oliver found it hard to estimate the size of his collection: 'I stopped counting a while back. My guess would be around 5,000, give or take 1,000. Right now, about 2/3 to 3/4 of that is hip-hop. The remainder is older soul/funk/jazz/Latin/rock/reggae. I also own about 200–300 CDs and probably around 200 45s.'

When he moved to LA in 2006, Oliver had to pack up all his records, and thought the collection was

> '… closer to 7,000 to 8,000 now. The main difference in the last five years is that I've turned far more attention to collecting Latin records – including boogaloo, salsa, cumbia – whereas I've barely added much to my hip-hop collection. I still have most of my rap records boxed and stored; they've been like that for two-and-a-half years and I've yet to miss them. That's probably quite telling.'

How do you treat/provide for their storage and use?

In 2002, the collection was in bookshelves: 'nothing custom but they work well for LPs. For my 45s, I have cardboard boxes especially designed for 7" records. I also have cabinets for my CDs.' In 2009, he still had the same set up, but 'I'm waiting to buy my first home and when that happens, I'm willing to invest in some custom shelving.'

He does not maintain a catalogue of the collection: 'Always meant to but never got around to it.'

How often do you currently purchase records, where, and why?

In 2002: 'with the advent of eBay, I suppose it's nearly a daily practice, though in the physical world, I visit a record store [mainly second hand] once a week on average.' Used stores were preferred because 'they are either 1) cheap or 2) specialized (rarely both) and almost 90 per cent of what I look for are older records that wouldn't be serviced by chain music stores.' The World Wide Web represented 'a blessing and a curse, opening up many new opportunities to find records but it's also negatively affected prices upwards because of increased demand on a still-limited supply. It's great if you're a seller but as a buyer, it's definitely emptying out pockets across the globe.'

Now, living in Los Angeles: 'the record stores down here and harder to get to, especially with a full time job. I might step inside an actual store once a month or so.' Online shopping continues, however, and the World Wide Web is now by far his main site for acquisitions, 'followed in distant second place by used record stores. It comes down to time – if I had more of it, I could invest in making more personal connections with sellers and dealers and that's probably where I need to move more towards but in terms of efficiency, online buying is so easy even if it's not so affordable.'

What are your preferred formats, and why these?

'Vinyl. Part of it is logistical ... most of the records I look for are only available on vinyl. But beyond that, I like the physical sensation of vinyl and the very fact that it represents a link to the past which is immediate and visceral. There's definitely an elitist snobbery to it – what I collect tends to be rare and therefore the vinyl is irrefutable proof of ownership in a way that doesn't translate in the digital media world. It's also part of a hip-hop aesthetic – DJs who turn into collectors are always supposed to favour vinyl since that's where hip-hop's sonic origins begin. I will say this much – CDs are quite convenient and I can't deny that. When I review albums for publications, I usually try to wrangle two copies of the album – one on vinyl for my library, the other on CD for review purposes.'

In 2009, it is now MP3s that are convenient:

'I still like CDs since they come with booklets and liners but usually, if it's an album I'm just reviewing, then all I need are the MP3s. But again, I'm just talking about utility. In terms of what is my preferred medium for ownership, it's definitely vinyl for certain records. I do like CD boxsets, usually because they come with great documentation. If the choice is between an album reissued on CD vs. the original vinyl, I prefer the original vinyl still. Old habits die hard!'

What are your main genre/performer preferences?

In 2002, hip hop patterned Oliver's record collection:

'hip-hop is what got me into music ... artists like A Tribe Called Quest, De La Soul, Public Enemy, etc. (all the late '80s/early '90s "Golden Era" artists). So far, that constitutes the bulk of my collection but these days, I spend a lot of time (and money) collecting older funk, soul and jazz from the '60s and '70s. This started because I was looking for the music that was sampled by hip-hop artists but since then, I've branched out into listening to all sorts of music from that era, not just what's been sampled. I'm attracted to all things funky which is a rather ambiguous category since it can apply across so many genres but that's the best way I can describe it.'

By 2009, he had

'... increased, substantially, my interest in Latin records and that's in inverse proportion to my interest in funky jazz songs which I used to collect much more in the early part of the decade. I very rarely add much to that genre and if anything, I've been selling off records in that vein. I've also developed a beginning interest in Northern Soul and sweet soul but haven't gone whole hog yet, mostly out of cost. These days though, I'm definitely less interested in collecting "funk" and much more into "soul" as well as Latin.'

The impact of the internet

In 2002–03, Oliver was one of the collectors who alerted me to the increasing impact of the internet on collecting. Commenting on this trend in 2009, he observed:

> 'The internet has drastically changed the landscape. These days, you have blogs that post entire albums – many of them rare or obscure – online for free. In a sense, it's created a new form of collecting mentality and competition – both in who can collect the most MP3s but more about who can post the most. Those sites (and by extension, bloggers) which put up the most/best material are the ones who have the top rep. So in a sense, it's not your collection that gets you props, it's what you share out of your collection.'

He also noted the decline of physical retail: 'That's very much transformed the traditional forms of record collecting; it requires a lot more footwork to find viable places in the physical (as opposed to online) world.'

Lisa Wheeler

Lisa Wheeler lives in Austin, Texas, where she is a media spokesperson. A long-time record collector, with her passion encouraged by her mother, Lisa's main current interest is in radio station compilations. Over the past two years, she has developed a website documenting this fascinating but neglected area of collecting. Lisa sees enthusiasm as central to record collectors and the collecting process. 'I think that's a fair categorization – I'm very enthusiastic about record collecting. That said, it's not an obsession with me. While I enjoy collecting records, there are many other interests in my life that are just as enjoyable.' Lisa's collecting has shifted toward a more selective, rather than a completist approach.

At what age did you begin buying records?

> 'The first record I remember buying was "ABC" by the Jackson 5, back in 1970. My grandparents gave me money for my ninth birthday – so I walked down to the TG&Y (a discount store) and bought it. Still have it. My mother collected records, and was the one who sparked my interest. When she was a teen she would go out and buy the latest hits of the day, on 45 (1955–58). When I was young she would carefully pull out her records and play them for me – not only did this introduce me to Elvis, the Everly Brothers, Ricky Nelson, etc., but it also exposed me to the world of music on vinyl.'

How many records do you own, in what formats, and how do you store them?

'I have maybe 10,000 of various formats, including over 500 radio station compilations. I prefer vinyl. There's really no reason, except that sometimes you can't teach an old dog new tricks. I have an office area with bookshelves. The records (and CDs) are stacked in the shelves, the 45s are in long boxes, stacked in a closet, nearby.'

'I've actually purged quite a few records, probably about 10,000, over the past few years. At one point it was all about possessing the vinyl – now that's just not the case. I don't "need" to have a record in my collection to complete me. I'm not being critical of anyone who does that, it's just not my thing, anymore. It just dawned on me that I was keeping records in my stash that I never even listened to, which was just asinine, to me.'

I was intrigued that Lisa had purged so many records, and asked why she had done so, and which she had deleted from the collection.

'The reason why I purged so many records is simple – I got bored. I went through my collection and thought, "Why did I buy this particular record, in the first place?" I had honestly forgot. Case in point – I had a massive Sex Pistols collection – over 60 albums, probably 30 45s, etc. I kept them stored in a box for years. I don't think I played [more than] a couple, ever. Then one day I rediscovered them. I played a few on my turntable and just kinda went "OK, whatever." So about a week later, I posted all of them on eBay – sold them all for about $700. I probably could have gotten more if I sold them individually, but I just didn't want to be bothered with it.'

'That kind of started me rethinking what else I had in this collection that I just "had to have" and "couldn't live without", at one time. To be honest, it's so easy to dub off a vinyl record onto a digital format, that I could take an album, dub off the one (or maybe two) songs I really liked, and ditch the record. Late last year I traded a guy 500 45s for 10 radio station albums for my website – I was thrilled. I would venture to guess that I've sold quite a few, but for the most part I simply give them to Goodwill [a US charity, thrift shop] or to friends. No regrets.'

How often do you currently purchase records? And where do you buy from?

'I don't obsessively seek records. If I happen to be out and about, I'll swing by a neighbourhood store, and see what's new. That said, if I'm on vacation, I will visit the local record stores. I've never re-mortgaged the house for a record – I know my limits. Some of my record collecting friends say I'm very frugal. I've passed up many a record, and have never had any regrets. You can be very blinded by those expensive "holy grails" out there – and while it's tempting, I've never paid more than I budgeted.'

'I'm all for buying local. Austin is blessed with many great record stores – plus the big convention here twice a year. I prefer these because they are so accessible. I do troll eBay – especially for additions to my radio station compilation collection. Every April and October the Austin Record Convention keeps me busy for three days – I think I save up for this, both financially and time-wise. I love this show. I've been going to this show for 25 years – I guess I'm officially a "regular". It's like going to school reunion and seeing old friends. I catch up with guys I haven't seen, sometimes in years, and it's a wonderful fellowship, of sorts. The dealers know me so well that they'll find me and say "I've got something for you". Last record show I had several dealers hold back radio LPs to show me, until I made it to their booths – of course, I bought them all!'

What are your genre and performer preferences?

'Well I kind of have blinders on with the radio station comps. I started the site two years ago, and it's been a lot of fun. That said, when I'm not trying to find additions to that collection, I love bluegrass and vintage country, and world music. I arrived late to the party when it comes to my discovery of bluegrass, world music, etc. I have no idea why, because these genres are brilliant. I guess when you are a certain age, you wear blinders when it comes to music. In the '70s it was all about rock and roll – and that pretty much clouded my listening habits for 30 years. One day my husband bought me a Cesaria Evora CD. He heard a song of hers on our local NPR radio station, and thought I would like it. It literally opened the door (and my ears) to this beautiful music. I didn't understand a word she was singing, but it really spoke to me. I got on kind of a Tuvan throat singing kick a while back – that was fun to explore. I really don't "collect". If I happen to hear something, I'll just pick it up – there's no ulterior motive, not like before (for collecting, reselling, etc.). Plain and simple, my musical tastes just "grew up".'

Has the internet and digital music influenced your collecting?

'I probably buy more iTunes than vinyl. I like the accessibility of the songs. It took me long enough to realize that I need to enjoy the music, instead of focusing on trying to find some physical possession.'

Collecting radio station compilations

'When I started collecting radio station compilations, I couldn't find a resource guide – so I designed my own website http://www.radiouseonly.com. Not that I design a website for all of my collections, but that's how I catalogue those particular pieces. The rest of my collection is not formally catalogued in any particular way.'

'Every summer I would spend with my grandparents, in Dallas. My favourite station there was KZEW, an album-rock station. One day, while shopping at a local Dallas record shop, I found a KZEW album, of radio bits and such, and bought it for my collection. I filed it away until about three years ago. I've always been a record collector. After rediscovering the KZEW album in a box, I started collecting radio station compilations. Before too long I had several hundred. I began to search on the internet for more information about these compilations, but found nothing – that's when I decided to create my own website, as a resource, of sorts.'

'These albums were a perfect fit for me – especially since my chosen career, for two decades, was radio; I'm incredibly nostalgic. These comps are literally a time capsule to the way radio once was – musically and visually. Quite a few of these albums feature pictures of DJs in their wide lapel suits and mutton chops of the time, to radio equipment, like reel-to-reel players, that are obsolete now at today's stations.'

'I'm all for the enjoyment of the hobby – once it stops being fun to me, I'll take up another interest. Life is too short for a boring hobby.'

Conclusion

I now want to draw together some general observations on record collectors, their collecting practices and the context within which these take place. I begin by situating record collecting and record collectors in relation to the various approaches to 'collecting' and the definition of 'collectors' present in the academic literature (and referred to in my Introduction). Reflecting their love of music, I regard the distinctive characteristic of record collectors as the use value they make of the collection, an emphasis that sets them apart from most other collecting constituencies. Looking across the characteristics exhibited by record collectors, it is not possible to sustain a unitary definition of them. Instead, given the differing emphases and practices taken on over time by record collectors, I argue for the notion of a 'career' in record collecting.

A broadly psychoanalytical perspective (Baudrillard, 1994; Muesterbeger, 1994) understands collecting as the result of childhood experiences, primarily sexual experience or its repression, creating sublimated needs and associated pathological behaviours, notably obsession. This overly reductionist characterization (see Grijp, 2006: Chapter 2) underpins the popular stereotype of the record collector as an antisocial individual, obsessed with collection size and so forth. I have found only limited support for this view. A few of the collectors I talked with exhibited – and indeed recognized in themselves – behaviours seen as less desirable and even pathological in relation to their collections. There are also examples of collectors who represent the popular image of the collector as avoiding personal relationships, and as relatively isolated individuals lacking social competence; however, this is certainly not true of the body of collectors this study is based upon. For instance, the great majority of the collectors I profiled in Chapter 7 were currently in long-term relationships, and four had children. The continued dominance of the negative image owes much to the dominant representation of the collector in popular media culture, and the tendency of the mainstream media to highlight examples of such stereotypes.

Also linked to a loose psychoanalytic approach, but with greater validity, is the widespread view of collecting as central to the construction and expression of personal identity. This is clearly present in the case of record collectors whose collections represent an assertion of their individuality and a form of musical cultural capital, presented through the various configurations of their collecting interests and practices. An aspect of this is the manner in which the collection works as a form of 'masquerade', providing a refuge from the everyday grind of much of daily life and comfort in times of increased anxiety.

Collecting is also frequently conceptualized as a form of consumption, often seen in ritualistic terms, with an accompanying set of meanings and value imbuing the collected objects and practices (Appadurai, 1986; Belk, 2001, Pearce, 1995). A key motif in such accounts is the manner in which ownership is conventionally divorced from use, and where the collected objects are reconstituted through the special status accorded to the collection. Instances of this are the mint stamp removed from its primary use as a means of paying postage, and the unread first edition book. Record collecting is obviously a form of consumption, with a set of attendant practices, but records differ from most collectibles in terms of the maintenance of their use value. While some record collectors will valorize the 'mint' condition recording, including sealed vinyl, most will make very regular use of the collection to provide a literal soundtrack to their lives. This is to emphasize the central place of pleasure and passion, the affective dimension of record collecting.

As I have shown, since the origins of record collecting during the 78 era, collectors have displayed a shared interest in sound recordings as significant cultural artefacts, an interest underpinned by notions of discrimination, musical canons and rarity. They also share the dominant characteristics of collectors more generally, albeit with particular inflections of these: the thrill of the chase; obsession, linked to accumulation and completism; at times a preoccupation with rarity and economic value; and a concern for cultural preservation. The last has frequently involved self-education and public scholarship, drawing on the collection as a resource. These traits are subsumed into collecting as a significant aspect of social identity, involving the acquisition and display of cultural capital, related to historical memory and overlaid with a patina of nostalgia.

The diversity of these motifs and practices, however, indicate that there is no 'standard definition of the record collector'. It is more appropriate to see a range of 'types', each of which is linked to particular collecting practices; these include the record collector as cultural preserver, as accumulator and hoarder, as music industry worker, as adventurous hunter, as connoisseur and as digital explorer. Further, the individual collector may exhibit different degrees of investment in combinations of these roles through their collecting lives. The collecting process and the attitudes of the individual collector towards it can take on different emphases over time, relating to combinations of increasing age, changing study commitments and employment, decisions about who and what to collect and the availability of sought-after recordings, and income and domestic circumstances.

A career in record collecting

Drawing primarily on the profiles in Chapter 7, it is possible to sketch a 'typical' career in record collecting, a composite biography of the record collector. In most cases, demonstrating the common disposition to collect during adolescence as a part of the establishing of personal identity and peer group cultural capital, the nascent record collector will acquire his or her first recordings as a teenager. He or she will then continue to expand this basis, while gradually extending their knowledge about artists and styles, along with the sites and practices associated with finding records. By this point, typically in their late teens and early twenties, the collector begins to regard their 'holdings' as moving past being simply an accumulation of records: it now warrants the status of 'a collection'.

In early adulthood, the passion for collecting and the knowledge gained from it facilitates a move into related vocational fields. This is very much the case with those working in the music industry full time, for example as musicians and DJs, in radio, as music journalists and in running record labels. Other collectors will engage in these activities on a part-time, 'hobby' basis, or as an aspect of their primary job (as with graphic designers who design record covers and suchlike). Then there are those collectors who become academics, primarily in media studies, sociology and music studies; they draw on the collection as a resource in researching, writing and teaching about popular music. Individual collectors will engage in several of these activities across their collecting lives: Hasse, for instance, has worked as a club DJ, a music journalist, a songwriter and an academic. Of course, such activities also supply a rationalization for collecting.

Collectors will become progressively more comfortable with being accorded the label 'record collector', and describing themselves as such. Aware of the negative stereotypes associated with record collecting (and collecting more generally), they will at times admit to some of these characteristics, especially the frequently obsessive nature of collecting, but seek to distance their own practices from the stereotype. In later years, their collecting emphases tend to move away from an element of accumulation and a concern with completism, more toward greater selectivity and musical discrimination. For most, there is a point of realization that one has 'enough' music; this may result in a downsizing and rationalizing of the collection.

The music preference of youth will sometimes be left behind, as genre and performer interests change. Attitudes toward formats also shift. Vinyl continues to be the collectable format, but there is frequently an acceptance of other formats as *collectable*, notably CDs and digital downloads – although they may not be considered genuine parts of the *collection*. With greater confidence in their knowledge and a desire to share and display musical cultural capital, collectors take up spaces and opportunities for the public display of the collection, engaging in various forms of collection 'show and tell'.

In the modern social order, fantasy and the desire for material goods/objects play a more complex and important role in culture than ever before (Campbell, 1987). The 'social practice' of record collectors provides an example of this, in the interwoven narrative of desire, compulsion and identification, alongside a love of music and notions of cultural and economic value that characterize many collectors' accounts of their passion. It is appropriate that the final word goes to a collector: 'I think there is a thread between all record collectors: one part nostalgia, one part fun past time, three parts music lover, and a grey area of strange obsession and hoarding behaviour that we try to ignore discussing' (Michelle Flannery).

Appendix 1
The collectors

As a long-time collector myself (see Appendix 2), I had been interested for some time in the popular conceptions of collectors and the collecting process. During late 1998 and early in 1999, as part of another project, I interviewed a number of people about their general involvement in popular music. Several considered themselves keen 'record collectors' and their interviews initiated a more focused attempt to contact and survey record collectors, at first through face-to-face interviews, then (increasingly) via an e-mail questionnaire. This was done initially through personal contacts, with many made at several popular music-oriented conferences (especially the IASPM conference at Turku, Finland, in July 2001). The response rate from those I approached personally was extremely high (roughly 90 per cent, after a bit of gentle nagging). This opportunity sample was extended with a more general call for responses through the IASPM e-mail list (10 August 2001). Many of those who contacted me and agreed to be interviewed also forwarded the questionnaire to other collectors, including some on collecting lists.

In all, I eventually received 67 responses (56 male; 11 female). Given that my interest was in gaining qualitative information and reflections, rather than quantifiable data, the articulate self-reflexivity apparent in many of the responses was ideal for my purposes. Several not only completed my questionnaire, but also provided me with useful references (and a few excellent records!). The interviews generated approximately 250 pages of transcripts. These provided the basis for an unpublished report, circulated to the interviewees for their information and comment, in 2003; at the same time I obtained permission to use their names in further publications.

Obviously, this was in no sense a 'sample', in the usual social science sense of the term. Rather, the group represents a self-identified group of record collectors, with access to e-mail, drawn very heavily from academia (half were then university teachers/graduate students). Given that collecting is generally common to all social classes, the primarily middle-class location of these collectors raises questions as to their typicality. Their emphasis on discrimination arguably may distinguish them from other collecting constituencies; for example, those more conscious of the size, rarity and economic value of their collections. The self-reflexivity demonstrated by my respondents also sounds a note of caution in relation to their ability to rationalize and justify their collecting. Further, while impressive in the scope of their musical interests they were primarily collectors of 'rock music', defined in the broadest sense of the term to include the blues, 1950s rock and roll, and its subsequent variants, such as rap, hip hop, reggae, heavy metal, indie/alternative music. Only a few included jazz or classical music among their collecting interests. In addition to this group, I have drawn on other published interviews with record collectors, along with those included in (largely unpublished) academic studies.

While this original group of interviews is obviously dated, it remains valuable for the insights it provides into record collectors and their practices, and underpins much of the book. I maintained contact with a number of these collectors, and in 2008 went back to some of them to see how their collections, views of the collecting process and the state of the 'hobby' had developed over the intervening years. A number of these collectors are profiled in Chapter 7. I also conducted further interviews, usually informally, with several people working in music retail and the music press (most were themselves record collectors).

Appendix 2
The author as collector

I am a long-time collector myself, primarily of postal history, but also of records, music books (mainly critical studies, consumer guides and biographies) and music magazines. In common with most collectors, my collecting began in early adolescence. I began collecting stamps when I was around 12 years of age; I was attracted by the romance and aesthetic appeal of many issues of stamps, and collecting them was a way into the history, geography and culture of various countries. I put these collections largely on hold and into storage while I was a student in my twenties, and then lived overseas. I returned to them more seriously in my mid thirties, when I had more disposable income and a settled domestic situation. I then usually described myself as a 'postal historian', since much of my interest was in the delivery of mail, and 'rates and routes'.

Gradually, I became much more 'serious' about the hobby, investing increasing amounts of time, money and effort. I also built up a fairly comprehensive philatelic reference library, joined a number of philatelic societies, and researched, wrote about and exhibited on the areas I was collecting in. Around 2000, my interest waned to a degree, in part because I had taken my main collections to as high a level as I could within my financial constraints; that is, the few items I did not have were both quite rare and extremely expensive. Over the next six or seven years I sold off several of the more valuable collections, partly to finance family overseas trips and household renovations. At the same time, however, I began several new collections, on areas which were challenging but where much of the material could be acquired reasonably cheaply. Today, I have around 80 albums and stock books of stamps and covers, covering six collections.

Glancing back at what I have just written, it strikes me as revealing that I chose to talk about my 'stamp collecting' before considering my record collecting. The former does indicate, however, my general approach to collecting, emphasizing systematic engagement, discrimination and the acquisition of knowledge as much as the collectible itself. I have never considered myself a 'serious' record collector, although I have at times owned several thousand recordings in various formats. So while I have a 'record collection', I consider myself a 'record collector' only in a relatively modest and discriminating way. I have regularly searched for particular records, but have rarely spent more than $30 on a recording, and usually considerably less. My aim has been to acquire the music itself. Further, influenced by music critics and notions of a popular musical canon, I sought to include 'the best' examples of performers and genres. I have been less bothered about condition (with vinyl, I regard a good playable state as sufficient in most cases); nor is my collecting generally concerned with completism or collection size.

I began buying records shortly after I began buying stamps, around age 14, when I developed a taste for British R&B and rock performers such as The Animals, The Kinks, The Who, The Pretty Things and, above all, The Rolling Stones. I saw many of these bands, and other international performers, when they toured New Zealand in the mid to late 1960s, and when I lived in London in the early 1970s. Some of their early work – the covers of R&B, soul and blues records from the United States – encouraged me to listen to and buy the original artists. In the mid to late 1960s, involvement in the 'counter culture' led me to listen to and purchase a good deal of 'psychedelic' music, which I continue to have an affinity for. Other major tastes emerging over the next 25 years have included folk rock, alt. country, progressive rock, jazz (mainly jazz piano) and punk rock. Until around 1990, nearly all my purchases were vinyl, and primarily as albums; since then, most have been on CD.

I have always actively traded records, usually for credit at second hand shops, culling out music I was no longer attracted to, and acquiring desired newer genres and performers. On two occasions, I have sold off large parts of my record collection. In late 1972 I was aware, from prices in several second hand record shops, that many mid to late sixties releases were already 'collectable'; accordingly, to raise money before I went overseas, I sold to a dealer (at a good price for that time) many of the albums I had from that period. Then in 2003, a major (and expensive) relocation led me to sell off about 1,200 vinyl albums, many of them of performers whose work I now had on CD compilations and reissues – this applied to much of my remaining rock, blues and punk on vinyl. I did keep a few of the more valuable albums, even though these are now rarely played. Currently I have around 1,200 vinyl albums (most carefully stored in the basement; the better items in the upstairs study), 840 CDs (including about a dozen boxed sets), and 220 audiotapes (though most are never played). My attempts to maintain a catalogue have always been cursory, and I don't currently have an up to date listing. I have a small amount of music in digital form on my computer, mainly to use with my teaching. I do, however, have access to a considerable volume of such music through my teenage children's iPods and iTunes collections.

Where I do consider myself a 'music collector' is in relation to my music magazines (see Chapter 6) and books. Here, I have been increasingly systematic in developing an extensive library of books and magazines on 'popular music', primarily but not exclusively, rock (and its various related genres) and blues. Unlike my recordings, I do maintain an up to date bibliography of my 'print music' collection, which has almost 1,400 items. This collection, and its maintenance and continued expansion, has been an essential resource for my work in popular music studies, my main academic area of research and teaching since the mid 1990s. This also, of course, supplies a rationale for the collection. It is underpinned by a fascination with 'music in print' and the pleasures of exploring the field through biography and historical studies. Indicative of this is the point that I shall maintain and draw on the collection (for research and writing) after I retire. I enjoy reading and thinking about music in conjunction with listening to it.

Appendix 3
Institutional collecting

The focus of this study is on the individual record collector, but it is worth noting that there is considerable record collecting undertaken by institutions. Individual record collectors are often involved with the development of institutional collections, as in the case of Peter Blecha and the Experience Music Project in Seattle (Blecha, 2005). While their motivations (for collecting) and practices have much in common with those of individual collectors, the emphasis in institutional collecting is more firmly on cultural preservation and display (for a useful introductory discussion see Belk, 2001: Chapter 4; also the contributions to MacDonald, 2006). Institutional collections frequently include sheet music and other printed music literature, in addition to recordings, musical instruments and popular music ephemera.

Several types of institutional record collections can be distinguished:

1. 'Traditional' style museums, especially those devoted to musical instruments; as with the Horniman Museum in London and the Sibelius Museum in Turku, Finland.
2. Sound archives, with collections of sound recordings and sheet music; for instance the Library of Congress and the British Library Sound Archive.
3. Public and university library specialized music collections, such as the University of Chicago Jazz Archive and the New York Public Library Performing Arts Center at Lincoln Center.
4. 'Rock museums', devoted to the history of popular music, which are part of the now prominent 'heritage industry'. Prominent examples in the United States include the Rock and Roll Hall of Fame (Cleveland), the Experience Museum (Seattle) and the Delta Blues Museum (Clarkesdale).

A form of institutional collecting is represented by The Hard Rock Café chain, with the world's largest collection of memorabilia, especially musical instruments. Also noteworthy is *The All Music Guide*, the world's largest digital archive of music, which represents the intersection of personal and institutional collecting.[1]

As do 'mainstream' museums, these all raise questions around the selection of the material for inclusion (which artists, periods, styles, artefacts) and the

---

[1]   See Brian Bowe, 'How a Small-town Music Fetishist Turned an Obsession into a Multimillion-dollar All Media Guide', *Metro Times*, 24 January 2007; online at www.metrotimes.com.

manner in which these are to be contextualized and displayed. This process of reconstructing the musical past, and institutional record collecting more generally, are worthy of further investigation, but this has not been possible here.

Bibliography

Aizlewood, John (ed.) (1994) *Love is the Drug*. London: Penguin.

Anderson, Ian (1977) *Rock Record Collectors Guide*. London: MRP Books.

Appadurai, Arjun (1986) *The Social Life of Things: Commodities in Cultural Perspective*. Cambridge: Cambridge University Press.

Bailey, Steven (2003) 'Faithful or Foolish: The Emergence of the "Ironic Cover Album" and Rock Culture', *Popular Music and Society*, 26 (2), pp. 141–60.

Bannister, Matthew (2006) *White Boys, White Noise: Masculinities and 1980s Indie Guitar Rock*. Aldershot: Ashgate.

Barrow, Steve and Dalton, Peter (1997) *Reggae: The Rough Guide*. London: The Rough Guides.

Basbanes, Nicholas A. (2001) *Patience and Fortitude : Wherein a Colorful Cast of Determined Book Collectors, Dealers, and Librarians Go About the Quixotic Task of Preserving a Legacy*. New York: HarperCollins.

—— (2002) *Among the Gently Mad: Perspectives and Strategies for the Book Hunter in the Twenty-first Century*. New York: Henry Holt and Company.

Baudrillard, Jean (1994) 'The System of Collecting', in John Elsner and Rodger Cardinal (eds) *The Cultures of Collecting*. London: Reaktion Books, pp. 7–24.

Becker, Howard (1982) *Art Worlds*. Berkeley, CA: University of California Press.

Belk, Russell W. (2001) *Collecting in a Consumer Society*. (2nd edn) London: Routledge.

—— (2006) 'Collectors and Collecting', in Christopher Tilley, Webb Keane, Susanne Kuechler-Fogden and Patricia Spyer (eds) *Handbook of Material Culture*. London: Sage, pp. 534–45.

Benjamin, Walter (1968; first published in German, 1931) 'Unpacking My Library: A Talk about Book Collecting', in *Illuminations*, ed. Hannah Arendt. London: Fontana Collins.

Bennett, Andy and Dawe, Kevin (2007) *Guitar Cultures*. Oxford and New York: Berg.

Bernardy, Cathy (2004) 'Goldmine: Music Collectibles Magazine Also Collectible', *Goldmine*, 1 October, p. 34.

—— (2006) 'Market Beat: E-Mail, Internet Radio, Web Sites, and Mail Catalog Auctions Work Together', *Goldmine*, 21 July, p. 53.

Betz, B. and Betz, P. (1966) *Literature of the Acoustical Era [1877–1925] of Sound Recording*. Albany, NY: School of Library Science, State University of New York.

Bierman, Stanley (1990) *The World's Greatest Stamp Collectors*. Sydney, OH: Linn's Stamp News.

Blake, Andrew (ed.) (1999) *Living Through Pop*. London and New York: Routledge.

Blancey, John (2008) *Beatles for Sale: How Everything They Touched Turned to Gold*. London: Jawbone Press.

Blanks, Harvey (1968) *The Golden Road: A Record Collector's Guide to Music Appreciation*. Adelaide: Rigby.

Blecha, Peter (2005) *Rock and Roll Archeologist: How I Chased Down Kurt's Stratocaster, the 'Layla' Guitar, and Janis's Boa*. Seattle, WA: Sasquatch Books.

Blom, Philipp (2002) *To Have and to Hold: An Intimate History of Collectors and Collecting*. Woodstock, NY: Overlook Press.

Bogle, Vicki (1999) 'Women Who Collect Records'. Graduate Research Paper. University of Auckland, New Zealand.

Bourdieu, Pierre (1984) *Distinction: A Social Critique of the Judgement of Taste* London: Routledge and Kegan Paul.

Brewster, Bill and Broughton, Frank (1999) *Last Night a DJ Saved My Life: The History of the Disc Jockey*. New York: Grove Press.

Bryant, E.T. (1962) *Collecting Gramophone Records*. London and New York: The Focal Press.

Campbell, B. (2001) 'Turn, Baby, Turn: Obsessions, Compulsions, Redemption and Satori in the World of Record Collecting', *Colorado Springs Independent*, 14 June. http://www.csindy.com/gyrobase/Content?oid=oid%3A3654.

Campbell, Colin (1987) *The Romantic Ethic and the Spirit of Modern Consumerism*. Oxford: Blackwell.

Cantwell, Robert (1996) *When We Were Good*. Cambridge, MA: Harvard University Press.

Cavicchi, Daniel (1998) *Tramps Like Us: Music and Meaning among Springsteen Fans*. Oxford: Oxford University Press.

Chanan, Michael (1995) *Repeated Takes: A Short History of Recording and Its Effects on Music*. London: Verso.

Christgau, Robert (1982) *Christgau's Guide: Rock Albums of the '70s*. London: Vermilion.

—— (1990) *Christgau's Record Guide: The '80s*. London: Vermilion.

Clayton, Martin, Middleton, Richard and Herbert, Trevor (eds) (2003) *The Cultural Study of Music: A Critical Introduction*. New York and London: Routledge.

Clifford, James (1988) *The Predicament of Culture: Twentieth-Century Ethnography, Literature, and Art*. Cambridge, MA: Harvard University Press.

Cohen, Stanley and Taylor, Laurie (1976) *The Theory and Practice of Resistance to Everyday Life*. Harmondsworth: Pelican Books.

Collis, John (ed.) (1980) *The Rock Primer*. New York: Penguin.

Cooper, Gregory (1993) *Collectable Compact Disc Price Guide*. Paducah, KY: Collector Books.

—— (1998) *Collectible Compact Disc Price Guide 2*. Paducah, KY: Collector Books; Schroeder Publishing.

Copeland, Peter (1991) *Sound Recordings*. London: British Library.

Corenthal, Michael G. (1986) *The Iconography of Recorded Sound 1886–1986: A Hundred Years of Commercial Entertainment and Collecting Opportunity*. Milwaukee, WI: Yesterday's Memories.

Crafts, Susan D., Cavicchi, Daniel, Keil, Charles, and the Music in Daily Life Project (1993) *My Music*. Hanover, NH and London: Wesleyan University Press.

Danet, Brenda and Katriel, Tamar (1994) 'Glorious Obsessions, Passionate Lovers, and Hidden Treasures: Collecting, Metaphor, and the Romantic Ethic', in Stephen Harold Riggins (ed.) *The Socialness of Things: Essays on the Socio-Semiotics of Objects*. Berlin and New York: Mouton de Gruyter, pp. 23–62.

Day, Timothy (2000) *A Century of Recorded Music: Listening to Musical History*. New Haven, CT and London: Yale University Press.

Dean, Eddie (2001) 'Desperate Man Blues', in Douglas Wolk and Peter Guralnick (eds) *Da Capo Best Music Writing 2000: The Year's Finest Writing on Rock, Pop, Jazz, Country, and More*. New York: Da Capo Press, pp. 76–97.

De Koningh, Micael and Griffiths, Marc (2003) *Tighten Up! The History of Reggae in the UK*. London: Sanctuary.

DeNora, Tia (2001) *Music in Everyday Life*. Cambridge and New York: Cambridge University Press.

DeRogatis, Jim (1996) *Kaleidoscope Eyes: Psychedelic Rock from the '60s to the '90s*. Secaucus, NJ: Citadel Press/Carol Publishing.

De Whalley, Chas (2007) 'Back to the Future: The Reissues Industry', *Record Collector*, A Special Report in Three Parts: June, July and August.

Dibbell, Julian (2004) 'Unpacking Our Hard Drives: Discophilia in the Age of Digital Reproduction', in Greg Weisbard (ed.) *This is Pop: In Search of the Elusive at Experience Music Project*. Cambridge, MA: Harvard University Press, pp. 279–88.

Discoveries for Record & CD Collectors Magazine. http://www.mondotimes. com/2/topics/5/entertainment/80/6578.

Docks, Les R. (2001) *American Premium Record Guide: 1900–1965*. (6th edn) Iola, WI: Krause.

Doggett, Peter (1987) 'How Record Collecting Has Grown', *Record Collector*, 100, December, pp. 16–18.

—— (1996a) 'Editorial', *Record Collector*, 200, April.

—— (1996b) 'History of Collecting', *Record Collector*, 200, April, pp. 39–56.

—— (1997) 'Rock Books', *Record Collector*, 212, April, pp. 35–57.

—— and Hodgson, Sarah (2003) *Christie's Rock and Pop Memorabilia*. New York: Billboard Books.

Dougan, John (2006) 'Objects of Desire: Canon Formation and Blues Record Collecting', *Journal of Popular Music*, 18 (1), pp. 40–65.

Eisenberg, Evan (1988) *The Recording Angel: Music, Records and Culture from Aristotle to Zappa*. London: Pan Books.

Elsner, John and Cardinal, Roger (eds) (1994) *The Cultures of Collecting*. London: Reaktion Books.

Fabrizio, Timothy C. (1999) 'Ordinary People: The Talking Machine in Real Life', *ARSC Journal*, 30, pp. 20–23.

—— and Paul, George F. (1997) *The Talking Machine: An Illustrated Compendium 1877–1929*. Atglen, PA: Schiffer.

—— (2000) *Discovering Antique Phonographs*. Atglen, PA: Schiffer.

Farrugia, Rebekah and Swiss, Thomas (2005) 'Tracking the DJs: Vinyl Records, Work, and the Debate Over New Technologies', *Journal of Popular Music Studies*, 17 (1), pp. 30–44.

Felton, Gary (1980) *The Record Collector's International Directory*. New York: Crown.

Fonarow, W. (2006) *Empire of Dirt: The Aesthetics and Rituals of British Indie Music*. Middletown, CT: Wesleyan University Press.

Fox, Alison (1988) *Rock and Pop: Phillips Collectors Guides*. London: Boxtree.

Frith, Simon (1996) *Performing Rites: On the Value of Popular Music*. Cambridge, MA: Harvard University Press.

Gabbard, Krin (1995) 'Introduction: The Jazz Canon and Its Consequences', in Krin Gabbard (ed.) *Jazz Among the Discourses*. Durham, NC and London: Duke University Press.

Garofalo, R. (2003) 'I Want My MP3: Who Owns Internet Music?', in M. Cloonan and R. Garofalo (eds) *Policing Pop*. Philadelphia, PA: Temple University Press, pp. 30–45.

Gay, Paul du and Negus, Keith (1994) 'The Changing Sites of Sound: Music Retailing and the Composition of Consumers', *Media, Culture and Society*, 16 (3), pp. 395–413.

Gellat, Roland (1977) *The Fabulous Phonograph, 1877–1977*. New York: Macmillan.

Gillies, Douglas (1966) *Collecting Records*. London: Batsford.

Glebbeek, Caesar and Noble, Douglas J. (1996) *Jimi Hendrix: The Man, the Music, the Memorabilia*. Limpsfield: Paper Tiger/Dragon's World.

Godbolt, Jim (1984) *A History of Jazz in Britain 1919–1950*. London: Quartet Books.

Goldmine. website: www.goldminemag.com.

Gracyk, Theodore (2007) *Listening to Popular Music: Or, How I Learned to Stop Worrying and Love Led Zeppelin*. Ann Arbor, MI: University of Michigan Press.

Granata, Chuck (2002) *45 RPM*. New York: Princeton Architectural Press.

Gregson, Nicky and Crewe, Louise (2003) *Second-Hand Cultures*. Oxford and New York: Berg.

Grijp, Paul van der (2006) 'Passion and Profit: Towards an Anthropology of Collecting', *Comparative Anthropological Studies in Society, Cosmology and Politics: Volume 3*. Berlin: Lit.

Gronow, Pekka (1983) 'The Record Industry: The Growth of a Mass Medium', *Popular Music*, 3, pp. 53–75.

—— and Saunio, Ilpo (1998) *An International History of the Recording Industry*, trans. Christopher Moseley. London and New York: Cassell.

Guterman, Jimmy (1992) *The Best Rock-and-Roll Records of All Time: A Fan's Guide to the Stuff You Love!* New York: Citadel Press.

Hamlyn, Nick (ed.) (1991) *Music Master Price Guide for Record Collectors*. London: MBC Information Services.

Hammond, John, with Irving Townsend (1977) *John Hammond on Record: An Autobiography*. New York: Penguin.

Hanel, Ed (1983) *The Essential Guide to Rock Books*. London: Omnibus Press.

Hayes, David (2006) 'Take Those Old Records off the Shelf: Youth and Music Consumption in the Postmodern Age', *Popular Music and Society*, 29 (1), pp. 51–68.

Herrmann, Frank (1999) *The English as Collectors: A Documentary Sourcebook*. New Castle, DE: Oak Knoll Press and London: John Murray.

Heylin, Clinton (1995) *Bootleg: The Secret History of the Other Recording History*. New York: St Martin's Press.

Hibbert, Tom (ed.) (1982) *The Perfect Collection*. London and New York: Proteus Books.

Hicks, Michael (1999) *Sixties Rock: Garage, Psychedelic, and Other Satisfactions*. Urbana and Chicago, IL: University of Illinois Press.

Hilbert, Robert (1988) *Winning Bids: Actual Prices Paid for Jazz and Blues 78 RPM Recordings*. Miami, FL: Pumpkin Productions.

Hill, Randall C. (1981) *The Official Price Guide to Collectible Rock Records*. Orlando, FL: House of Collectibles.

Hillis, Ken and Petit, Michael, with Nathan Scott Epley (eds) (2006) *Everyday eBay: Culture, Collecting and Desire*. New York and London: Routledge.

Hills, Matt (2002) *Fan Cultures*. London and New York: Routledge.

Hornby, Nick (1995) *High Fidelity*. London: Random House.

Hoskins, Janet (1998) *Biographical Objects: How Things Tell the Stories of People's Lives*. New York and London: Routledge.

Hosokawa, Shuhei and Matsuoka, Hideaki (2004) 'Vinyl Record Collecting as Material Practice: The Japanese Case', in William W. Kelly (ed.) *Fanning the Flames: Fans and Consumer Culture in Contemporary Japan*. New York: State University of New York Press, pp. 151–68.

Hull, Geoffrey P. (2004) *The Recording Industry*. (2nd edn) New York and London: Routledge.

Hunter, Seb (2004) *Hell Bent for Leather: Confessions of a Heavy Metal Addict*. London and New York: Fourth Estate.

IFPI (2006) 'Global Digital Music Sales Triple as a New Market Takes Shape', available at http://www.ifpi.org.

Inglis, I. (2001) '"Nothing You Can See That Isn't Shown": The Album Covers of the Beatles', *Popular Music*, 20 (1), pp. 83–98.

Johnson, William W. (compiler) (1954) *The Gramophone Book: A Complete Guide for All Lovers of Recorded Music*. Issued by the National Federation of Gramophone Societies. London and New York: Hinrichson Education.

Karp, Marilynn Gelfman (2006) *Caught in the Act of Collecting*. New York: Abrams.

Kay, Hilary (1992) *Rock'N'Roll Collectables: An Illustrated History of Rock Memorabilia*. London: Pyramid Books/Octopus Press.

Kelso, Jonathon (2007) 'The Influence of the Internet and Digitization on Record Collecting', Paper for Media Studies Honours, Victoria University of Wellington, Wellington.

Kenney, William Howland (1999) *Recorded Music in American Life: The Phonograph and Popular Memory, 1890–1945*. New York and Oxford: Oxford University Press.

King, A. Hyatt (1963) *Some British Collectors of Music*. Cambridge: Cambridge University Press.

Kirshenblatt-Gimblett, B. (1999) 'Objects of Memory', in Barbara Hensen (ed.) *Exploring Culture and Community for the 21st Century'*. Ipswich, QLD: Global Arts Link.

Krebs, Gary M. (1997) *The Rock and Roll Reader's Guide*. New York: Billboard Books.

Kuhns, Barbara (2000) 'Bob Hyland: A Pioneer Record Collector's Early Collecting Experiences', *The Old-Time Herald – A Magazine Dedicated to Old-Time Music*, 7 (5), August–October, pp. 24–6.

Laing, Dave (1985) *One Chord Wonders: Power and Meaning in Punk Rock*. Milton Keynes: Open University Press.

Leibowitz, Alan (1980) *The Record Collector's Handbook*. New York: Everest House.

Lejeune, Patrick (2008) *The Bootleg Guide to Disco, Acetates, Funk, Rap and Disco Medleys*. Netherlands: Discopatrick Press.

LeMahieu, D.L. (1988). *A Culture for Democracy: Mass Communication and the Cultivated Mind in Britain Between the Wars*. Oxford: Clarendon Press.

Leonard, Marion (2007) *Gender in the Music Industry: Rock, Discourse and Girl Power*. Aldershot: Ashgate.

Lewis, Lisa A. (ed.) (1992) *The Adoring Audience: Fan Culture and Popular Media*. London: Routledge.

Loescher, Greg (1999) 'A Brief History of Goldmine Magazine', *Goldmine*, 8 October, 25th Anniversary Issue, pp. 38–43.

Lopez, Paul (2002) *The Rise of a Jazz Art World*. Cambridge: Cambridge University Press.

MacDonald, Sharon (2006) *A Companion to Museum Studies*. Malden, MA: Blackwell.

Marsh, Dave (1989) *The Heart of Rock and Soul: The 1001 Greatest Singles Ever Made*. New York: Plume/Penguin.

—— and Swenson, John (eds) (1984) *The Rolling Stone Record Guide*. New York: Random House/Rolling Stone Press.

Marsh, Graham and Callingham, Glyn (eds) (2003) *Blue Note Album Cover Art: The Ultimate Collection*. San Francisco, CA: Chronicle Books.

Marshall, Lee (2003) 'For and Against the Record Industry: An Introduction to Bootleg Collectors and Tape Traders', *Popular Music*, 22 (1), pp. 57–72.

—— (2005) *Bootlegging: Romanticism and Copyright in the Music Industry*. London: Sage.

Martin, Paul (1999) *Popular Collecting and the Everyday Self: The Reinvention of Museums?* London and New York: Leicester University Press.

Maycock, Stephen (1994) *Miller's Rock and Pop Memorabilia*. London: Miller's/ Reed.

McCourt, Tom (2005) 'Collecting Music in the Digital Realm', *Popular Music and Society*, 28 (2), pp. 249–52.

Milano, Brett (2003) *Vinyl Junkies: Adventures in Record Collecting*. New York: St Martin's Press.

Millard, Andre (1995) *America On Record: A History of Recorded Sound*. Cambridge: Cambridge University Press.

Miller, Chuck (2004) *Warman's American Records: Identification and Price Guide*. (2nd edn) Iola, WI: Krause.

Miller, Daniel (1998) *A Theory of Shopping*. Cambridge: Polity Press.

—— (2006) 'Consumption', in Christopher Tilley, Webb Keane, Susanne Kuechler-Fogden and Patricia Spyer (eds) *Handbook of Material Culture*. London: Sage, pp. 341–54.

Montano, Ed (2003) 'Collecting the Past for a Material Present: Record Collecting in Contemporary Practice'. MA Dissertation. Institute of Popular Music Studies, Liverpool University.

Morrison, Craig (1996) *Go Cat Go! Rockabilly Music and Its Makers*. Urbana and Chicago, IL: University of Illinois Press.

Moses, Morton (1936) *The Record Collector's Guide: American Celebrity Discs*. New York: Concert Bureau, College of the City of New York. [An updated version was published by Dover Publications, New York, in 1949.]

—— (1977) *Collectors Guide to American Recordings, 1895–1925*. New York: Dover. [A further update of Moses 1936, 1949.]

Muesterberger, Werner (1994) *Collecting. An Unruly Passion: Psychological Perspectives*. Princeton, NJ: Princeton University Press.

Muggs, Joe (2007) 'Re Enter the Dragons', *WORD*, 54, August, pp. 41–3.

Neely, Tim (1996a) *Goldmine Price Guide to Alternative Records*. Iola, WI: Krause.

—— (1996b) *Goldmine Price Guide to 45 RPM Record*. Iola, WI: Krause. [2nd edn 1999.]

—— (1999) *Goldmine Record Album Price Guide*. Iola, WI: Krause.

Negus, Keith (1996) *Popular Music in Theory*. Cambridge: Polity Press.

Neumann, Mark and Simpson, Timothy A. (1997) 'Smuggled Sound: Bootleg Recording and the Pursuit of Popular Memory', *Symbolic Interaction*, 20 (4), pp. 319–41.

Nevins, Richard (2006) Booklet accompanying *The Stuff That Dreams Are Made Of*, 2-CD set, Yazoo.

North, Adrian and Hargreaves, David (2008) *Social and Applied Psychology of Music*. New York: Oxford University Press.

Oliver, Paul (2003) 'Song Collecting', in John Shepherd, David Horn, Dave Laing, Paul Oliver and Peter Wicke (eds) (2003) *The Continuum Encyclopedia of Popular Music, Volume One: Media, Industry and Society*. London and New York: Continuum, pp. 43–6.

Osborne, Jerry (1976) *Record Collecting Price Guide*. Orlando, FL: House of Collectibles.

Parsonage, Catherine (2005) *The Evolution of Jazz in Britain 1880–1935*. Farnham: Ashgate.

Pearce, Susan (1995) *On Collecting: An Investigation into Collecting in the European Tradition*. London: Routledge.

—— (ed.) (1997) *Experiencing Material Culture in the Western World*. London and Washington, DC: Leicester University Press.

—— (1998) *Collecting in Contemporary Practice*. London: Sage.

—— and Martin, Paul (2002) *The Collector's Voice: Critical Readings in the Practice of Collecting, Volume 4: Contemporary Voices*. Aldershot: Ashgate.

Pettit, Emma (2008) *Old Rare New: The Independent Record Shop*. London: Black Dog.

Plasketes, George (1992) 'Romancing the Record: The Vinyl De-Evolution and Subcultural Evolution', *Journal of Popular Culture*, 26 (1), pp. 109–22.

Propes, Steve (1973) *Those Oldies but Goodies: A Guide to 50s Record Collecting*. New York: Macmillan.

—— (1975) *Golden Goodies: A Guide to 50s and 60s Popular Rock & Roll Record Collecting*. Radnor, PA: Chilton.

Pruter, Robert (1997) 'A History of Doowop Fanzines', *Popular Music and Society*, 21 (1) (Spring).

Rab, George (2007) 'At the Cutting Edge with Bolan', *Record Collector*, October, pp. 81–4.

Rabinowitz, Harold and Kaplan, Rob (eds) (1999) Foreword by Ray Bradbury. *A Passion for Books: A Book Lover's Treasury of Stories, Essays, Humor, Lore, and Lists on Collecting, Reading, Borrowing, Lending, Caring for, and Appreciating Books*. New York: Three Rivers Press.

Rare Record Price Guide (2002). (6th edn) London: Parker Publishing.

Ratneshwar, S., Mick, David Glen and Huffman, Cynthia (eds) (2000) *The Why of Consumption: Contemporary Perspectives on Consumer Motives, Goals and Desires*. London and New York: Routledge.

Record Collector: Serious about Music. London: Diamond Publishing Limited. Website: www.recordcollectormag.com.

Rees, Tony (1985) *Rare Rock: A Collector's Guide*. Dorset: Blandford Press.

—— (1995) *The Vox Record Hunter*. London: McCelland & Stewart.

Regev, Motti (2003) 'Rock Aesthetic and the "Pop-Rockization" of Popular Music', in Keith Negus and David Hesmondhalgh (eds) *Studies in Popular Music*. London: Arnold.

—— (2006) Editorial Introduction, *Popular Music* 25 (1), pp. 1–2.

Reynolds, Simon (2004) 'Lost in Music: Obsessive Record Collecting', in Greg Weisbard (ed.) *This is Pop: In Search of the Elusive at Experience Music Project*. Harvard, MA: Harvard University Press, pp. 289–322.

Sandvoss, Cornel (2005) *Fans: The Mirror of Consumption*. Oxford: Polity Press.

Schloss, Joseph Glen (2004) *Making Beats: The Art of Sample-Based Hip-Hop*. Middletown, CT: Wesleyan University Press.

Schwartz, Roberta Freund (2007) *How Britain Got the Blues: The Transmission and Reception of American Blues Style in the United Kingdom*. Aldershot: Ashgate.

Semeonoff, Boris (1949) *Record Collecting: A Guide for Beginners* (With a Chapter on Collecting Jazz Records by Alexander Ross). Chislehurst: Oakwood Press.

Shepherd, John, Horn, David, Laing, Dave, Oliver, Paul and Wicke, Peter (eds) (2003) *The Continuum Encyclopedia of Popular Music, Volume I: Media, Industry and Society*. London and New York: Continuum.

Shirley, Ian (2008) '200 Rarest UK Albums', *Record Collector*, 355, November, pp. 46–71.

—— (2009) *Rare Record Price Guide 2010* (*Record Collector Magazine*) (10th edn) London: Diamond.

Shuker, Roy (2004) 'Beyond the "High Fidelity" Stereotype: Defining the (Contemporary) Record Collector', *Popular Music*, 23 (3), pp. 311–30.

—— (2005) *Popular Music: The Key Concepts*. (2nd edn) London and New York: Routledge.

—— (2008) *Understanding Popular Music Culture*. London: Routledge.

Smith, Giles (1995) *Lost in Music*. London: Picador.

Smith, Sid (2002) *In the Court of King Crimson*. London: Helter Skelter.

Soderbergh, Peter (1983) *Dr. Record's Original 78 RPM Price Guide*. Des Moines, IA: Wallace Hampton.

Solly, Bob (2000) 'The Birth of Rock'n'Roll Collecting', *Record Collecting*, 200, April, pp. 55–6.

—— (2007) 'Playing for Keeps: Top 50 Elvis Collectables', *Record Collecting*, September, pp. 68–70.

Stanley, John (2002) *Miller's Collecting Vinyl*. London: Octopus.

Steffen, David J. (2005) *From Edison to Marconi: The First Thirty Years of Recorded Music*. Jefferson, NC: McFarland.

Steffens, Roger and Pierson, Leroy Jodie (2005) *Bob Marley and the Wailers: The Definitive Discography*. Kingston and London: LMH Publishing.

Sterne, Jonathon (2003) *The Audible Past: Cultural Origins of Sound Reproduction*. Durham, NC: Duke University Press.

Straw, Will (1997a) 'Sizing Up Record Collections: Gender and Connoisseurship in Rock Music Culture', in Sheila Whiteley (ed.) *Sexing The Groove: Popular Music and Gender*. London: Routledge, pp. 3–16.

—— (1997b) 'Organized Disorder: The Changing Space of the Record Shop', in Steve Redhead et al. (eds) *The Clubcultures Reader: Readings in Popular Culture Studies*. Oxford: Blackwell, pp. 57–65.

Strong, Martin C. (1998). *The Wee Rock Discography*. Edinburgh: Canongate.

Styven, Maria (2007) 'The Intangibility of Music in the Internet Age', *Popular Music and Society*, 30 (1), pp. 53–74.

Symes, Colin (2004) *Setting the Record Straight: A Material History of Classical Recording*. Middletown, CT: Wesleyan University Press.

Tarmarkin, Jeff (2004) 'Former Goldmine "Head Honchos" Reminiscence', *Goldmine*, 1 October, p. 18.

Taylor, Paul (1985) *Popular Music since 1955: A Critical Guide to the Literature*. London: G.K. Hall.

Thompson, Dave (2002) *The Music Lover's Guide to Record Collecting*. San Francisco, CA: Backbeat Books.

—— (2007) 'Cassettes Survive Against All Odds', *Goldmine*, 28 September, pp. 16, 35.

—— (2008) 'Complete Collector: Celebrating the Birth of the Bootleg Recording', *Goldmine*, 20 June, p. 14.

Thompson, Emily (1996) 'Machines, Music and the Quest for Fidelity: Marketing the Edison Phonograph in America, 1877–1925 (Part I)', *Antique Phonograph News*, November–December, pp. 3–9.

Thompson, Stephen (1994) 'Record Collecting, 1974–1994', *Goldmine*, 14 October, pp. 180–81.

Thornton, Sara (1995) *Club Cultures: Music, Media and Subcultural Capital*. London and New York: Routledge.

Tilley, Christopher, Keane, Webb, Kuechler-Fogden, Susanne and Spyer, Patricia (eds) (2006) *Handbook of Material Culture*. London: Sage.

Tosh, David (2008) 'In the News: Treasures Await Record Convention Attendees', *Goldmine*, June, pp. 10, 67.

Toynbee, Jason (2000) *Making Popular Music: Musicians, Creativity and Institutions*. London: Arnold.

Tuchman, Mitch; photos by Peter Brenner (1994) *Magnificent Obsessions: Twenty Remarkable Collectors in Pursuit of Their Dreams*. San Francisco, CA: Chronicle Books.

Vale, Vivian and Juno, Andrea (eds) (1993) *Incredibly Strange Music, Volume 1*. San Francisco, CA: Re/Search Publications.

—— (eds) (1994) *Incredibly Strange Music, Volume 2*. San Francisco, CA: Re/Search Publications.

'Vinyl Frontier' (2007), *WORD*, August, p. 43.

Von Appen, R. and Doehring, A. (2006) 'Nevermind the Beatles, Here's Exile 61 and Nico: A Canon of Pop and Rock Albums from a Sociological and Aesthetic Perspective', *Popular Music*, 25 (1), pp. 21–40.

Welsh, Walter and Burt, Leah (1994) *From Tinfoil to Stereo: The Acoustic Years of the Recording Industry*. Gainesville, FL: University Press of Florida.

Whitburn, Joel (1988) *Billboard: Top 1000 Singles 1955–1987*. Milwaukee, WI: Hal Leonard Books.

Willis, Paul, Jones, Simon, Canaan, Joyce and Hurd, Geoff (1990) *Common Culture: Symbolic Work at Play in the Everyday Cultures of the Young*. Milton Keynes: Open University Press.

Index